POLARIZED AND DEMOBILIZED

DANA EL KURD

Polarized and Demobilized

Legacies of Authoritarianism in Palestine

HURST & COMPANY, LONDON

First published in the United Kingdom in 2019 by
C. Hurst & Co. (Publishers) Ltd.,
41 Great Russell Street, London, WC1B 3PL

This paperback edition first published in 2022 by
C. Hurst & Co. (Publishers) Ltd.,
New Wing, Somerset House, Strand, London, WC2R 1LA

A Cataloguing-in-Publication data record for this book
is available from the British Library.

ISBN: 9781787388246

This book is printed using paper from registered sustainable
and managed sources.

www.hurstpublishers.com

Published in collaboration with The Arab Center for Research
and Policy Studies, Doha, Qatar.

Dedicated to Dad, Luai, and Qais Rauf—I hope I make you proud

CONTENTS

ACKNOWLEDGEMENTS

This book has been in the making for a few years now, and of course nothing is achieved in a vacuum. Without the support of many people at various points in this manuscript's existence, I would not have been able to complete the task and actually see it in print.

First, to those who facilitated the original fieldwork: thank you to my dissertation advisor Dr Zoltan Barany for his support throughout graduate school. The obstacles were many, but I was able to complete the PhD thanks to him. Thank you also to my entire committee for the feedback on the original project from which this book was developed.

Secondly, I would like to thank my uncle Dr Abdallah Al-Kurd for giving me access to the PA's institutions and helping me throughout my fieldwork stays. Thank you also to the rest of my extended family for opening their homes to me and hosting me whenever I stopped by—especially my grandmother, Najah al-Tahhan. Palestine will always be home thanks to them.

At Birzeit University, I owe a debt of gratitude to Dr Ghada al-Madbouh and Dr Helga Baumgarten for hosting me in their departments and giving me access to the Birzeit student population. It was also especially comforting to commiserate with Dr Ghada about fieldwork and being an Arab in academia whenever we saw each other–I very much appreciated the support and camaraderie. Thank you also to Dr Murad Shaheen, Dr Tariq Dana, and Dr Emad Bishtawi for giving me access to their classes and being generous with their time.

At the Palestinian Center for Policy and Survey Research, I would like to thank Hamada Jaber for facilitating my research and tolerating my many emails and constant changes in schedule. Thank you also to the researchers at PCPSR, especially Waleed Ladadweh for his help with the data.

I would also like to thank the employees of the Palestinian Authority's institutions that made time for me to interview them. They provided extensive information, and I could not have written the dissertation without their expertise. In Palestinian society today (particularly within the diaspora, far removed from realities on the ground), it is easy to dismiss those who work for the PA as traitors and collaborators with the Israeli occupation. It has in fact become common to dichotomize reality: traitors and collaborators on one end, and heroes and resistance on the other. But I would like to make it clear here that while PA leadership bears a lot of responsibility for the situation Palestinians are in today, this blame is not equally shared. This book is not intended as an exposé of the Palestinian Authority. Those who work within the PA, even some of the decision-makers, are not traitors or collaborators. They are victims of their circumstances, often having given their lives and futures for the Palestinian cause. The PA provides them with their only chance at normalcy after years of Israeli repression. This book tells the story of how members of the PA became divorced from their own people in spite of their intentions.

As I worked on transforming this into a book project, I was supported by my supervisors and colleagues at the Arab Center for Research and Policy Studies. In particular, thank you to Dr Mohammad al-Masri for encouraging me to submit this manuscript as a part of the Arab Center book series, and for giving me the time and space to complete the revisions. Thank you also to all my colleagues who attended my seminar on this project or have seen various parts of it, and who have provided feedback throughout the past two years.

I would also be remiss if I did not thank the Project on Middle East Political Science, particularly the organizers and attendees of the POMEPS book workshop in November 2018. Getting detailed feedback on my manuscript at that crucial time helped prepare it for the review process, and I am very grateful for the opportunity. Thanks also to Dr Amaney Jamal, Dr Nathan Brown, and Dr Sean Yom for being generous with their time and giving consistently helpful feedback.

At Hurst, thank you to Farhaana for her patience with me throughout the publication process. Thank you to OUP for sending this out to anonymous reviewers, and thank you to those reviewers for their input. The feedback significantly strengthened the final product.

Last but not least, I would like to thank my family. Thank you to my father, Saed Kurd, for encouraging me to complete my PhD, and playing a pivotal role in my academic career. I am where I am due to his sacrifices and hard work. Thank you to baby Qais for brightening my life and putting everything in perspective. And, most importantly, I would like to thank my partner and colleague Luai Allarakia. Both his academic and logistical advice were invaluable, and I am deeply grateful to him for his love and encouragement. Truly, this book would not exist if not for him.

INTRODUCTION

DELAYED STATEHOOD; PALESTINE BEFORE
AND AFTER THE OSLO ACCORDS

Ayed is a political activist from a modest background. He grew up in a West Bank village under occupation and did not have the opportunity to emigrate for work or higher education. He was in his late teens when the first intifada erupted in late December 1987. As a member of Fatah's political arm, Ayed organized protests against the occupation. For his efforts, he was imprisoned for thirty years in Ofer military prison. But in the late 1990s, Ayed's luck turned around. As part of a deal with the Israeli government, the Palestinian Authority (PA)—the new Palestinian government—was able to secure Ayed's release.

Ayed returned to Palestinian society but soon realized that much of the conditions of occupation remained exactly the same. He attempted a return to activism and was involved for some time in organizing protests and sit-ins. He could not, however, find institutional support for his activism. There were few organizations in place to facilitate coordination, and Ayed felt like he was getting nowhere. The PA itself did not seem interested in supporting such actions and encouraged him to take a bureaucratic position in its interior ministry instead. Facing economic hardship and unable to find alternative work, Ayed agreed. Today, Ayed talks of the past and looks at his personal situation as symptomatic of the Palestinian struggle. "We come here and pretend to work," he says, "but we are only pencil pushers." He is unhappy with the PA's policies but can do little to challenge them, especially because he is dependent on them as a source of income.[1]

1

This pattern of stagnation is not exclusive to Ayed; Palestinian society as a whole struggles with this general malaise. Before 1994, Palestinians were highly politicized and organized, despite a sustained loss of land and military occupation. Many Palestinians participated in a number of organizations in their daily lives—organizations that arose organically and functioned on the basis of democratic practices. This not only had to do with the highly educated nature of Palestinian society but also the reaction of Palestinian society to the effects of the Israeli occupation.[2] Palestinians organized themselves in order to better provide services to their communities and coordinate effectively in seeking their political objectives. Many of these organizations were highly responsive to their members, and the overall nature of Palestinian civil society was democratic and robust. Thus, when the first intifada erupted in the late 1980s, a strong civil society was one of the main reasons that Palestinians were able to sustain a diffuse, mostly non-violent uprising despite the heavy cost imposed on them by Israeli repression. The first intifada was locally organized and effective in its objectives and sustained itself for four years. Although coordinated with the Palestinian Liberation Organization (PLO), a representative of the Palestinian people in the diaspora, local forces took the lead in organizing the uprising.

Following the intifada, the PLO entered into talks with the Israeli government and international powers including the United States and European nations. From these negotiations, the Palestinian National Authority emerged as a governing entity, intended to facilitate the transformation of the occupied Palestinian territories into a viable state within five years. Considering the context in which the PA was created—one that featured a highly organized population with a robust civil society—it should have been the case that the PA would develop in a democratic and responsive manner in accordance with the society it governed. Indeed, the development of democracy was a key objective according to the PA's leadership and its international donors. As it turned out, however, the actual trajectory of the PA's political development drastically departed from this objective.

Over time, the PA grew more authoritarian and began to erode the democratic underpinnings of Palestinian society. For example, scholars have noted the effect that the PA had on civil society organizations: civil society organizations became less effective, more isolated, and reported lower levels of trust among members.[3] Throughout the 1990s, the PA served to coopt Palestinian institutions. Where cooptation did not work, the PA used repression. Palestinians began to recognize that the authoritarian nature of the new regime hindered their ability to mobilize.

When the five-year deadline for statehood passed, Palestinians launched a second intifada. This uprising was very different from the first in terms of character and outcomes: it was much less organized and achieved few of its political objectives. The disorganized nature of the second uprising also meant greater violence, as groups within Palestinian society found it harder to coordinate on common strategy and sanction spoilers.[4] The PA's authoritarian nature seemed to have widespread implications for how society functioned and the political stagnation that has characterized Palestinian society since 1994.

International patrons were heavily involved throughout this process. The EU, Israel, and the United States were all engaged in setting the parameters of development and imposing pressure when the PA attempted to stray from their objectives. For instance, when the Islamist party Hamas won a plurality in the legislative elections of 2006, the United States urged the outgoing party to launch a coup and prevented the democratically elected members from taking power.[5] The United States in particular was also heavily involved in funding the PA's security projects, and the EU provided technical support for the PA's bureaucracy. When international patrons did not get their way, sanctions would follow and the PA's funds would be withheld. In certain circumstances, Israel would intercede militarily and assassinate or imprison members of the PA's leadership. Over time, Palestinians have found themselves in a state of gridlock, as the PA's institutions have ceased to function as intended, and the grassroots organizations that once mobilized Palestinians have disappeared from the scene.

How did the PA demobilize society, when years of Israeli occupation had failed to do the same thing? I argue that the PA's repression is more effective and more damaging. The PA more successfully demobilized Palestinians because it is an indigenous authoritarian regime rather than an external occupier. Despite Israel's greater resources and international backing, the PA was able to utilize its ties within society and covert authoritarian strategies to accomplish what Israeli repression was unable to do: polarize and demobilize the Palestinian population.

Crucially, the PA developed in an authoritarian fashion largely as a result of international involvement. International involvement, led by the United States, encompassed a wide range of behavior including foreign aid and diplomatic pressure. This involvement created a disjuncture between the PA and Palestinian society. As a result, the Palestinian leadership was insulated from its domestic constituency, consumed with addressing international pressures rather than negotiating with Palestinian society. This insulation strengthened authoritarian practices. Not only did the role of international patrons become a polarizing issue among the public but so too did the practice of authoritarianism itself. My research demonstrates that certain authoritarian strategies used by the PA increased societal polarization. Rising polarization, in turn, affected a number of key outcomes, including patterns of mobilization and the capacity for collective action.

This dynamic is not unique to the PA. Across the Arab world, repressive regimes backed by international support have been able to polarize opposition forces and demobilize their societies. International involvement is a highly salient variable in the region. Where the interests of international patrons have been at odds with the interests of the domestic public, regimes deduce that accountability to their publics—or for certain segments of their publics—is no longer viable. Overall, international involvement that results in the insulation of the regime, thus facilitating the increased use of authoritarian practices, has profound societal consequences.

This project

This book seeks to examine the effect of repression on demobilization in societies characterized by high levels of international involvement. Specifically, I will delineate the types of authoritarian strategies that are effective and outline the causal mechanisms at work. This overarching goal has informed the project's research questions: (1) What demobilizes a once-mobilized society? And (2) How does international involvement amplify or suppress these dynamics? I use the context of the Palestinian case to illustrate and answer these questions as it allows us to examine how international involvement has affected state–society relations and long-term social cohesion. It also helps us appreciate how authoritarianism, assisted by international involvement, affects polarization and people's behaviors.

The PA as a case study is useful for a number of reasons. First, the PA's development has been overwhelmingly affected by external, mostly American, influence and involvement; thus, the international dimension is a highly salient factor. Second, the Palestinian territories provide an interesting case of a society that is no longer as highly mobilized as it once was, which offers an insight into the dynamics that have made this change possible. Most importantly, this case actually provides a unique opportunity to examine how a regime can restructure society from the *inception* of a state-building project, however flawed initially and despite its later failure. When discussing these processes in well-established states with entrenched regimes, it is often difficult to isolate the most important factors at work, and even more difficult to ascertain their individual effects. But, since the PA was created relatively recently, data on various aspects of its development are widely available.

Specifically, an examination of the PA's effect on Palestinian society serves as a heuristic case study, as it helps identify new causal paths and mechanisms regarding the effect of particular types of repression on demobilization.[6] By identifying the causal path, this case study can then be used to make inferences about similar cases in which the same patterns are discernible. This can serve as a building block for future studies on this topic and can help us re-examine many cases in a new light, particularly cases within the Middle East in which international involvement has played a key role in shaping regimes. Thus both the theory presented here and the findings of this research will be relevant to cases across the region while also providing context to those concerned with the condition of Palestinian society and its political development.

This research builds on the literature that examines international–domestic linkages and the consolidation of authoritarianism. However, it goes further in that it not only highlights the existence of this relationship but also deduces the long-term behavioral implications in the societies within these states. Thus the first contribution of this research is to explain how state–society relations function in highly "penetrated" environments and their impact on social cohesion and mobilization in the long term, with a focus on the micro-foundations of this dynamic.[7] Accordingly, this book will help contribute to our understanding of how particular forms of authoritarianism, assisted by international involvement, have an effect on polarization and subsequent political engagement.

It is of course well recognized that the PA is an atypical case, since it is not a full state. The "state-building" project encouraged by the international community following the Oslo Accords had other objectives, such as the outsourcing of Israeli repression, and has by all measures failed to establish an actual state. However, previous studies have found it useful to assess the PA within theories on authoritarian regimes and state–society dynamics since the Palestinian administration can be considered a "governing authority" for all intents and purposes in the areas it has agreed to govern—an authority that possesses coercive capacity over the people it governs.[8] Thus the case of the PA can certainly be used to build and assess theories in a way that generates generalizable knowledge.

This is not to imply that we should ignore the role of the Israeli occupation, however. On the contrary, as the upcoming chapters will show, the Israeli occupation plays a large role in the dynamics of international involvement and increased authoritarianism in the Palestinian territories. Where it is relevant, Israeli policies and repression are examined and analyzed. Nevertheless, the focus of this project is on the PA as an indigenous regime, rather than on the Israeli occupation. This is because people react very differently to an occupying power versus an indigenous authoritarian regime.

Before Oslo

Before delving into new research, it is important to contextualize the Palestinian dynamic by reviewing governance and social cohesion throughout the different periods of recent Palestinian history. This overview will include three main time periods: from 1967 to 1994, before the Oslo Accords; from 1995 to 2005, following the Oslo Accords; and from 2006 to the present day, following the consolidation of the PA.

Since the creation of Israel in 1948, Palestinians have lived a fractured existence, separated by a number of borders and governed by a variety of administrative entities. Palestinians who escaped the effects of the 1948 Nakba and remained inside the newfound State of Israel found themselves under military rule, with severely curtailed rights as second-class citizens of the new Jewish state. Palestinians who fled the 1948 attacks found themselves refugees spread over Syria, Lebanon, Jordan, Egypt, and Iraq, among many other places. Each refugee community adapted to its host country's regulations and particular societal dynamics, often with explosive results. Finally, Palestinians in the remainder of historic Palestine—the territories of the West Bank and Gaza—found themselves under Jordanian and Egyptian rule respectively. From 1948 to 1967, the territories developed on different tracks.

This all changed following the 1967 war, when a preemptive strike by Israel led to the destruction of the Egyptian Air Force and Arab armies found themselves in complete disarray. Israel then went on to occupy the Sinai Peninsula of Egypt, the Golan Heights of Syria, the Shebaa Farms of Lebanon, and most importantly for our purposes, the West Bank and Gaza. For Palestinians within the territories, the 1967 war had the odd effect of unifying their existence under a single administration—that of the Israeli military occupation. This was the time when settlements were introduced into the territories, their growth angering Palestinians whose lands were confiscated to house new settlements. Settlers were also often armed and supported by the Israeli army, thus causing greater amounts of violence. US–Israeli ties also deepened during the same period,[9] providing military and diplomatic support for Israeli policies in the occupied territories. However, US involvement in Palestinian politics was less relevant at this moment in time. The United States and its allies were instead heavily involved on the Israeli side of the equation, supporting Israeli crackdowns and incursions with increased military aid and arms sales.

Palestinians in the Israeli-occupied territories faced severe restrictions on their ability to organize politically. The Israelis banned the PLO, which had been founded in 1964 as a liberation movement, and Palestinians faced repeated cycles of repression when they attempted to coordinate in the pursuit of political ends. This included military detention, home demolitions, deportation, and extrajudicial killing if they were caught protesting. As a result, the PLO began operating mostly outside the occupied territories. Its leadership organized the diaspora refugee communities of Jordan, Lebanon, and other Arab states. Since the PLO's numerous factions operated predominantly in other countries, they became embroiled in regional politics and conflicts. Different factions within the PLO eventually received funding and support from various regional powers.[10] This created a certain level of division and ultimately resulted in the PLO's actions proving ineffective in the diaspora. At the same time, the Palestinians on the ground in the occupied territories were somewhat insulated from this dynamic. Although they attempted to coordinate to some degree with the PLO, that they were under a direct and highly repressive military occupation meant they had to rely on grassroots organizations, which may have shared affiliation with the PLO but were locally based and operated at a local level. This gave Palestinians in the territories some degree of independence, flexibility, and dynamism.

This independence allowed the Palestinians in the occupied territories to organize the first popular uprising, the intifada, with a high degree of coordination on objectives and tactics. The first intifada was sparked by years of repressive Israeli policies, including Yitzhak Rabin's "Iron Fist" policy, which created untenable living conditions for Palestinians.[11] When protests ignited spontaneously in the Gaza Strip following an attack by the Israel Defense Forces (IDF) in Jabalya refugee camp, the grassroots organizations within Palestinian society leapt into action by organizing a shared non-violent strategy of boycotts, strikes, and protests to pressure the Israeli occupation and hold it accountable on the international stage. There was a good deal of coordination between the different groups, and they shared the same preferences in terms of objectives and strategy.[12] Polarization was minimal: Palestinian politics at the time could not be characterized as having two main "camps" or some central division. Moreover, political leadership on the ground was highly responsive. Leadership often reacted to popular pressure in order to achieve a high degree of participation in the activities of their groups.

The various grassroots organizations formed the Unified National Leadership of the Uprising (UNLU), which was responsible for coordinating the intifada for the years that it lasted. UNLU emerged with the support and involvement of Fatah, the Popular Front, the Democratic Front, and the Palestinian Communist Party.[13] At the time, these were the major political parties at work in the occupied territories, and it is significant that they were all represented within the UNLU. The high levels of cohesion meant that, for most of the intifada, those who took part in the uprising adhered to the principles set forth by UNLU. Fragmentation, and the growing power of Islamist resistant groups, did not occur until the main thrust of the uprising came to an end after 1991.

After Oslo

In 1994, these dynamics shifted. That year, the Oslo Accords were signed between the PLO and the State of Israel in order to begin the process of providing statehood for Palestinians in the West Bank and Gaza. Although international powers had been involved in the Palestinian–Israeli conflict before 1994, the level of international involvement in internal Palestinian dynamics and politics increased markedly after the creation of the PA. The intention behind the PA was that it would control particular areas of the West Bank and Gaza and prepare the groundwork for a full takeover of these territories in 1999. The territories were divided into Areas A, B, and C, with the PA exercising the greatest autonomy over Area A, sharing jurisdiction with the Israeli government in Area B, and having no control over Area C. The issue of Jerusalem was left for negotiations at a later date. In the meantime, Israel divided the areas of Jerusalem into J1 and J2, with J1 areas under the direct control of the Israeli Jerusalem municipality. Today, most Palestinians (55 percent of the population) live in Area A, although it contains only 18 percent of the territory. Comparatively, 41 percent of Palestinians live in Area B (20 percent of the territory), and approximately 1 percent of Palestinians live in Area C (62 percent of the territory). This excludes residents of East Jerusalem.[14]

Following the Oslo Accords, the PA's institutions grew and took over the public sphere, making the grassroots organizations that had existed before the

PA's creation increasingly irrelevant. Members of the PLO returned to Palestine for the first time in decades and took part in the state-building project by serving as bureaucrats and administrators. Tensions arose between the returnees and the local leadership to some degree, as many noted administrative positions and salaries, as well as access to economic opportunities, were distributed based on personal connections rather than merit.[15] Nevertheless, the PA's new political class used the aid and directives coming from external powers, particularly the United States and the EU, to begin building state infrastructure immediately.

Throughout this early stage of development, international patrons provided aid and training to the PA across a wide array of institutions, including security forces, economic initiatives, and infrastructure development. In fact, as multiple sources involved in the negotiations and ensuing aid packages note, aid was seen as crucial to developing public support for the institution of the PA and the peace process. But, although economic growth took place to some degree, the underlying issues facing Palestinians worsened. The occupation continued to have a huge effect on living conditions and the human rights of Palestinians, but none of the international aid provided to the PA did anything to resolve that reality.

Instead, US and European aid served to stall political development and perpetuate particular internal conflicts. Some scholars note that the PA during this time had a negative effect on civil society, stunting its growth.[16] This came not only as a result of the PA's heavy-handed, often repressive relationship with dissenting voices but also because conditional foreign aid served to empower particular groups in society over others.[17] Dissident voices, or groups that took a critical position on the Oslo Accords and state-building process, were often ineligible to receive foreign aid or PA support. Groups that wanted to benefit from this largesse had to reorient their goals and criticisms in order to better suit international patrons. The critical role of civil society was thus neutralized during this time period.

The administration of Yasser Arafat, the PA's president at this time, also utilized the state-building project to build patronage networks within Palestinian society. This was a way in which the PA could incorporate societal support for the state-building project as well as neutralize possible opposition. As a result, employment through the PA became a primary source of income for a large segment of the Palestinian population. Arafat was also the head of Fatah, a secular center-right party in Palestinian politics. Fatah had always dominated the Palestinian political scene, but during this time it consolidated its control over the PA's institutions as well.

Although foreign patrons worked with the PA to set up institutions in conjunction with the goals of the Oslo Accords, there was some degree of tension between Arafat and the United States.[18] The United States complained of the lack of professionalization in PA institutions and noted that Arafat would often support or at least tolerate resistance against Israeli incursions and attacks. The Palestinian political leaders involved with the PA during this time period note that Arafat was a pragmatist: he viewed the Oslo Accords and the ensuing state-building project as merely one tool or pathway among a variety of other tools available to the PLO. If the objectives of the Oslo Accords and the state-building project did not achieve gains for Palestinian liberation, he was not necessarily committed to pursuing them further. As such, he tolerated Islamist organizing during this time and did not eschew armed resistance against Israel when conflict arose. Thus, during Arafat's reign, US pressure was constant and often antagonistic. The United States and its allies threatened to cut off aid whenever Arafat proceeded in a direction they disagreed with, and Arafat often had little room to maneuver.

Donors, and the United States in particular, emphasized a "good governance" framework in a way that was incompatible with Palestine's economic and political conditions. As Mushtaq Husain Khan argues, "viable" states with functioning economics are a precursor to democracy and accountability.[19] However, the nature of the Oslo Accords and its economic equivalent—the Paris Protocol—meant that the PA was almost entirely constrained in its ability to build a functioning state economy. Indeed, it seemed the Oslo Accords were intended by design to manifest a Palestine that was underdeveloped and dependent on Israel. As such, Palestine's situation vis-à-vis Israel can be described as "asymmetric containment," meaning Israel ensured its security by making sure Palestine was kept controlled and vulnerable.[20] In such an environment, Khan notes, it is easier to understand why Palestinian elites were more likely to pursue "short-term predation" rather than long-term interests. Thus, as Anne Le More succinctly argues, the situation in Palestine before the second intifada cannot be blamed on any single Palestinian actor.[21] To argue that Arafat was to blame for economic and political outcomes—such as corruption or an increasingly powerful executive—would be to ignore that these outcomes were inevitable given the way the Oslo Accords were designed.[22]

Palestinian statehood was meant to be declared in 1999, but the deadline came and went with no Palestinian state in sight. Palestinians continued to suffer under direct occupation—even Area A, supposedly under PA jurisdiction, often faced Israeli incursions. Increased military activity frequently went hand-in-hand with increased settlement activity and provocations. Arafat's administration had to find some solution to this situation. Thus, the Palestinian leadership attempted negotiations with its Israeli counterparts at Camp David in July 2000 under the auspices of US mediation. But these negotiations failed. Scholars argue that the Oslo Accords deferred discussion on key issues on which Palestinians and Israelis held incompatible views.[23] As a result, when the time came to have these final negotiations, the Oslo Accords fell apart. The PA could not declare Palestinian statehood, and Arafat had to face growing opposition at home. Even PLO factions under Fatah control were quickly splintering off.

This anger over deferred statehood led to the second intifada. Not only were conditions for Palestinians not improving but Israeli politics had shifted markedly to the right as a result of elections that brought Ariel Sharon to power. Sharon was more hardline and right wing than his predecessor Ehud Barak. He supported the growth of settlements and launched a number of provocative actions such as invading the Al-Aqsa mosque during prayer time.[24] Coupled with IDF attacks in Gaza, these provocations led to an outpouring of protest and violence in what we now call the second intifada.

The second intifada was markedly different from the first in that there was no unified leadership, and grassroots organizations did not direct strategy as they had in the past.[25] Palestinian groups engaged in violent tactics, and even parts of the PA, such as the police in certain areas, splintered off and actively resisted the Israeli occupation. Fatah's militant wing did the same. Although Arafat did not direct the intifada, he did not call for its end. Foreign patrons, particularly the United States, criticized Arafat's tacit support of the protests. When Arafat was attacked militarily by the Israeli army, and put under siege in his compound in Ramallah, the United States immediately began looking for alternatives within Arafat's circle to push to power after his death.[26] In doing so, the United States became embroiled in internal Palestinian politics, supporting particular political figures and refusing to engage with Palestinian demands even if it meant intifada eruptions or a president under siege for years. Arafat remained under siege in his compound until his death in 2004.

The second intifada gradually tapered off with very little political gain for the Palestinian people. Mahmoud Abbas, a Fatah party member with US support, came to power following Arafat's death. Given the breakdown of PA institutions during the intifada, with some Palestinian security forces taking up arms against the Israeli army, international donors were keen on "professionalizing" the PA to avoid such an occurrence in the future. The days of

Arafat's pragmatism, and view of the PA as a means to an end, would soon be over. As such, the PA's institutions underwent a structural shift from 2005 to 2009, particularly with the appointment of Salam Fayyad to the position of prime minister in 2007.

Fayyad was an American-educated economist, with credentials and an outlook that won the support of international donors.[27] He focused on "professionalizing" the PA (i.e. purging the PA's institutions of overly political or critical voices). Palestinian scholars often argue that this professionalization essentially "de-politicized" the Palestinian public.[28] Fayyad also undertook extensive security-sector reform with US support and training. This resulted in the dismantling of militant groups, particularly those affiliated with Fatah, as ex-militants were incorporated into the PA's patronage networks.[29] And finally, Fayyad purported to focus on economic growth by developing investment opportunities such as the new city of Rawabi in the West Bank, as well as facilitating loan programs for the Palestinian middle class.[30]

The Palestinian territories today

The "professionalization" of the PA and Fayyad's overall reforms help to explain the stagnation of the Palestinian state-building project we see today. Fayyad's reforms on the economic front were criticized as misguided given that the Israeli government would often withhold critical payments to the PA and cause financial crises.[31] In such a context, economic investment was unlikely to succeed. The issues plaguing Palestinians were also not easily resolved by focusing energy on the availability of bank loans or investment opportunities in new expat cities. Settlements continued to expand into areas of the future Palestinian state, and the occupation continued to restrict Palestinian freedoms. In short, the political aspirations of the Palestinian people were put on hold with band aid economic solutions—solutions that eventually amounted to very little.

Under Abbas, the PA consolidated its control over Palestinian politics and society with increasingly repressive tactics. Palestinians are now more dependent than ever on PA salaries and services. Even segments of society that had traditionally opposed the state-building project have been silenced, either by cooptation into the PA's patronage networks or through direct repression. Specifically, Abbas's brand of authoritarianism is "based on networks of business and technocratic elite," underscored by "centralized control over the security branch" and a high degree of coordination with the Israeli government.[32] As such, Palestinian elites are interested in stability and fear political change that may affect their role in the status quo. Concurrently, Israeli governments have become increasingly right wing and intransigent, and fruitful negotiations that attempt to go beyond the status quo have seemed less possible as a result. Throughout this process, international patrons and the United States in particular supported Abbas's authority.

Following the second intifada, the United States and its allies ratcheted up their involvement in a partisan way by first demanding legislative elections in 2006 and then moving to isolate the Islamist opposition party Hamas after its victory. In this manner, the United States and its allies essentially strengthened Abbas's party internally while weakening the opposition. The Palestine Paper leaks following the episode confirmed that the US and UK intelligence services had already planned to support a crackdown on Islamist opposition movements prior to any election victory.[33] The main Islamist party, Hamas, had gained traction in the Palestinian territories mostly in reaction to the PA's disappointing policies. Hamas's insistence on the right to resist the Israeli occupation, as well as its refusal to accept a two-state solution, meant it posed a risk to continued Israeli control over the occupied territories. Thus the United States and its allies supported a crackdown on the Islamist party despite it winning fair and free elections and pledging moderation. It is important to note that the United States supported the crackdown in the West Bank because it saw political repression as a means of increasing security and assuaging Israeli demands for an end to resistance.

Over time, US involvement created "camps" in Palestinian politics: the pro-Oslo Accords and security coordination camp allied with the United States, and the anti-status quo opposition camp. Political groups across the political spectrum once worked together during the first intifada. And before the complete restructuring of the PA in 2007, there were tacit agreements between the PA and Islamist opposition in times of crisis, and therefore coordination to some degree. Since 2007, however, political elites from different parts of the political spectrum have instead been completely at odds. They have expended large amounts of energy and time in conflict with each other rather than in coordination around issues related to the Israeli occupation.[34]

Furthermore, it is clear from the increased political repression in Palestinian territories that US involvement has created a situation in which political elites feel increasingly unaccountable to public opinion. First, with US support, Abbas has been allowed to overstay his term limits. Moreover, the Palestinian National Council, a representative legislative body that acts as a check on the executive committee of the PLO, has not convened since 1996, and PA officials have made no move to rectify this situation. Specific institutions within the PLO's structure intended to maintain accountability are now generally defunct. At the same time, American "technical assistance" in the security-sector reform process has helped to facilitate two trends: first, increasing coordination between the PA and Israel and, second, increasing authoritarian conditions and political repression within the Palestinian political landscape in service of that goal.

To facilitate increased security coordination, the PA spends a full third of its budget on its security apparatus and employs over 80,000 people.[35] To put this in comparison, there is one security/police officer for every forty-eight Palestinians, whereas there is one officer for every 384 Americans. As another, more shocking point of comparison, East Germany, considered the quintessential police state, had only one police officer or employed informant per sixty-six East Germans.[36] Many Palestinians today complain about the "police state" conditions in the West Bank specifically, as journalists, students, and dissidents are targeted and repressed.[37]

Moreover, when PA officials are asked about governance in the territories today, answers are often in support of repression. For instance, PA officials interviewed by the author would often claim that Hamas and other opposition groups are foreign implants or traitors.[38] "There is a difference between democracy and making trouble," one official said, implying that the repression activists faced was well deserved.[39] Many other officials concurred with this statement and went further to say Palestinians were unfit for democracy; therefore it was in the best interest of Palestinians to remove Hamas from power. Finally, every PA official interviewed confirmed that they had to acquiesce to US policy preferences, which were often in support of these types of crackdowns. Thus it becomes clear from these statements the involvement of international powers bred authoritarian conditions to some degree, by both openly supporting crackdowns or creating the conditions by which one group is strengthened at the expense of the other. And even though reconciliation between Hamas and Fatah may be in the works at the time of this writing in 2019, these conflicts linger and are in no way resolved.

Chapter outlines

This brief overview of recent Palestinian history has highlighted the role of international involvement in increasing authoritarianism and weakening societal cohesion and mobilization in Palestinian society. This project argues that these processes are linked, and Chapter 1 outlines a theory through which to understand the mechanisms and dynamics at work. Chapter 1 will situate the theory within the literatures on international involvement, repression, and mobilization, as well as deduce the main empirical implications of this research. These empirical implications will be the focus of this study. This chapter is particularly useful to readers from political science interested in the theoretical debates that this book addresses.

The remaining chapters address the empirical implications and are of interest to a political science audience as well as those interested in the Palestinian issue more generally. In the second chapter, entitled "Americans Have Taught Us: There Is a Difference between Democracy and Creating Problems," I answer the following question: What effect does international involvement have on the preferences of the Palestinian leadership versus the preferences of the Palestinian public? In answering this question, I present evidence for the first argument of this book: that international involvement has had an impact on how the PA functions *as well as* the PA's relationship to society. In particular, I provide empirical confirmation that international involvement creates a divergence between political elites and the societies they purport to present. I utilize a mixed-method approach to assess this question. First, I analyze interviews with political elites, working within the regime and thus directly targeted by many forms of international involvement. I provide evidence of how elites do not prefer democracy and accountability, and that their positions are at odds with public opinion on the subject. To address the public opinion component, this chapter also utilizes a nationally representative survey with an experimental component. I provide empirical evidence of how international involvement may affect domestic preferences conditionally, depending on where individuals place themselves in relation to the regime. I also provide evidence of a divergence in preferences across the elite–public line as a result of international involvement. The chapter concludes with the implications of this finding: that international involvement has caused the PA to develop in an authoritarian manner given the way in which its political leadership has become insulated from public opinion.

In the third chapter, entitled "The Legacy of Repression," I turn to the main focus of this book: the effect of the PA's growing authoritarianism on Palestinian society. Specifically, I ask: What is the effect of the PA's authoritarian strategies on polarization within society? And how does such polarization affect collective action? I present evidence for a two-stage theory of authoritarianism and its effect on societal outcomes, arguing that (1) PA authoritarianism generated polarization, and (2) that this polarization has subsequently affected social cohesion and capacity for collective action. I provide evidence for this argument by utilizing experiments conducted in the Palestinian territories at Birzeit University. I couple this data with qualitative evidence including interviews with activists in the West Bank from across the political spectrum, as well as a case study of Islamist opposition groups from 1994 until the present day. Using both types of data is useful because experimental methods isolate the causal impact of particular variables, and the qualitative evidence helps to outline the causal mechanisms at work in this particular case.

The results of Chapter 3 confirm the theory that the PA's authoritarian strategies exacerbate polarization within society. This polarization in turn affects the ability and willingness of different segments to coordinate on a common task. In particular, "exclusionary" repressive strategies generate greater levels of polarization than "inclusionary" cooptation strategies. Moreover, the qualitative evidence shows that Islamists, one of the more repressed political factions in the West Bank, are much more insular and less willing to cooperate with others.

In the fourth chapter, "Demobilizing a Mobilized Society," I provide further evidence of the dynamic highlighted above. Specifically, I use this chapter to outline the impact of PA authoritarianism on political mobilization. I focus on protests in the West Bank using an original dataset on daily protests at the neighborhood and village level. I also capitalize on the variation in control of the PA over the Palestinian territories, since the PA's level of control varies based on the Oslo II/Interim Agreements of 1995. This variation, over a homogeneous population, makes it possible to isolate the effect of the PA's authoritarianism on mobilization patterns. I couple the quantitative data analysis with a qualitative assessment of the protest movements before and after Oslo. I find that mobilization has declined systematically in places where the PA has more direct control, even though Palestinians in those areas are more densely populated and have greater access to resources. Counterintuitively, political mobilization today is actually more prevalent in areas under direct Israeli occupation, despite Israeli repression. The findings suggest the PA has a direct role in this dynamic as a result of its authoritarian practices. Overall, the chapter helps demonstrate how authoritarian strategies have inhibited social cohesion and led to a decreased capacity for mobilization.

Finally, in the fifth chapter, I apply the results of my assessment to two additional cases. This chapter, entitled "The Effect of International Involvement across the State Sovereignty Spectrum," demonstrates the generalizability of the overall theory of international involvement and its societal effects. I look at the case of Iraqi Kurdistan and Bahrain, both of which lie further on the spectrum of state sovereignty. I look at the role of international involvement, particularly American involvement, in the development and trajectories of these additional cases and provide evidence of the theory's empirical implications outside of Palestine.

In the conclusion, I briefly summarize the findings and outline the contributions of this research to the study of international–domestic linkages and authoritarianism more broadly. I will also address opportunities for future research on the subject. Finally, I will provide some analysis and predictions for the future of the Palestinian cause.

1

A THEORY OF INTERNATIONAL INVOLVEMENT AND ITS SOCIETAL EFFECTS

An introduction to the research

As we saw in the introduction, this book looks at the effect of externally backed authoritarianism on demobilization processes and particularly the impact of externally backed repression on social cohesion and mobilization. This helps to explain how the PA, supported by the United States and other patrons, succeeded in demobilizing Palestinian society in a way Israel was never able. This is despite the fact that Israel was also the recipient of extensive American backing. The difference, I argue, lies in the type of repression at work.

To address the many literatures that speak to this topic in an ordered manner, I will break down the various relationships embedded in the dynamic between international involvement, authoritarianism, and demobilization by moving from micro-level implications to macro-level implications. Thus, I will begin with the main topic of this book: a review of the research on mobilization and how it is affected by authoritarianism and different types of repression. I will then add the discussion of the international dimension and how international involvement or penetration has an impact on authoritarian practices as well as, subsequently, societal-level dynamics.

Why do societies mobilize, and what affects their success?

For the purposes of this study, mobilization can be defined as individuals challenging political authorities by engaging in political action through a variety of methods. The most visible form of mobilization is the protest. Demobilization, on the other hand, is here defined as "official termination or significant alteration of the formal institution engaged in challenging authorities; departure of individuals from relevant organizations; termination of or significant reduction in dissident behaviors; or a fundamental shift in the ideas of the challenger away from what was earlier established."[1] However, before we can understand how society becomes demobilized, it is important to review the literature on why people engage in political action in the first place.

The political science literature provides a wide range of explanations for why people mobilize or engage in political action (either violent or non-violent). Many of these explanations fall into the realm of rational choice in that they presume individuals engage in political action after a cost–benefit analysis. For instance, some argue that people might mobilize and engage in political action as a result of selective incentives. This concept suggests that individuals must gain some private benefit from their participation; consequently, the implication is that the group benefit is not enough to facilitate participation.[2] This implies that explanations for mobilization essentially boil down to whether the benefits outweigh the costs for each individual, and that other motivations—ethnic tension, emotions, and so on—are to some degree epiphenomenal.

Another vein of literature focuses on the concept of grievance, or the idea that people mobilize in response to frustrations with the status quo. One such explanation is the idea of "relative deprivation." The argument with this theory is that individuals with high expectations that are not met by their current political contexts are more frustrated, which leads them to be the likely participants of mobilization. A corollary to this general argument is that those with higher levels of education and low achievement are likely to fit this description.[3] The relative deprivation literature thus again focuses on individual, psychological explanations for mobilization.

However, scholars have noted that while relative deprivation theory perhaps explains psychological motivations for mobilization, it may not capture the whole story. In particular, it does not address the structural conditions in which these individuals live and the strategies available to them. For that reason, scholars have developed theories of "resource mobilization."[4] This cluster of work argues that grievances are not a necessary or a sufficient condition for social movements of any form. Rather, the availability of individuals with resources—time, money, labor—was a much more salient determinant. Access to institutions/centers of power, media, information, money, and elite structures is crucial to the emergence of mobilization.[5] Education in particular leads to greater access to these resources, as well as fostering a sense of national interest, civic duty, and providing greater organizational capacity.[6] Material conditions are key to such explanations, though again they fall into the cost–benefit analysis framework.

For the authoritarian context specifically, the literature often assumes that the sheer threat of force and/or the denial of clientelistic benefits (i.e. material costs at the individual level) are enough to limit political mobilization that may challenge the regime. For example, Amaney Jamal discusses the manner in which civil society organizations became polarized, and then supportive of the PA's authoritarian regime, as a result of clientelistic benefits.[7] The failure of social movements and collective action has also often been attributed to contexts of extreme repression, because such a context has an impact on the cost–benefit analysis at the individual level.[8]

However, in order to be the case, this would mean that significant political mobilization will only occur in cases where exogenous shocks limit the state's capacity for repression, or structural conditions change in such a way as to weaken the ability of the regime to coopt.[9] While this may be true to some degree, explanations that focus on proximate costs of mobilization can only adequately explain a limited subset of cases. They do not illuminate, for example, the conditions that make mobilization possible *despite* these proximate costs.[10]

The reason these explanations remain incomplete is precisely because they rely on proximate costs, at the individual level. But, as the historical record shows, repression or cooption alone cannot control political mobilization entirely. Additionally, the effect of such proximate strategies is not necessarily clear: certain studies have shown that repression, for example, may in fact backfire and increase political mobilization.[11] Other studies have shown that, with particularly strong social ties, groups can even overcome severe repression despite the high cost it imposes.[12] Thus what is missing from these explana-tions is an understanding of how regimes control or limit political mobiliza-tion not just by increasing *individual* costs but by fundamentally altering interactions at a societal level.[13]

The social movements literature has provided some insight on the dynamics of successful political mobilization. Success has been attributed to the "struc-ture" of political opportunities or constraints, the opportunity costs of rebel-lion at the individual level, the forms of organization available to citizens, as well as the processes that "frame" issues and turn opportunity into action.[14] Finally, the threat of community sanctions can push individuals both to participate and cooperate in pursuit of a larger goal.[15] Alternatively, where social networks have become weak and communities have become more fragmented and polarized, these sanctions are no longer credible from the community at large. Overall, as Hahrie Han notes, "motivation to act … is not formed in isolation; instead, it is the product of myriad social interactions."[16] As such, the role of social cohesion, and not just individual considerations, may also be crucial in determining the scope and effectiveness of mobilization.

I define social cohesion as a sense of "collective purpose."[17] I disaggregate that concept to mean the capacity for collective action and intergroup cooperation between different segments of society, fueled by shared preferences. I argue that without understanding the role of social cohesion, our explanations cannot account for the conditions under which societies with high levels of political mobilization may become *de*mobilized. And this is important to consider because, as Ruud Koopmans notes, while much has been written about social movements, an "explanation of protest decline is perhaps the weakest chain in social movement theory and research."[18]

Polarization and demobilization

Demobilization has been studied to some degree, with two main schools of explanation: those that focus on internal dynamics of groups, and those that focus on external dynamics and their effect on groups. Internal dynamics include polarization, fragmentation, lack of trust, and fatigue. External dynamics include the impact of different forms of repression, which can be categorized as either covert or overt.[19] Repression can include strategies such as resource deprivation, problem depletion (i.e. convincing the audience of a social movement through propaganda that their existence is irrelevant), and outwitting. These techniques that "kill from the outside" are often effective alone, but they can also have an effect on the internal dynamics and trust levels within social movement organizations. This can lead to dynamics that kill a social movement "from the inside." According to Christian Davenport, these dynamics can include "burnout, factionalization and polarization, lost commitment, membership loss, and rigidity."[20]

Davenport argues that democracies rely more regularly on covert rather than overt repression, unlike authoritarian regimes. This is because authoritarian regimes can utilize overt repression to a greater degree, including strategies such as "overwhelming" organizations with brute force. Importantly, because Davenport examines both internal and external dynamics, his greatest contribution is linking both internal and external sources of failure within social movements in his explanation of demobilization.

For our purposes, Davenport's focus on the role of polarization in demobilizing groups is crucial. He writes: "we know very little about factionalization, how it develops, and what factors are associated with it."[21] Indeed, scholars have long pointed to polarization as one of the key mechanisms that facilitates demobilization. Eric Hirsch notes that

> polarization is often seen as a problem since it convinces each side that their position is right and the opponent's is wrong; this makes compromise and negotiation less likely ... Since it leads each side to develop the independent goal of harming the opponent, movement participants may lose sight of the original goal.[22]

I define polarization at the societal level by three main characteristics. First, each group should be homogenous internally along some lines (i.e. ethnically or ideologically). Second, there should be a high degree of heterogeneity across groups. Finally, the number of groups is often small, as the most polarized societies frequently have only two main groups bifurcating the public sphere.[23]

The reason polarization is key to our understanding of the Palestinian case, and this argument, is that it has profound and long-term effects on societal dynamics and development. Hyper-polarized societies function differently from more moderate societies.[24] This is especially true in the context of authoritarianism: where societies are highly polarized, effective challenges to the regime become less likely. It is for that reason that authoritarian regimes often capitalize on these divisions in order to maintain control more effectively.

But polarization is just one mechanism, among a large number, that Davenport explores. Thus, while his work is invaluable for outlining the various external and internal pressures that social movement organizations face, he does not delve into great detail on each of these mechanisms. His assessment is that polarization is one of many factors, and his work does not elucidate the causal impact of polarization specifically, or what leads to polarization independently of other concurrent effects and aside from the mixture of overt and covert repression that any government might engage in at some point. He also examines polarization among social movement organizations in a very specific context (i.e. the United States in the 1960s and 1970s). Much of his theoretical analysis stems from the unique experience of the cases he examines, as social movement organizations operating in a moderately democratic context.

Overall, while the mobilization literature offers a basis for understanding the dynamics of successful collective action or successful demobilization, it has been criticized for its broad assertions and lack of falsifiability. The theories discussed within this literature attempt to combine structural conditions with micro-level decision-making, as well as external and internal dynamics as in the case of Davenport, but often include an excess of possibly relevant variables, as a result of which they often arrive at highly contingent explanations. There is less of a focus on identifying the variables that act as mechanisms, the relevant antecedent conditions, and which variables are merely confounders. Moreover, the causal impact of different varieties of repression, which have an effect on polarization and fragmentation, is not fully explored in this literature.

The impact of authoritarianism on society

Authoritarian regimes have a pressing need to control or repress any significant mobilization. Obviously, authoritarian regimes vary in their *degree* of authoritarianism, but the strategies they use are quite similar.[25] All authoritarian regimes utilize some mixture of cooptation and repression to achieve their objectives. In "softer" authoritarian regimes, cooption may be used to a larger degree than repression, in the form of large ruling parties, extensive patronage networks, and other related methods.[26] Some less developed or more violent authoritarian regimes often do not have these institutions at their disposal and so more readily rely on their repressive capacity to inhibit mobilization and engagement.[27]

Authoritarian regimes must engage in processes of consolidation in order to be durable. Consolidation is defined as "a deliberate state project to improve a regime's capabilities for governing society."[28] In other words, consolidation is the process through which the threat of regime breakdown is weakened by "establishing the conditions that make persistence likely" with the use of self-reinforcing mechanisms.[29] Consolidation also refers to an *increase* or *improvement* in the regime's capacity for control over a variety of realms (territory, opposition, population, etc.), rather than just persistence.[30] Consolidation does not assume regimes are immune to collapse: exogenous factors may always shift and play a role in weakening regimes. Consolidation simply means, holding all else equal, that persistence becomes more likely given increased control over internal dynamics.

The mechanisms of authoritarian consolidation are important to consider if we are to understand the manner in which these regimes become robust, as well as the long-term effects of such robustness on the societies they govern.[31] These include cooptation of possible opposition, controlling individuals and organizations through coercive force, and directing the political mobilization of the masses.[32]

One crucial mechanism in authoritarian consolidation is cooption of elites and the creation of a ruling coalition. Milan Svolik defines this process as "authoritarian power-sharing."[33] To establish a mostly uncontested authoritarian regime, robust institutions must be created to channel elite pressure in a way that does not challenge the regime overall. Alternatively, a contested autocracy does not feature these types of safeguards. Thus one must examine the process by which a ruling coalition is created, with particular focus on which groups in society are included, in order to understand the dynamics of authoritarian consolidation. This book argues that one such factor that may affect which groups are included in the regime's coalition, and in what manner, is the role of international involvement.

The second mechanism important to authoritarian consolidation is the establishment of control over society. Previous literature has examined the success and failure of "authoritarian control," but only in relation to the coercive apparatus of the regime. For example, in situations where the coercive apparatus begins to pose a threat to the regime itself, authoritarian control is considered to be failing.[34] In situations where the regime has subordinated its coercive apparatus, authoritarian control is said to have succeeded. However, it is not only the coercive apparatus of the regime that needs to be controlled; society itself poses a threat to the regime if not adequately managed. These attempts at societal control may have a profound impact on how societies organize and how segments of society relate to each other, as the coming chapters will show. And, as the next section will discuss, exogenous factors may affect how authoritarian regimes engage in these strategies—exogenous factors such as forms of international intervention.

International involvement and authoritarianism

This book argues that international involvement has an effect on how authoritarianism is practiced in certain states, as well as a regime's subsequent attempts to control society. I outline the literatures on the impact of international involvement in the sections below.

International–domestic linkages

The strategic choice approach in the international relations literature has facilitated a serious rethinking of international and domestic linkages.[35] One of the main assumptions of this approach is that strategic interactions at one level translate to another in a coherent fashion. This means that in order to understand certain domestic level dynamics, researchers ought to examine how the international dimension affects outcomes.[36] This is also in line with the "second-image reversed" concept, whereby the international sphere may affect domestic level outcomes.[37] The strategic choice approach further builds on this insight because it entails a disaggregation of certain environments (e.g. disaggregating the state level to examine both regime and societal interactions).[38]

Similar developments have also occurred in the field of comparative politics. For instance, Robert Putnam argues that domestic (regime) actors often play a "two stage game" in which they seek to account for both public and international pressures.[39] Building on this insight, comparative politics scholars have highlighted the effects of international involvement on a number of issues: democratization,[40] diffusion of liberal policies,[41] and human rights issues.[42] International involvement here means a range of state behavior, including foreign aid, diplomatic pressure, and sometimes direct military intervention.

In the study of the Arab world in particular, scholars have noted how international involvement helps to stall democracy under certain conditions[43] or affects public opinion during elections.[44] Some research has also alluded to the idea that the impact of international involvement is key to understanding certain social outcomes. For instance, scholars have pointed out that international involvement can have an impact on political engagement, particularly mobilization, in the domestic sphere.[45] It can help determine the type of mobilization that becomes prevalent at the domestic level, as well as the efficacy of said mobilization.[46] But the literature that exists on the societal effects of international involvement remains to be unpacked, both theoretically and in terms of empirical testing. How does international involvement affect regime behavior and subsequent societal dynamics? How are state–society relations affected in "penetrated" societies?[47] Such a research frontier, especially in the context of the Middle East, will help refine existing theories of international–domestic linkages by further disaggregating the domestic arena.[48]

International involvement and preference formation

As the previous section shows, the literature broadly agrees that international involvement affects regime dynamics, but the effects on regime versus societal-level dynamics are not synonymous. I define involvement as the way in which a powerful state imposes a hierarchical relationship with another, less powerful, client state.[49] By imposing this hierarchy, the powerful state becomes an important actor in the decision-making processes of the client state's regime. This involvement can be "democratizing," in the sense that it influences certain regimes to liberalize and become more accountable. It may be ambivalent, especially if the penetrated state is not a significant priority for the external power. Or, it may be "autocratizing," in the sense that it consolidates the client state's power and insulates it from domestic pressures.[50]

Research shows that international involvement can change the preferences of regimes in a variety of ways. Martha Finnemore, for instance, illustrates the ways that international "society" can affect national interests through the proliferation of certain norms.[51] More recently, Susan Hyde has demonstrated that election monitoring in authoritarian or semi-democratic states changes regime behavior, on the margins.[52] Election monitoring in this case has a distinct effect on regime behavior and induces greater compliance. Other examples include state entry/compliance with the Convention against Torture or the International Criminal Court (ICC).[53] Becoming a member of the ICC, for example, can lead states to "credibly commit" and take tentative steps toward reducing violence. On the other hand, ratification of the Convention against Torture can be a small way to cede to domestic opponents while still maintaining a certain level of repression. Overall, what these studies show is that international involvement can clearly change regime preferences and behavior at the domestic level, even if not always in the direction that is expected.

International involvement can also change preferences at the public level. Research on political motivations and beliefs has shown that preferences do not arise only from internal, mental calculations. Preferences can also emerge from changes in the environment around an individual, and subsequent changes to that individual's preference structure.[54] In terms of the political environment, this logically includes changes to the domestic political context as a result of international involvement.

Previous research has shown, for example, that preferences for democracy can be informed by the role of international involvement. In the case of "democratizing" involvement, through the use of foreign aid and democracy promotion programs targeted at civil society, research has found that publics become more amenable to democracy over time.[55] On the other hand, when the role of international involvement is "autocratizing" in the sense that international patrons overturn democratic elections or enforce penalties, publics may become more anti-democratic and prefer stability to democracy.[56] Other research on specific types of involvement has found that the endorsements of international powers during elections can polarize society based on their aversion to the endorser.[57] In such surveys on the subject, pre-existing cleavages within society determined opposition or support of the international power. Some behavioral research has also reached the same conclusions.[58] Therefore, international involvement may act as a moderating factor on the preferences of domestic publics, especially in cases where such involvement is made more salient and direct.

Principal–agent framework

The effect of international involvement on elite–public dynamics can be best characterized using the principal–agent framework. Scholars have previously argued that international patrons can disrupt the "feedback loop" between the domestic regime and society. Domestic regimes begin to answer to patron interests rather than societal pressures. International involvement thus causes a principal–agent problem, and a divergence in the interests of elites/regime participants (agent), and the society they purport to represent (principal). A principal is defined by the ability to both grant and revoke authority to and from the agent.

The principal–agent dynamic creates both moral hazard and adverse selection problems as a result of incomplete information. Moral hazard problems arise when the agent pursues goals that are not in line with a principal's preferences. Adverse selection, on the other hand, is when the agent uses information unavailable to the principal in order to pursue goals adverse to the principal's interests. But the traditional principal–agent dynamic is not always the most accurate model of certain relationships on the international stage. In the case of international patrons and societal pressures on a single agent (i.e. the regime), we have a dynamic of "multiple principals."

In this particular case, the principals include both international patrons and society. International patrons can withdraw support for domestic regimes (financial or otherwise), impose sanctions, and take military action. Society can take advantage of institutions to vote agents in and out of power, or use the threat of mass mobilization to grant/revoke authority. These varying dynamics create a situation of multiple principals, divide society into different groups, and affect society's relationship to political elites—as we shall see in Chapter 2.

The effects of American involvement

This book focuses on American involvement as the most salient form of international involvement in the Middle East and Palestine specifically. Although many countries are heavily involved with one another, and linkages between them can be highly important, the United States in particular poses a different caliber of international involvement altogether. The role and breadth of US involvement is wholly different from the involvement of other nations—even including regional hegemons.

First, the United States is an international hegemon, to the point that many scholars define the United States as a unipolar power, or an empire.[59] Without delving too deeply into the nuances of these definitions, it becomes clear from such work that scholars recognize the very different role the United States plays in the political trajectories of other nations. The United States is not merely a strong state but an overwhelming one.[60] As a result, the nature of US involvement cannot be compared with other powers also involved in Palestine, such as the EU, Japan, or the Gulf states.

The scope of US involvement is also above and beyond any other nation in the world. Take, for instance, the military engagements of the United States: conservative estimates pin the number of US military bases around the world at 800.[61] In the Arab world specifically, the United States is known to have over 50,000 troops in the Egypt, the Levant, and the Gulf.[62] Moreover, the United States has historically shaped the trajectories of regions as a whole. For instance, throughout the Cold War, Europe was entirely shaped by the United States, even with vigorous competition from the Soviet Union. The United States "remade" many of these nations in the post-war order in a manner that has defined modern-day Europe.[63]

Before the end of the Cold War, the United States and its allies had a mixed record of supporting democratic movements. The calculation boiled down to the region in which the movement took place and whether or not such a movement would affect US strategic interests.[64] In regions where the United States had a large stake, it often worked to preserve authoritarian status quos rather than support democratic movements that posed a threat to American hegemony. Regions such as South America or the Middle East suffered from the heavy-handed role of the United States, which bolstered authoritarian regimes, and in many respects increased overall militarization of the region.[65] These strategic calculations were justified as the natural response to a bipolar environment, to contain the Soviet Union and its allied states.

After the Cold War, and the neutralization of the Soviet threat, the effect of US involvement should have shifted. And indeed, the literature on this topic often assumes American involvement today to be more positive, in service of upholding a liberal world order.[66] In some cases, research does in fact corroborate this claim. For example, political liberalization in certain regions has been found to increase as a result of US foreign aid.[67] Western influence can also assist in the diffusion of democracy through coercion of domestic regimes, or indirect support to oppositional forces.[68] Moreover, some research argues that transition to democracy is more likely in the first place where Western "linkages" are widespread and Western "leverage" is more prevalent.[69] Such studies often test their theories with cross-national empirical data and make claims about general trends.

That is not to say that these general claims have not been challenged, however. Sean Yom, for instance, argues that American involvement creates non-durable regimes plagued by civil unrest.[70] Other scholars examining some democratization programs in detail have noted that these sometimes fail in their implementation.[71] While useful for their technical insight, these studies tend to focus too narrowly on the outcomes of specific programs and have less to say about the effect of Western involvement more generally. This is especially the case when it comes to research on regional variations.

Scholars who have assessed the differentiated effects of involvement in certain regions have noted that international factors may not always be conducive to democratization and/or consolidation across the board.[72] But it is often argued that linkages with *other* authoritarian states are the driving factor for authoritarian persistence.[73] When Western intervention is examined, a negative impact is noted only when the focus is on direct military intervention or the unintended consequences of foreign aid.[74] For example, work within this literature has examined how international involvement can strengthen a regime's coercive apparatus through military aid, or bolster the regime economically.[75] In another vein, some studies point out that some types of food aid, debt forgiveness, or other types of foreign funding have adverse effects on mobilization and democratization.[76] The most recent assessments of USAID democracy spending indeed found that these programs are effective worldwide—except for in the Middle East. The failure is then tied to the authoritarian nature of Middle Eastern regimes and the fact that aid was found to bolster the economic interests of these states.[77]

Furthermore, in studies on the Arab world, scholars point to the rise of political Islam—in interaction with Western involvement—as having a negative effect on the average citizen's preference for democracy. Specifically, the argument goes that in an increasingly unstable economic context, citizens find it too costly to support democratic reforms, despite individual support for democratic tenets. US foreign policy exacerbates these conditions by sending mixed signals to Arab populations about the feasibility of true democracy if Islamists come to power.[78] Overall, it becomes clear that the societal effects of Western involvement, beyond direct military intervention, remain understudied. They often focus on specific programs, such as in the case of Jason Brownlee's work, and do not examine the mechanism of societal demobilization.[79] Thus, US intervention and democratization efforts are examined too narrowly, with a focus on regime-level outcomes and less focus on long-term changes to state–society dynamics.

The United States and its allies no longer function in a Cold War environment, and yet much of the same calculations persist in the post-Cold War world when it comes to highly strategic areas. In locations with high strategic value, such as the Middle East, US involvement prioritizes autocracy over democratic development as a way of maintaining stability and control.[80] This is especially the case because, as Osamah Khalil notes, American foreign policy in the region has largely been shaped by neo-conservative forces, particularly since 9/11.[81] Forthcoming work shows the manner in which the United States helps to strengthen "collaborationist" regimes, providing financial support and a source of legitimacy, in the context of the Middle East.[82]

The United States in Palestine

In the case of Palestine, the United States has been heavily involved in a variety of ways. Particularly with the use of aid as both a carrot and a stick, the United States has been able to shape the development of the PA and impose its preferences on the Palestinians.[83] Before 1993, US aid was focused on the concept of "quality of life," intended to separate economic concerns from political conditions.[84] Then, after 1993, US aid shifted from humanitarian assistance to "development" aid.[85] In the name of "peacebuilding," the United States fostered a system in which the interim conditions following the Oslo Accords, which should have ended in 1999, persist to this day. Indeed, some scholars liken the US role to "maintaining a colonial peace" or even conducting a "counterinsurgency" operation.[86]

The exact amount of aid from Western sources, including the United States, is not entirely clear or traceable.[87] As Mandy Turner notes:

around 40 donor countries and dozens of UN and other multilateral agencies have provided aid and "experts" to the OPT [i.e. the occupied Palestinian territories]. This has taken the form of two kinds of aid: the first is for humanitarian activities (which includes emergency response, reconstruction, relief and rehabilitation, and disaster prevention and preparedness), the second is for peacebuilding (which includes the wider governance and development aspects that are supposed to follow directly on from reconstruction in the relief to development continuum, i.e., building infrastructure and services, government and civil society assistance, as well as private sector development).[88]

Nevertheless, what is undeniable is that the United States in particular is the "largest bilateral donor" to the PA, with the value of aid from 1993 until today reaching close to 8 billion dollars.[89]

The United States has specifically focused on funding the PA's security-related institutions, in strict coordination with the Israeli occupation.[90] From 1993, the CIA was involved in training and vetting security forces. This involvement increased after 2006.[91] The United States intended to ensure that members of the decision-making cadre were adherents of the idea of maintaining Israeli security in exchange for a continuation of the two-state peace process. As such, despite the fact that the PA suffers from a variety of pressing humanitarian and economic concerns, it still allocates over 30 percent of its budget to the security sector alone.[92] This aggrandizement of the security sector through funding and training has led many to refer to the PA as a "police state," and a subcontractor of the occupation.[93] For instance, when the 2006 elections brought Hamas to power, the United States was the key driver of funneling aid to the office of the President specifically in order to facilitate the funds necessary for Fatah's attempted coup.[94]

Moreover, the United States has a large effect on other donors and international institutions and their capacity to engage in their missions.[95] Turner, for instance, reports how the United States creates a "difficult operating environment" for UN agencies to conduct their business, not only by defunding key agencies such as the United Nations Relief and Works Agency for Palestine Refugees in the Near East (UNRWA) but also by subjecting these institutions to "microscopic enquiry and critique." As such, UN officials proceed with a great deal of caution and self-censorship regarding the conflict and the needs of Palestinians, ensuring that the root causes of the stagnant situation in the occupied territories remain unaddressed.[96] EU funders faced a similar dilemma. Before the 2006 legislative elections, the EU had attempted to remain "technocratic" in its funding decisions, such as those involving infrastructure. After

2006, however, the EU also diverted aid to President Abbas directly in coordination with US efforts to bypass the new Hamas government.[97]

For these reasons, the focus of this book is the effect of US involvement. Not only does the literature support such a focus but the primary data collected from this particular case supports the contention that the United States plays a particularly important role in Palestinian politics.

Summary of concepts

Below is a summary of concepts discussed in this chapter. In the next section, I will outline my theory on the effect of internationally backed regimes on micro-level decision-making and the long-term effect of such a dynamic on society.

Table 1: Summary of concepts

Term	*Definition*
Polarization	When the political views of individuals in society are increasingly defined by their affiliation with a certain political group, and those groups are increasingly divergent
Demobilization	"official termination or significant alteration of the formal institution engaged in challenging authorities; departure of individuals from relevant organizations; termination of or significant reduction in dissident behaviors; fundamental shift in the ideas of the challenger away from what was earlier established"[99]
International involvement	Pressure from external powers, in the form of material incentives (or threat of withdrawal) and direct involvement in the decision-making of governmental institutions
Social cohesion	Enhanced intergroup cooperation and capacity for collective action and cooperation, fueled by shared preferences

Theoretical argument

The literatures outlined above highlight the debate around the effect of authoritarianism on social cohesion, the causes of demobilization, and how international involvement may amplify these dynamics. From this debate, it becomes clear that international involvement, particularly on the part of the United States, does not always facilitate democracy or accountability. Under certain conditions, such involvement can in fact exacerbate authoritarian conditions. This is the case because American involvement in particular can vary in its effect across regions. Thus, in regions where democracy is not seen as a strategic interest, the international power plays a role in facilitating authoritarian conditions.[100] Specifically, the United States affects the domestic sphere by polarizing publics around its role, insulating regimes from their publics, and facilitating an increase in authoritarian practices and strategies.

The United States facilitates authoritarian conditions because the outcome of democracy is likely to be opposed to international intervention. In the Middle East particularly, the United States fears the outcome of the actual democratic process for two main reasons: it has brought Islamists into power in the past and/or it may bring those to power who are interested in challenging the status quo on Israel's role in the region.[101] If we look at the Palestinian case, and specifically the 2006 Palestinian elections, we see these dynamics replicated. For these reasons, the effect of American involvement in the Middle East today is helping to consolidate and empower authoritarian regimes. This is in stark contrast to the American role throughout the Cold War period in particular regions, such as Eastern Europe, where Western interests aligned with democratic movements. However, it is similar to American involvement in other regions during and after the Cold War, such as in Latin America, where the United States and its allies overturned democratic movements that may have been antagonistic to US foreign policy.[102]

Although similar arguments have been made elsewhere, this dynamic has yet to be explored in full. Yom, for instance, talks about how international involvement increases repression in particular Middle Eastern regimes but argues that this *weakens* regimes in the long term. He also does not fully explain *why* international patrons choose to support regimes in this manner. Like Brownlee, Yom points to foreign aid as the main causal mechanism driving the relationship between increased international intervention and authoritarianism. As much of the literature points out, however, foreign aid is not necessarily always damaging or "autocratizing."[103] The relationship between foreign aid and regime-level outcomes depends largely on both the regional context and preferences of the international hegemon in that time period. Finally, neither Yom nor Brownlee accounts for the mechanism of societal demobilization—a phenomenon intimately connected to the state–society dynamic both authors allude to but do not elucidate fully.

Experts have also argued that American involvement and hegemony is underpinned by the objective of "elite incorporation" into the US-led world order. In order to achieve its interests, the United States relies on particular types of domestic elites, specifically those with ties to the United States, in order to propagate its agenda.[104] In so doing, the United States disrupts the "feedback loop" between domestic regimes and their societies, as political elites begin to answer to patron interests rather than societal pressures.[105] Although elites should be playing a "two-level game" (i.e. addressing international pressures while negotiating with their own societies), what is actually happening is that the elites are being insulated from their domestic audiences.[106] I argue that, as a result, international involvement causes a principal–agent problem and a divergence in the interests of regime participants and the society they purport to represent. The principal–agent problem, as previously defined, is the divergence that arises when one actor is responsible for decision-making on behalf of another actor.[107] This leads to my first hypothesis:

H1: *International involvement will cause a divergence in elite and public preferences.*[108]

If domestic political factions exist that are unfavorable to the international patron, the patron also has an incentive to aggrandize the role of non-democratic elements within the regime. Scholars have previously noted that in cases where radical political elements exist within society, international patrons have allied themselves with authoritarian regimes at the expense of representative democracy or accountable institutions. Over time, true democracy or accountability was made to seem "infeasible" to individuals within these countries because it was clear that the international patron would not approve of its results, and would readily overturn them.[109] These dynamics occurred even if it meant keeping large segments of the population unrepresented within the regime's institutions.[110] This effect of international involvement causes a shift in the public's preferences, especially for those who are directly affected by the threat of sanctions. Certain case studies have previously noted that affiliation with certain sectors of the economy breeds a low capacity for collective action.[111] Specifically, in the context of threat from international sanctions, the sectors affected most are those who are affiliated with the regime going out of power, or those tied to the patron's foreign aid.[112] Thus my second hypothesis is that:

H2: *Members of society will have divergent preferences for democracy and accountability based on their affiliation with the regime.*

As for the effect of international involvement at the societal level, there are two interrelated outcomes: polarization and declining mobilization. First, an international patron helps to facilitate infrastructural power for the regime that would otherwise stem from society itself.[113] For example, the ability of the regime to provide services in most states stems from the capacity of the regime to tax effectively.[114] This is one manifestation of infrastructural power. If a regime is unable to tax (or control its territory, or any other manifestation of infrastructural power), then it can be said that the regime presides over a "weak state" and will likely face competitors.[115] Therefore, regimes must establish and maintain the institutions necessary to use infrastructural power successfully.

In a scenario where an international patron is heavily involved, infrastructural power is generated for the regime without subsequent dependence on society. Under normal circumstances, a regime must incorporate wide segments of the population in order to achieve an effective level of infrastructural power. When an international patron supplies the necessary resources for regime durability, this allows the regime to become much more selective in its representativeness and provision of services. A patron can also provide resources to strengthen the indigenous regime's coercive capacity and allow the regime to target particular groups within society that pose a threat. The case study literature on the Middle East abounds with examples of how opposition movements become polarized and fragmented as a result of particular authoritarian strategies.[116] In this way, the practice of authoritarianism in and of itself, bolstered by international support, has the effect of increasing polarization within society. The polarizing divide lies between those that are included in the regime's services and whose interests are represented, and those who are targeted by the regime instead.[117] By allowing regimes to be unrepresentative of large portions of society without fear of backlash, we can expect the following:

H3: *Authoritarian strategies, such as cooptation and repression, will generate polarization.*

I argue that polarization has the subsequent effect of limiting political mobilization. This argument stands in contrast to the argument made by Yom, who claims that external involvement and support create long-term problems in state–society relations and, ultimately, lead to weak regimes plagued by increasing political unrest. Yom uses the cases of Jordan, Iran, and Kuwait to make this argument. According to Yom, Iran and Jordan are examples of countries with external patronage and varying levels of unrest, and Kuwait is an example of a country that lacks a main patron and has thus attained greater legitimacy.

However, it could be argued that regimes in Jordan and Kuwait have only become more authoritarian over time, despite waning American involvement or interest. In Jordan, mass protest is not common, nor particularly dangerous to the regime's longevity. Yom states, for example, that the protests that erupted in Jordan in 2018 were non-threatening to the regime, with protestors making it clear that their activities were a plea to their government rather than an attempt to subvert the ruling family.[118] While protests may occur periodically or once a decade, they are often ineffective and never reach the level of coordinated mobilization with attainable demands.

Similarly, political opposition is often resolved through international support of the regime, or through severe crackdowns. In Jordan, recent protests dissipated following regional economic support to offset protester demands.[119] Moreover, it is difficult to reconcile the image of Kuwait as a more responsive authoritarian system when, since 2010, there has been a terminal decline in the country's proto-democratic structure. For instance, opposition figures found themselves in lengthy court proceedings facing jail time after their protest activities in the parliament.[120] On top of that, Kuwait has only ever survived due to external patronage. The United States has developed strong military coordination with Kuwait and intervened following Iraq's invasion of the country in 1990, precipitating the First Gulf War. Regional proxies of the United States, such as Saudi Arabia, have also stepped in regularly to resolve Kuwait's economic and security issues.

Overall, Yom's argument may be explanatory for certain time periods in the history of the Jordanian and Kuwaiti states. But an assessment of the historical record shows that, even if we were to agree that American involvement or interest in these countries has waned, the legacy or effect of American involvement has persisted. As a result, authoritarian dynamics have continued in these countries and limited the capacity for collective action and mobilization over time.

Thus, unlike existing literature on this topic, I argue that externally motivated polarization *limits* political mobilization by weakening social cohesion. Previous work has found that strong communities can facilitate engagement and mobilization through the use of "social sanctions."[121] However, in cases where the regime polarizes society, the potential for communities to serve this function is weakened dramatically. Therefore, I expect that:

H4: *Where international influence has created a polarizing regime, political mobilization will decline.*

The potential for communities to sanction is weakened as a result of exacerbated coordination problems. Specifically, as societies become more polarized, the cohesion necessary for effective mobilization begins to decline. In a cohesive community, the overall interest of its members is more readily discernible, and when action is deemed necessary, mobilization can be achieved. In a context of high polarization, similar interests may not exist, although individuals may come from the same community and live under similar conditions. If some segment of the population finds mobilization to be within their interests, it is not clear that this sentiment will be shared by a necessary plurality. Moreover, the social structures necessary to "sanction" members into action are not available in a polarized society: after all, effective sanctions must involve the threat of being sanctioned by the community *at large*. If the community is divided on whether mobilization is necessary, sanctions will not be effective. Therefore, in the event of attempted mobilization around a shared interest, the classic free-riding problem will occur. I characterize this mechanism as a "coordination problem" because polarization limits the ability of people to agree on shared interests and allows free-riding to occur more easily. This can be considered a long-term outcome. Over time, such a dynamic reinforces demobilization.

Finally, the relationship between state and society determines whether internationally backed authoritarian conditions will have a demobilizing effect or not. At first glance, it may seem that international support for authoritarian conditions does not play a large role in determining the level of polarization and the presence or absence of mobilization. For instance, American support of the Israeli government, and its military occupation of the West Bank and Gaza, has been ongoing for decades. In terms of its scope, American support for Israel is certainly much greater than the support received by the PA. Nevertheless, when the Israeli government controlled the Palestinian territories directly, it was unable to produce the levels of polarization and demobilization that characterize Palestinian society today. Palestinians were still able to organize and mobilize effectively prior to 1994, in fact garnering concessions in both the first and second intifada, despite severe Israeli repression in the occupied territories. So what explains the variation between Israeli repression and PA repression, if both are backed to a large extent by American support?

Work on repression in democratic contexts may provide the answer here. Davenport argues that democratic regimes are more likely to rely on covert rather than overt tactics. Covert tactics, he says, lead to infiltration of opposition movements and thus reduced trust and polarization.[122] As such, Davenport expects there to be "more challenges in democratic countries than in autocracies, and for social movement organizations in democratic systems to display greater variability in survival rates."[123] In work on Palestine specifically, Silvia Pasquetti notes that Palestinian communities within Israel—i.e. with Israeli citizenship and theoretically a part of the state—are characterized by high levels of distrust and polarization. She juxtaposes this dynamic with Palestinian communities within the West Bank, particularly those in refugee camps. In these areas, Palestinians are much more cohesive and share high levels of trust vis a vis Israeli repression.[124]

Israel is by no means democratic or liberal in its treatment of its Palestinian citizens.[125] However, the relationship of Palestinian citizens of Israel with the Israeli state is markedly different from the relationship of Palestinians in the occupied territories to the Israeli state. They are, at the end of the day, told they are citizens. They have access to particular institutions of the state, and recourse to the law, in a way that Palestinians under military occupation do not. Moreover, the state has much more access to *them*, meaning that the Israeli state is better at surveilling and infiltrating Palestinian communities within its boundaries than it is in the territories. This explains why the Israeli state relied on more overt action in the occupied territories and more covert actions within the state's boundaries. As Davenport notes, states rely on more covert action when they have greater knowledge of the social movement and rely on overt action when they need to repress the movement but know less about its inner workings. Palestinians in the occupied territories thus reacted differently to overt repression and were faced with fewer attacks on trust and internal cohesion. Ultimately, they faced an external enemy—and their behavior reflected as much. They were able to adapt and "code" their political engagement as "social engagement."[126] Overall, they were able to organize effectively despite Israeli repression.

Similarly, the PA has a very different effect on Palestinians in the territories than the Israeli occupation does. The PA is again by no means democratic or liberal, but it is an indigenous regime. People who work within the PA's bureaucracies represent a sizable portion of the population. The relationship of Palestinians in the territories to the PA is thus one of shared background and, theoretically, shared objectives. At some point in the past, many of these same leaders were part of the PLO, and to some degree accountable to their Palestinian constituency. Thus, when faced with repression from the PA, Palestinians in the occupied territories are likely to be much more divided in their response, for the reasons highlighted above. Moreover, the PA, as an indigenous regime with high awareness of its own society, can rely on more covert repression. For one, the "coding" of political engagement as social engagement that Jamal speaks of, which was effective in circumventing Israeli repression, is not as effective with an indigenous regime such as the PA. The PA is more likely to recognize what such engagement actually means and react accordingly. Its cooptation mechanisms will be more effective at infiltrating society and imposing control on mobilization activities. Finally, when an indigenous regime uses overt repression selectively, this also creates in-group and out-group dynamics. This leads to greater polarization than an external occupation's repression is likely to achieve.

Thus, I build on Davenport's important work on the topic of demobilization, as well as the insights from the case study literature on Palestine, to make the distinction between indigenous or internal authoritarian strategies and the authoritarian strategies imposed by an external enemy. I differ from Davenport in that I argue regime type is not necessarily the explanatory factor here; rather, the nature of state–society relations within a given space determines if international support will be polarizing or not. Indigenous repression has a very different effect from external repression. This helps to explain why American and international support of Israel did not lead to the levels of polarization and demobilization in the Palestinian territories we see today, whereas support of the PA succeeded in polarizing Palestinian society and harming mobilization efforts. Although the focus of this book is the PA and the occupied territories, I will turn in the final chapter to the dynamics within Palestinian communities inside Israel to demonstrate how, over time, state–society relations have shifted there as well, changing patterns of mobilization in the process.

The theory outlined above can help highlight the role of international involvement in facilitating authoritarian conditions in client states. Moreover, this theory can help explain some of the societal implications of this dynamic—i.e. how authoritarian regimes can transform and control political engagement and mobilization—in a way that turns engaged citizens into authoritarian subjects. As previously mentioned, studies on authoritarianism often focus primarily on regime institutions and/or elite bargaining and

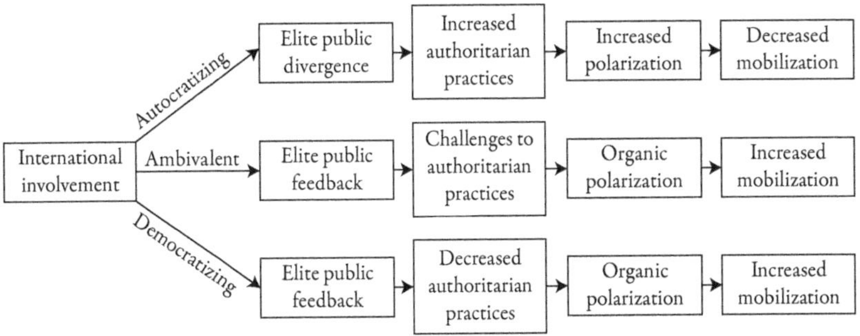

Figure 1. Causal diagram showing the role of international involvement in authoritarianism, polarization, and mobilization

power-sharing. Rarely has the relationship between the regime and the public been unpacked in the literature, especially with a focus on the impact of the international context. This is a gap this theory would seek to redress.

This project's causal outline

Figure 1 outlines a visual representation of the theory presented in the previous section, with some key additions. The theory presented here discusses autocratizing international involvement. But international involvement is not only one type, as previously mentioned. Autocratizing international involvement has a different effect from ambivalent or democratizing involvement. As such, American involvement has had a different effect on political development in regions where democracy served American strategic interests. In those cases, US involvement was democratizing. This meant that civil society organizations were supported to some degree in their efforts against particular regimes, and this led to some democratization success (for example, across the Eastern bloc). In other cases, US involvement was ambivalent. Where strategic interests were easily replaceable despite the fall of an ally regime, the United States acquiesced to popular demand and did not overtly support authoritarian leaders.[127] This ambivalence gave space for civil society in those countries to mobilize and pressure their regimes effectively.[128] Regimes may still repress or cling on to power in the context of pressure, but their capacity to do so will suffer significantly. The international legitimacy afforded to the regime, as well as the material support through weapons and aid, may no longer be available. As such, the regime is made more susceptible to being overthrown. While I recognize that these types of international involvement exist, the bulk of this project aims to explore the causal chain that emerges from autocratizing involvement.

Figure 1 also shows that polarization does not have a unidirectional effect on mobilization. In the case of autocratizing international involvement, polarization leads to demobilization. This is because polarization is generated through authoritarian strategies and practices, which are externally backed. This external backing means the regime has greater capacity to engage in such practices without consequence, leading to extreme levels of polarization and declining social cohesion. However, this is not the case across the board. In cases where international involvement is democratizing or ambivalent, polarization or hyper-partisanship may still exist as a result of particular historical legacies. The impact of authoritarianism does not disappear overnight, after all. Nevertheless, international forces that have become ambivalent to regime change no longer function as a polarizing force in domestic politics.

More importantly, polarization in and of itself does not cause the failure of democratic transitions. Indeed, scholars who study Latin America have argued that polarization may in fact be necessary for the democratic process, as it creates partisanship and helps build clear party platforms.[129] This helps institutionalize the democratic process and channel opposition into formal institutions. In the absence of international opposition to the democratic process, opposition groups can compete in the domestic political sphere and gain or lose support organically based on what they can offer to society. In this scenario, political groups cannot remain niche: they must create broader coalitions and appeal to at least a plurality of the population to have success electorally.[130] As such, this helps create more cross-cutting preferences and moderates political positions. Finally, it also helps make opposition group capacity more symmetrical, given that the international patron is no longer tipping the scale in favor of one over the other. These dynamics are not replicated in the case of autocratizing involvement.

In our case, the causal chain has various mediating variables.[131] It begins with autocratizing international involvement, which causes a divergence between elite and public preferences (Chapter 2). International involvement/support for the regime substitutes for the domestic regime's organic infrastructural power and legitimacy. This leads to rising authoritarianism and polarization, both around the role of the international patron and around the regime (Chapter 3). These variables in turn lead to a decline in social cohesion, defined as a sense of "collective purpose."[132] In this book, I disaggregate that concept to mean the capacity for collective action and cooperation between different segments of society, fueled by shared preferences (explored in Chapter 4).

It is also important to note here that while I utilize a causal diagram for the sake of clarity, this by no means implies that the variables outlined in the diagram are the only variables that are important in understanding the Palestinian case. Causal diagrams are used to identify the independent variable(s) of interest and the causal mechanisms—the links—between those variable(s) and the outcome. This does not mean that all interesting events/variables need to be included in the causal diagram—only the most relevant according to the theory in question.[133] Thus, for instance, when I make the claim that international involvement leads to polarization between certain segments of Palestinian society, this is not to say that polarization would not have emerged along different lines had international involvement not been so intrusive. Instead, what I am claiming is that the particular degree and form of polarization we see today can be linked to the type of international involvement we see in the Palestinian case.

2

"AMERICANS HAVE TAUGHT US: THERE IS A DIFFERENCE BETWEEN DEMOCRACY AND CREATING PROBLEMS"

Palestinians have long complained that their leaders are unaccountable and unrepresentative. Activists describe Palestinians as existing in a perpetual state of rejection—angry over the status quo, but also suspicious and cynical of the opposition that exists. This is particularly the case today, when the popularity of Hamas has also declined despite initial support for its claim to political power. Overall, there is palpable stagnation in the Palestinian political sphere.

Officials within the PA voice a similar sense of cynicism and frustration, but in the opposite direction. Many are frustrated with the status quo and with the PA's political position domestically and internationally, and, most importantly, they express frustration with society: "No one wants to sacrifice anymore," said one PA official, "there is no sense of national unity or struggle." A number of officials complained that they were in thankless positions, with Palestinians simply not understanding the constraints the PA faced.

Take, for instance, the chain of events following the 2008 Israeli war on Gaza. Outrage over the level of destruction and a high civilian death toll led to the production of a report by the United Nations Fact Finding Mission on the Gaza Conflict (known as the Goldstone Report), highlighting Israeli crimes and violations. But instead of pursuing this line of attack at the United Nations, the PA succumbed to US pressure to withdraw support for the report. While Abbas was praised by US and UN officials as a "partner for peace," demonstrations erupted in the territories against this decision, and a number of Abbas's ministers resigned in protest.[1] Clearly, there was—and remains—a disjuncture between what the international community sees as best for Palestinians versus what Palestinians believe is in their interest.

What explains this state of affairs? How have elite and public positions/preferences become this divergent? The first link in the causal argument described in this chapter looks at the effect of international involvement on elite and public preferences. The chapter consequently examines the effect of international involvement on individual preferences for democracy and accountability in the Palestinian territories. I argue that this involvement affects elite and public opinion in various ways.

I define international involvement as pressure from an external power in the form of material incentives (or threat of withdrawal) and direct involvement in the decision-making of governmental institutions. This encompasses a wide range of state behavior: in the case of Palestine, it includes the strategic use of aid and diplomatic pressure on the part of the United States and its allies.[2] This chapter seeks to assess whether international involvement has an effect on domestic preferences, at both the regime and public level, within the Palestinian territories. The PA has been targeted by various forms of international involvement since its inception. Today, on a number of dimensions, international involvement remains highly salient. Moreover, the question of democracy in the Palestinian territories remains unresolved and up for public debate.

I accomplish this task by utilizing experimental methods at both the political elite and public level. For the purposes of this book, I define political elites as those working within the PA's bureaucracy with some level of decision-making power over policy and thus directly targeted by many forms of international involvement. All the people I interviewed were "elites" by this definition in that they held some authority and direct contact with US policymakers, including the US security coordinator's office. I interviewed them on the questions of democracy and accountability to assess how such involvement affects their preferences given their proximity/relation to the governing apparatus. For the sake of comparison across the state–society line, I also utilize a nationally representative survey with an experimental component to address public opinion. The survey experiment given at the public level tests individual preferences for democracy and accountability while taking into account various forms of international involvement.

In this manner, I provide empirical evidence of how international involvement may affect domestic preferences conditionally, depending on where individuals place themselves in relation to the regime. I also provide evidence of a divergence in preferences across the state–society line as a result of international involvement. Rather than assume certain dynamics about the state–society relationship while only empirically assessing one half of it, this chapter will provide a look at the effect of international involvement at both levels using comparable metrics. In this way, I will prove the first link in the main causal argument: international involvement has a notable impact on elite and public preferences regarding political accountability. Specifically, it has the effect of making elite and public preferences diverge, thus separating political elites and the leadership further from the Palestinian public.

I focus on American involvement because the United States in particular is heavily involved in internal Palestinian politics and development. As is the case with US involvement across the region, this involvement can range from foreign aid, "endorsements" of certain policies, or direct pressure in the form of military action. But other than assumed effects, there has been little empirical work to show how this involvement may shape, or change, the preferences of different segments of society. Moreover, there has been little work on the conditionality of this effect—specifically, examining the effect of international involvement on preferences for certain policies, depending on the individual's position in society.

And this is not an unimportant question to address. Not only is the link between international involvement and domestic implications often ignored but, when it is examined, it is assumed to be working at the regime level alone. However, there is no reason to assume this is the case. International involvement targeted at state-level institutions or the political regime surely has implications that affect the societies these states purport to govern. Therefore, international involvement may have a profound impact on state–society relations, as well as the preferences and behaviors of individuals within those two spheres. These effects may be differentiated along pre-existing lines (i.e. where members of society place themselves in relation to the state). In that sense, international involvement complicates the traditional principal–agent dynamic between the regime/elites and the public.

From patron to public: what we know about international involvement and its effects

The effect of elites on public opinion

While the nature of an external intervention can inform how domestic publics react to international involvement, scholars have also noted the role of the political elite in creating other types of cleavages. Elites are particularly important to the shaping of public opinion and subsequent preferences. As noted by John R. Zaller, elites can affect how information is processed and what is made salient to the public. They do this in two ways: (1) by providing new information that is then evaluated by the public, or (2) providing heuristics for individuals to receive information quickly (i.e. based on whether they agree with the elite on other attitudes and opinions).[3]

In studies of elite effects on polarization in the American context, elites play a role in polarizing the public across specific issues. This particularly works on those considered the most well informed.[4] Research specific to the Middle East has also found the role of elites to be highly significant. For instance, Lisa Blaydes and Drew A. Linzer show that preferences can become polarized in countries where elites are purposely exacerbating ideological divides within society.[5] They speak in particular about the Islamist–secular divide and link elite exacerbation of this divide to greater anti-Americanism in public opinion. Amaney Jamal and Sarah Bush also point out that regime support or opposition is a major divide within Middle Eastern countries and affects individual opinions on international involvement.[6] Thus, in such cases, individual preferences toward international involvement are shaped according to political affiliation and elite influence.

Particularly in the Arab world, where democratic systems by and large do not exist, publics interact with political elites much more directly than in democratic countries. Political elites have a large influence on the opinions of certain segments of the public, and opposition to/support of the political regime can often be the main divide within society. This is because political interactions in authoritarian states are often not mediated, in a significant sense, by institutions such as meaningful political parties or legislatures.[7] Thus, particularly in the Middle East, there is evidence to suggest that elites can directly affect domestic preferences in a bifurcated way.

The argument posed in research thus far has been that elites in autocracies can create polarization by creating two "camps": part of the public reflects elite opinion, and the other part opposes it. This informs the assumption made in much of the literature that looks at polarization, namely that patterns of pro- and anti-democracy sentiment found in the public will be reflected to some degree among elites as well.[8] However, there is no empirical evidence to prove that public preferences and elite preferences mirror each other, or that public preferences stem from the effect of elite persuasion alone. It could indeed be the case that anti-democratic elites affect a significant portion of the public's preference for democracy, because of their effect on individual strategic calculations. Or, alternatively, international involvement may affect public and elite preferences differently. As a result, public and elite preferences for democracy may actually diverge.

How international involvement affects elites and their societies

Given what we know about preference formation at the elite and public level, we can derive specific implications for the interaction between preference formation and international involvement. First, as previously mentioned, scholars have argued that international patrons can disrupt the "feedback loop" between the domestic regime and society.[9] Domestic regimes begin to answer to patron interests rather than societal pressures.[10] I argue specifically that international involvement causes a principal–agent problem and thus a divergence in the interests of elites/regime participants (agent) and the society they purport to represent (principal).[11]

When there are multiple principals at work, expectations differ from a traditional principal–agent relationship. For one, information problems are particularly exacerbated with multiple principals, increasing the possibility of moral hazard and adverse selection problems. Second, in this scenario, principals with more power and resources have a greater impact on the agent.[12] International patrons would thus have much more influence on the agent's behavior than society, which lacks coercive capacity in the traditional sense. This dynamic of multiple principals, and power imbalances between them, leads to the first hypothesis:

H1: *International involvement will create a principal–agent problem, demonstrated by a divergence between regime (agent) and public (principal) preferences.*

This divergence pertains to preferences for democracy and accountability, as well as other national objectives.

However, the effect of international involvement on regime/elite preferences is conditional on the patron's preferences—particularly because the international patron in this case is the "stronger" principal and therefore its objectives are more greatly weighted. Preferences here include three possibilities: a preference for democracy, a preference for stability, or a mixed preference. When the preferences of principals align, the agent has less room to pursue independent objectives.[13] Thus, in the first scenario, if the patron has an incentive to advance democracy and accountability in line with domestic preferences, then such an objective should pressure the regime and its participants to prefer democracy. This is especially the case when their regimes, and thus their positions, are beholden to external support. In the case of "democratizing" international involvement, we should expect to find that elites prefer democracy when international patrons signal a preference for democracy.

On the other hand, in the second scenario, if the international patron prefers stability, involvement may not necessarily be "democratizing." For example, if domestic political factions exist that are unfavorable to the international patron, the patron would have an incentive to aggrandize the role of non-democratic elements within the regime. Scholars have previously noted that in cases where radical political elements exist within society, international patrons have allied themselves with authoritarian regimes at the expense of representative democracy.[14] In this context, patrons prefer stability, even if that entails authoritarianism.

The dynamic of multiple principals would suggest that agent autonomy would increase when principal preferences are heterogeneous, such as the scenario described above. However, this is under the assumption that there is an equal distribution of power between principals. In the case of international involvement, that is not the case. When an international patron (the stronger principal) favors stability over democracy in contradiction to public preferences, regimes (their agents) have more space to pursue independent action—but only from the weaker principal (i.e. from their publics). In many cases, that independence entails becoming more authoritarian and less accountable. Therefore, we also have reason to believe that elites will prefer democracy less when international patrons signal a preference for stability. This is indeed the case in the context of the Middle East, and Palestine specifically, where US interests are tied to maintaining stability rather than allowing those who may oppose American foreign policy to come to power.[15]

In the case of the third scenario, mixed or countervailing preferences (as in the case of mixed signals from one of the principals), expectations are not so clear. Across the Arab world, for instance, many regimes (as well as their publics) note a democratizing *rhetoric* on the part of international patrons such as the United States. However, this is not necessarily matched with democratizing policies. For instance, American officials were vocal about their support for democracy before the 2006 Palestinian legislative elections and pressured Fatah officials (i.e. the ruling party) to run elections.[16] Nevertheless, the United States rejected the election results that brought Hamas to power and punished voters through economic sanctions. Elites are particularly affected by these opposing pressures: on the one hand, they are exposed to democratizing rhetoric that may delegitimize their positions among the public, but on the other they are forced to pursue authoritarian practices to ensure opponents of the international patron do not come to power. Thus we arrive at the second hypothesis:

H2: *In the presence of both democratizing and autocratizing pressure, elites will react negatively to democratizing pressure.*

This is the case given that elites in this position know the consequences of democracy would incur retribution from international patrons. There is also the issue of opposing principal preferences: when there is a power imbalance between both principals, the patron will exert the stronger impact. But when the patron (i.e. the stronger principal) is itself sending mixed signals, as in the scenario described above, this gives space to the weaker principal, the public, to exert some pressure.[17]

The effect of international involvement on public opinion may also be conditional and simultaneously interact with elite preferences. Agents are actors in and of themselves; thus, there are situations in which agents (in this case, the regime) can influence the preferences of the principal (in this case, the public) using their more complete information or level of expertise.[18] When international patrons prefer democracy, they affect their agent (the regime) and its preferences. However, the regime can in turn affect its other principal (the public), which often has less complete information and resources in comparison with the international powers. In this way, it becomes a case of one principal affecting another through a common agent. For this particular scenario, if international involvement is "democratizing," then public opinion may also reflect a preference for democracy over time.[19]

In the case of "autocratizing" international involvement, the opposite may be true. Scholars have previously noted that when international patrons favor stability over democracy, democracy was made to seem "infeasible" to individuals within these countries.[20] International patrons, such as the United States, often prefer foreign policy continuity; for this reason, patrons may support authoritarian regimes to avoid upheavals that come with regime change.[21] Thus, in this scenario, supporting stability becomes tantamount to supporting authoritarianism. Moreover, it becomes clear to citizens that the international patron would not approve of true democratic results and would readily overturn them.[22] Such "autocratizing" international involvement would likely cause a shift in the public's preferences. Thus there is some evidence to suggest that, under certain circumstances, public opinion may reflect preferences for stability if the international patron favors stability.

However, this may not be true for all segments of the population. For the sake of parsimony, we aggregate large groups into single actors in our models, but in reality principals and agents are not single actors. The public, as a single principal, is not a uniform body, and disaggregating the different groups that make up a "single" principal is useful in some cases. In the case of international patrons backing authoritarianism, it is useful to disaggregate the public in order to see how such influence affects groups conditionally.

The historical record is saturated with examples of mass protest in support of democracy despite the lack of encouragement internationally.[23] Thus a shift in public opinion (in support of stability even if authoritarian) may in fact be conditional on the proximity of individuals to the regime. Specifically, this should be the case for those who are directly affected by the threat of sanctions. This means international involvement should only affect those who are affiliated with the regime going out of power or those tied to foreign aid (such as those employed by the regime, or those whose salaries are funded by the international community). Therefore, I argue that:

H3: *Members of the public will have divergent preferences for democracy based on their affiliation with the regime. Those with little affiliation with the regime will be less affected by international involvement in their preferences for democracy.*

This fits with the idea that elite opinions are reflected at the public level, at least to some degree. But it also addresses the fact that international involvement disrupts state–society relations and causes a divergence in preferences between elites and certain segments of their public. To assume a direct correlation between elite and public opinion in the case of international involvement is to assume such involvement has little domestic effect, which, as this chapter will illustrate, is a false assumption to make. Moreover, that regimes have multiple principals, some of which are more powerful, has a profound impact on the behavior of these regimes and their relation to their weaker principals.

Two-level data on Palestinian elites and the Palestinian public

To analyze the dynamics outlined above, I utilized a combination of original qualitative and quantitative data, at both the elite and public level, in the

Palestinian territories. At the elite level, I conducted interviews with decision-makers within the PA. I conducted interviews with thirty-five members of the Ministry of Interior, the police force, and the PLO Executive Committee. Some, but not all, of these elites held positions that entailed international cooperation. I asked them open-ended questions on their positions within the PA, the development of the PA over time, and the effect of international involvement on that development. Combined with the survey data at the public level, these interviews will help elucidate general preferences for or against democracy and accountability among the elite in comparison with the public.

At the public level, I conducted a nationally representative survey of 1,270 people across the Palestinian territories, from every city, suburb, and neighborhood. This portion of the project was conducted in conjunction with the Palestinian Center for Policy and Survey Research, which guaranteed balance on relevant covariates (gender, age, etc.). The sampling frame utilized geographic breakdowns of the West Bank and Gaza, around existing governorates, to collect the sample. The target population was the adult population in the Palestinian territories. The survey asked a number of questions on Palestinian politics, as well as a battery of demographic questions. I also included an experimental component on the role of international involvement. Such survey experiments are often used to analyze differential effects of the independent variable in question, while randomizing the treatments in order to isolate the independent variable's effect from other confounders.

In this case, the survey experiment was used to analyze whether certain forms of international involvement affect people's preferences for democracy and accountability. This experimental component included two treatments and one control condition. The treatment conditions primed respondents with information on either "autocratizing" international involvement, or "democratizing" international involvement, and then asked them a question on their preference from democracy. The control condition, on the other hand, contained innocuous phrasing, designed to avoid priming respondents with any information relevant to international involvement. In this way, we can compare the results of those who had the control condition with those who had the treatment conditions and ascertain whether international involvement indeed has an effect on people's preferences.

There is some question as to the validity of this survey analysis, of course, given the tenuous nature of concepts such as "democracy" and the difficulty of ranking preferences (i.e. the "importance of" something). The validity of such a survey is in question since it is difficult to ascertain whether these concepts mean the same thing to different respondents.[24] Does the evaluation of how important democracy is to a person involve something concrete, such as policy outcomes or specific leaders (i.e. the performance of democracy)?[25] Or does it mean something larger, such as the importance of liberalism and democratic institutions? The range of "support" or "importance of" democracy can be very abstract to very concrete, and some scholars argue that such a wide gambit of meanings invalidates results. Moreover, many argue that the operationalization of such a large question using a simple ranking system cannot possibly capture the nuances of what support for democracy really means.[26]

However, robustness checks of these types of surveys find that such questions on support/importance of democracy can be considered a "summary indicator," with a number of different parts that do not necessarily need to be weighted equally.[27] The parts can range from the more concrete to the more abstract. Moreover, while conceptions of democracy may vary by group, there is no reason to believe that *within group* understandings of such a concept are wildly different.[28] Thus, if analyzing *across* samples, survey questions on support for democracy may need to be analyzed more rigorously. However, in a single sample, *within* group analysis, it can be assumed that conceptions of democracy are overall similar across respondents. This does not mean that causal mechanisms can be explicated using survey analysis alone, so it is true that nuances may not be captured. But with a multi-method approach, using both qualitative and quantitative analysis, this chapter will address both the causal relationship, as well as the mechanisms that facilitate it.

Using this data, criticisms notwithstanding, I will be able to examine what types of international involvement have an effect on public preferences for democracy and accountability. Specifically, I will be able to analyze under what conditions international involvement has an effect, and on what segments of the public. I will then be able to match those results with the information I collected from decision-makers/elites within the PA and analyze whether there are crucial differences first between different segments of the population and then between the elite and public levels as the theoretical argument would suggest.

Background on international involvement in Palestine

The Palestinian territories have technically been under Israeli occupation since 1967, and prior to that under Jordanian rule. In many ways, this occupation persists to this day. However, following the 1994 Oslo Accords, the Palestinian territories were given some level of independence in certain pockets of the territories. Since then, these pockets have been governed by the PA and the Israeli occupation forces concurrently. Despite ongoing occupation, the PA has been involved in a quasi-state-building process, creating many vestiges of a state and sovereign rule since its creation in 1994.

Throughout this state-building process, the international community was heavily involved in infrastructural and financial assistance to the PA. In particular, the United States, the EU, and to a lesser extent Arab allies, were involved with the development of physical infrastructure (such as police stations, ministries, etc.), as well as training programs for PA leadership and bureaucrats in order to build governance skills and provide logistic support. The CIA in particular has been implicated in supporting the PA with extra-legal wiretapping schemes, in addition to the training the PA's "Preventive Security" receives from the US intelligence services on a regular basis.[29] In sum, the PA heavily relies on the financial assistance of "donor" countries, as well as the approval of their international patrons. Without such support, the PA's institutions would grind to a halt.

The period following the legislative elections in 2006 is a good example of this. Hamas, the Islamist party considered a terrorist organization by the United States, won a plurality in the elections and assumed power in the ministries and in the parliament. Although by all accounts a free and fair election, the results were shocking to the American establishment and did not suit its overarching goal of creating a collaborationist regime in the Palestinian territories. As a result, the United States and its allies withdrew financial support for the PA's institutions. This meant that the salaries of all PA employees were withheld for months. It also eventually led to a coup attempt by the outgoing leadership (in Fatah), encouraged by the United States. This resulted in intra-Palestinian violence and fragmentation of the Palestinian territories into Gaza and the West Bank, each with its own governing apparatus. The episode following the elections is only the most recent example of how dependent the PA is on the assistance and approval of international patrons, and especially the United States.

Although Palestine seems like a special case, given its status under occupation and its heavy reliance on international support, the dynamics are actually generalizable to the larger Middle East. First, it has already been mentioned that the United States has particularly significant involvement in regimes around the Middle East specifically. If international involvement on the part of the United States and its allies indeed affects elite–public divides, as well as public opinion, then this should be the case in many other parts of the Arab world. Moreover, other countries around the Arab world are also heavily reliant on American financial and/or strategic support. Whether through military support that strengthens the ability of the regime to deal with both internal and external opposition, or through conditional aid programs that help regimes provide services, countries around the Arab world are not very different from the Palestinian territories when it comes to the scope of international involvement. As such, despite the unique dynamic posed by the ongoing question of statehood and occupation, the relationships discussed in this chapter are relevant to broader application, as we shall see in later chapters.

Empirical analysis

Survey analysis: public preferences for democracy and accountability

To assess the arguments related to public-level dynamics, I used survey data that tested whether people's preference for democracy (the dependent variable) was affected by various forms of international involvement (the independent variable). The dependent variable was operationalized by a question on the respondent's preferences for democracy and accountability, in which the respondent ranked its importance from (1) highly important to (5) not at all important. The English translation of the question can be found below:

> Treatment A: At times, following free and fair elections in the Middle East, some factions are unhappy with the results. Foreign powers such as the United States and EU have supported action against the winning factions, leading to coups and sometimes civil war.
>
> *How important is democracy and accountability to you? Rate from 1 to 5, 1 being the highest.*
>
> Treatment B: At times, following free and fair elections in the Middle East, some factions are unhappy with the results. Foreign powers such as the United States and EU have supported the winning factions anyway, providing financial aid and technical assistance.
>
> *How important is democracy and accountability to you? Rate from 1 to 5, 1 being the highest.*

The treatments included mention of accountability and not just the concept of democracy because of the peculiarity of the Palestinian case. The PA is a non-sovereign entity under occupation and has had a tumultuous and polarizing experience with elections (i.e. the 2006 legislative elections and ensuing coup). Thus the survey treatments mentioned accountability to pinpoint the particular characteristic of democracy relevant to this study. Asking solely about democracy without identifying the relevant characteristic that this study focuses on might have triggered particular biases and widened the scope of what democracy means in this case given the history of Palestinian elections.

The forms of international involvement were operationalized as the randomized treatments of the experiment (autocratizing versus democratizing versus control). The data also included a number of indicators and demographic questions in order to control for possible confounders. Specifically, the data included indicators of refugee status, employment, education, income, and governorate/location.[30] These factors affect political outlook and preferences in the case of Palestine in particular. Also, to account for certain political factors, I controlled for political affiliation, secularism, connection to the PA, and views on the peace process. Political affiliation accounts for all the major political groups in Palestinian politics. The secularism measure was included to capture those with ideological positions on the role of Islam in politics, which may have a large impact on their preferences for democracy (given Hamas's success in Palestinian elections). Finally, the peace process variable can be considered a type of "status quo" measurement. Those who support the peace process are, in essence, supportive of the current status quo under the PA. On the other hand, those who reject the peace process are essentially rejecting the PA's continued existence in its current form, including the legitimacy of its public officeholders.

Given that the dependent variable, preference for democracy, is an ordinal variable, an ordered logistic regression model is the most useful model in this case. I reversed the ranking order for ease of interpretation and ran two models for the two segments of the sample: those who work for the PA and those who do not. The relationship of the individual to the regime can be considered a moderating variable (i.e. a variable that affects the direction and/or strength of the relationship between the independent and dependent variables). In this case, many other confounding variables may affect an individual's preferences for democracy and accountability (the dependent variable). However, the manner in which international involvement in particular affects their preferences is *moderated* by a specific third variable: the relationship of the individual to the regime. Thus, by splitting the sample, we can account for this moderating variable and see if preferences for democracy are fundamentally different for members of the population if they are engaged in the PA's institutions.[31] A summary of the models can be found below:

Table 2: Summary of Models 1 (PA-affiliated) and 2 (not PA-affiliated)

	Model 1	Model 2
	PA affiliated	*Not PA affiliated*
Democracy		
Autocratizing	−0.271	0.013
	(0.359)	(0.134)
Democratizing	−0.601*	−0.115
	(0.345)	(0.136)
Secularism	−0.437*	0.138
	(0.229)	(0.096)
Refugee	0.192	0.042
	(0.294)	(0.119)
Education	0.205*	0.132***
	(0.117)	(0.044)
Employment	0.557	0.043
	(0.635)	(0.114)
Poverty Line	0.054	0.078
	(0.174)	(0.053)
Political Affiliation	−0.053	−0.030***
	(0.038)	(0.013)
Location Type	0.157	0.116
	(0.205)	(0.084)
Governorate	0.081**	0.024
	(0.035)	(0.015)
Peace Process	−0.539***	−0.269***
	(0.181)	(0.065)
N	182	1,084
LRchi2(11)	25.04	44.20
Prob > chi2	0.009	0.000

* $p<0.05$; ** $p<0.01$; *** $p<0.001$.

To check the robustness of both models, I dropped the control variables one by one to see if a specific variable was driving the results. In Model 1, results hold up only if education levels and poverty levels are accounted for. In Model 2, there were no differences from the main independent variables (i.e. the autocratizing and democratizing treatments), either in statistical significance or direction, no matter which control variable was included or excluded. Interested readers can refer to the appendix for details.

Clearly, there is a difference between those who are connected to the PA versus independent respondents on the question of democracy and accountability. In the first model with those connected to the PA, only "democratiz-ing" international involvement had any significant effect on preferences for democracy. But, interestingly, such "democratizing" international involvement made respondents *less* likely to rank democracy as important. These results were consistent no matter the inclusion, exclusion, or combination of control variables. Thus we can confirm hypothesis 3 that members of the public will have divergent preferences based on their affiliation with the regime.

On the other hand, if respondents were not connected to the PA, interna-tional involvement had no effect on their preferences for democracy and accountability. These results run counter to what the literature expects. Previous studies have made the argument that international involvement has a large impact on public opinion and the preferences of the public for democ-racy, in a way that implies uniformity. What these results make clear, however, is that such a relationship is not accurate unless we control for a major mod-erating factor: the position of the respondent in relation to the regime and its institutions. In this survey, such a connection was directly accounted for. As a result, we can indeed see clear differences between people's preferences depending on their position in relation to the regime. Certain types of inter-national involvement have an impact but only if respondents are tied to the regime's institutions in a meaningful way. This confirms the hypothesis that those unaffiliated will be less affected; in fact, what we see here is that for the general public, unconnected to official institutions, international involvement primes have no effect at all.

The control variables capturing education and views on the peace process were also statistically significant. Those who were more educated were more likely to value democracy in both the PA-affiliated and non-affiliated groups. On the other hand, the more a respondent opposes the peace process (and implicitly, the status quo of the Palestinian statehood question), the less sup-port they expressed for democracy and accountability. Again, this was the case across the entire sample. In the PA-affiliated group, the variable capturing secularism had a negative effect on democracy scores. The more secular, the less likely to express a preference for democracy and accountability. Given the particular antagonism between Hamas and Fatah in this case, it makes sense that those respondents who identify as specifically secular are less likely to express a preference for democracy and accountability. Democracy and accountability, after all, would bring Hamas to public office.

In the non-affiliated group, political affiliation was highly significant statis-tically, meaning the political party/group that respondents identified with had a significant effect on their preferences for democracy and accountability. The lack of significance on this variable in the PA-affiliated group is most likely a reflection of the fact that those affiliated with the PA are predominantly from one political party (Fatah). The breakdown of political affiliations, and their effect on the dependent variable, can be found below.

Table 3. Preferences for democracy by political affiliation

Popular Front for the Liberation of Palestine	−0.653
	(0.658)
Fatah	−0.895
	(0.589)
Hamas	−1.167**
	(0.595)
Democratic Front for the Liberation of Palestine	−0.234
	(0.726)
Islamic Jihad	−1.217*
	(0.697)
Fida	−1.084
	(1.090)
Al-Mubadara	−1.596**
	(0.684)
Mustaqbal al-Islami	−1.013
	(0.670)
Mustaqbal al-Watani	−0.573
	(1.645)
Salam Fayyad's party	−1.188**
	(0.589)
Unaffiliated	−0.705
	(0.939)
N	1084

* p<0.05; ** p<0.01; *** p<0.001.

Predictably, affiliation with Islamist parties such as Hamas and Islamic Jihad has a significant effect on preferences for democracy and accountability. Affiliation with those groups has a negative effect on preferences for democracy, according to this data, which is understandable given their previous experiences with the democratic process. The same can be said for groups that have separated themselves from the main ruling party within the PA, mainly al-Mubadara and Salam Fayyad's Third Way party. Both parties are made up of ex-PA members, dissatisfied with the status quo and the rhetoric of state-building with little results.[32]

To further examine differences between those connected to the regime versus those who are not, I also analyzed whether their preferences for democracy and accountability differed in magnitude (measured, as mentioned above, with an ordinal scale from 1 to 5). I ran an analysis of variance (ANOVA) test to determine whether there are differences in democracy preferences between the two treatment conditions and the control group, without splitting the sample between PA-affiliated respondents and non-affiliated respondents. The results are in Table 4 below. To follow up on that analysis, I ran a t-test to see if there are differences between the two treatments (autocratizing versus democratizing) only. Results are in Table 5 below. We can conclude from both tests that without accounting for the respondent's relationship to the regime, there is no statistically significant difference between treatment groups in terms of their democracy preferences. The experiment itself has null results without accounting for control variables, such as in the full regression models included above, or accounting for the main moderating variable (the respondent's relation to the regime).

Table 4: Pooled sample ANOVA testing

Treatment	Mean	Std. Dev.	Freq.
Autocratizing	2.495	1.170	430
Democratizing	2.569	1.191	430
Control	2.497	1.233	410

F value 0.53 Prob>F 0.587.

Table 5: T-test between treatments

	Democratizing	Autocratizing
Mean	2.569	2.495
SD	1.192	1.170
SE	0.057	0.056
N	0.430	0.430
P value	0.3585.	–

In sum, this analysis examines differences among the public itself. To ascertain whether there are also differences between the elite and public level, I examine the qualitative data collected through elite interviews in the next section.

Interview analysis: elite preferences for democracy and accountability

In order to assess the effect of countervailing international pressure on the preferences of elites, I conducted semi-structured interviews with PA officials. These interviews included open-ended questions designed to give respondents space to provide as accurate a description of their opinions as possible. I mainly focused on two key issues: the role of international patrons in their specific work and how important they believe democracy and accountability is to the overall objective of the PA.

First, on the role of international involvement generally, practically every single government official I interviewed regarded international patrons as crucial to their work. They often emphasized that US involvement in particular was especially important. Other states, such as members of the EU or Arab states, are considered "very limited" without the United States and, more importantly, American approval.[33] Opinions on this role were very mixed. Some expressed that "American hegemony is the crucial problem,"[34] and that their role was an autocratizing one because the United States was highly "undemocratic"[35] in the region. Others, however, claimed that American involvement is "the only way we [the PA] advance."[36] But overall, the PA was characterized as a "hostage" to international patrons.[37] Thus, interviewees agreed that the effect of such involvement—whether autocratizing or democratizing—was undeniable.

When asked to explain further how the United States and other patrons are crucial to the direction of their work, the interviewees outlined a number of key mechanisms. Specifically, interviewees argued that patrons are able to set the agenda and control the political process through the use of: (1) targeted funding and, (2) training programs. First, with regard to targeted funding, many government officials complained that American programs (through USAID and other organizations) attempt to impose issues/objectives "unsuitable for Palestinians" in their current stage of national liberation.[38] There is often little need for the programs that the United States funds, but PA officials feel obliged to take part in them for political reasons. For instance, officials cited programs on gender equality and environmental preservation as being less useful. Moreover, such targeted funding is never a "blank check," PA officials note, but is politically motivated and intended to target certain echelons of the PA.[39] As a result, such targeted funding creates pockets of corruption and clientelistic practices.[40] According to officials, targeted funding is a means by which the United States reorients the PA from focusing on the threat of

Israeli occupation to focusing on internal opposition.[41] Overall, many view the effect of such programs as having "killed the popular struggle."[42]

Furthermore, many such programs funded by the United States involve training programs in particular. These programs are intended to develop the logistic skills of officials involved in the state-building project in terms of understanding their respective roles within the bureaucracy. Ideally, such training would allow for clear demarcations of authority, separation of power, and oversight mechanisms. However, many PA officials regard these training programs as a means for political indoctrination or cooptation.[43] For instance, PA officials often mentioned that the syllabus/agenda of training programs for officials from the Ministry of Interior were amended by American officials if they included discussions of the Israeli occupation or popular mobilization.[44] When PA officials would insist, the United States would refuse to proceed with the training.

Another example involves Lieutenant General Keith Dayton, the US security coordinator for Israel and the PA. Dayton was heavily involved in the PA's decision-making processes and (at the time) Prime Minister Fayyad had to coordinate extensively with Dayton while implementing his reforms. Officials who refused to work within Dayton's parameters were effectively sidelined and given early retirement.[45] It is important to note that these parameters did not center on issues of corruption, bureaucratic competence, or the like but on the *political views* of the PA officials receiving training.[46] In fact, American officials would check with Israeli intelligence on each member of the PA that was being called for training before the commencement of the program. Those previously involved in protests, for example, were rarely included as a result.[47]

A group of retired bureaucrats pointed out that "forced retirement" had become the preferred tactic of Dayton and his allies within the Ministry of Interior. PA officials who refused to coordinate with Dayton fully or refused to limit training programs to particular employees found themselves at the receiving end of a gradual lay-off. Some of these incidents involved attempting to discuss political concerns and challenges in training, rather than keeping things purely "managerial" in scope.[48]

Thus it becomes clear that the United States has a profound effect on the objectives and considerations of elites and decision-makers. The involvement of international patrons, through a number of mechanisms, is not a negligible effect. Decision-makers within the PA take seriously the limitations imposed upon them by these patrons, in particular the United States. Moreover, the United States plays a specifically autocratizing role in this case: its limitations create pockets of corruption, aggrandizes individuals further and further removed from public opinion, and sidelines opposition. So, when we move on to the question of democracy and accountability, and how important it is to decision-makers versus the public, the results are to be expected. Often citing the fear of international involvement, respondents within the PA overwhelmingly found democracy a second-order priority, if a priority at all.

Moreover, officials would often claim that Palestinians are "not ready," "not qualified," or "unsuitable" for democracy.[49] "We must become like Sweden [in terms of economic development] before we can start asking for a democracy," one security official said. Rationalizations for this position included the "tribal culture" present in the Palestinian territories,[50] the lack of an educated populace,[51] or the threat of "extremism."[52] This point was repeated by numerous PA officials: if democracy was practiced, they claimed Palestinians would turn to extremists "such as Hamas or ISIS."[53] Many officials argued there is no space for any religion in a democracy; thus, given the presence of religious groups in Palestine, democracy was surely a premature notion.[54] Some also made the argument that democratic practices at the local level, or during the 2006 parliamentary elections, only served to fragment Palestinian society.[55] Therefore, democratic practices and accountability do more harm than good, and should not be an objective of the PA especially while under occupation and facing "internal threats." As one bureaucrat succinctly put it: "Americans have taught us that there is a difference between democracy and creating problems."

A recurrent theme in responses was also that international patrons often express democratic sentiments, but concurrently do not accept what democracy would entail. For instance, a number of respondents cited American pressure prior to the 2006 legislative elections as a case in point. "It was the Americans who forced us to have elections. We [Fatah] knew we weren't ready," one respondent claimed.[56] "Hamas would have controlled the West Bank," another respondent admitted, "they were popularly supported."[57] Thus, when elections occurred and the American-allied Fatah lost, the United States imposed sanctions that destabilized the territories. This episode has clearly had a profound effect on how elites respond when asked about democracy or accountability. Elites recognize international patrons may employ a certain pro-democracy *rhetoric*, but their *actions* lie in a completely different camp (in this case, actions that indicate a preference for stability and maintenance of the status quo). "Why didn't the US accept the election results?," many countered when asked about democracy in the territories. "It's clear they don't really want democracy, and they pressure us to do other things."[58] The mismatch in rhetoric and action on the part of international patrons may explain why "democratizing" international involvement has a *negative* effect on preferences for democracy and accountability among PA-affiliated respondents. Such involvement is generally associated with instability and international backlash. "We cannot judge the PA for its lack of democracy when political issues remain unresolved," said one official, "and Americans make it hard for us to solve anything."[59]

Specifically in the Palestinian case, PA-affiliated respondents also recognize that "democratizing" involvement would likely lead to a turnover, with Hamas at the helm. Judging by the historical record, this would be a development the American establishment would consider too abhorrent to uphold. For that reason, Palestinian elites as well as PA-affiliated respondents in the general public react negatively to international involvement, even when the rhetoric is "democratizing." Those unaffiliated with the PA do not have the same loyalties and are not concerned with Fatah remaining or leaving office (even if they do not necessarily support the Islamist parties). Their livelihoods are not tied to American support as directly as those affiliated with the PA.

Discussion

The differences between elite and public preferences thus become clear. While democracy and accountability is generally important to certain segments of the public, even under autocratizing international pressures, elites convey a very different calculation. As the theoretical argument proposed by this chapter suggests, elites in Palestine are concerned with wholly different pressures from the publics they represent. This is a direct result of international involvement, through the various mechanisms outlined in the empirical analysis. International involvement, particularly via the United States and its allies, therefore creates a principal–agent problem between elites and the societies they represent. This consequently confirms the first argument of this chapter.

The role of international patrons can of course vary case to case, as previously noted. However, in the case of the PA, it becomes clear via the qualitative analysis that the role of the United States and its allies is decidedly autocratizing even as the rhetoric is democratizing. Nevertheless, the United States does not prioritize democratic practices; rather, it creates pockets of corruption and facilitates the aggrandizement of groups within the PA unaccountable to their publics. Thus the autocratizing role of international patrons in this case leads elites to prioritize stability and express little support for democracy and accountability overall despite supposedly democratizing rhetoric. This confirms the second argument of this chapter. Elites reported democracy and accountability as being a low priority and made a number of arguments as to why their society was "unsuitable" for democratic practices.

On the other hand, public opinion, as the theoretical argument notes, is conditional on the relation of the individual to the political regime. The statistical analysis of the nationally representative survey corroborates this claim. Preferences for democracy and accountability differed, according to the position of the respondent in relation to the regime and its institutions. Those who were affiliated with the PA mirrored elites to some extent in that they considered international involvement important to their preferences. Alternatively, international involvement (either autocratizing or democratizing) had no significant effect on those individuals with little or no relation to the regime. This corroborates the claim that international involvement has an effect *in interaction with* the relation of the individual to the regime. To put it another way, the relationship of the individual to the regime moderates the effect of international involvement. This implies that not only do various types of international involvement create a principal–agent problem between elites and their public but that such involvement also fragments the public itself.

These results help to explain the divergence between Palestinian leadership and Palestinian society, as well as the mutual frustration described in the interviews and the beginning of the chapter. Results also highlight the divergence that exists in society itself. Crucially, the involvement of countries like the United States in the PA's decision-making processes helps to explain this dynamic. In the next chapter, we will link this elite–public and societal split to the polarization we see in Palestine today.

3

THE LEGACY OF REPRESSION

"They are traitors," one official said to me as we sipped coffee in his Ramallah office. Leaning forward, lowering his voice conspiratorially, he continued, "You know Hamas members take all their orders from the *murshid* [supreme guide of the Muslim Brotherhood] in Egypt right? They are not a group concerned with Palestine alone. To them, Afghanistan is the same as Palestine."[1]

This was not an uncommon response from Fatah-affiliated people I spoke to while conducting interviews in the West Bank. Many expressed their distrust of Hamas and the motivations of the opposition. But these sentiments were not limited to Fatah operatives alone. People from across the political spectrum referred to their political opponents as "traitors" and often questioned their true intentions. A common refrain was that Hamas/Fatah/third parties were backed by the Americans and the Israelis, either overtly or covertly. No matter whom I spoke to—whether officials in the PA or activists or people in regular conversation—this sense of deep mistrust and fragmentation was palpable.

The previous chapter showed the manner in which international involvement generated polarized public opinion around preferences for democracy and accountability. It also showed how affiliation with the PA regime had a large effect on whether or not international involvement was a salient factor in determining preferences. Clearly, the PA itself has an effect on society and creates two "camps" comprising those who are affiliated with the regime and those who are not. These two groups do not have congruent preferences, even though they live under the same system and face much the same challenges.

In this chapter, I examine the next step of the causal argument by examining whether the split in Palestinian society uncovered in Chapter 2 has an effect on political behavior. By many accounts, the PA has become increasingly authoritarian. Aside from regular violations against personal freedoms and the use of heavy-handed cooptation mechanisms, the PA has also ignored overdue elections.[2] Concurrently, Palestinian society has become increasingly polarized and unable to mount successful opposition, neither to the unpopular PA nor to the occupation. However, the link between the PA's own authoritarian strategies, and subsequent polarization and coordination issues within society, has not been fully explored. Therefore, the main questions of this chapter are: What is the effect of the PA's authoritarian strategies on polarization? And how does that polarization shape social cohesion?

Polarization is defined at the public level as a growing adherence to partisanship, where group affiliation increasingly defines policy preferences across a wide array of issues. While polarization at the party level has been addressed quite extensively, the debate on public-level polarization is ongoing. We know that particular conditions can generate polarization in society and that authoritarian contexts generate preference falsification and an inhibited ability to coordinate. But we do not yet have any research to link the two processes together. I argue that increased polarization is in fact linked to retrenched authoritarianism: authoritarian practices *generate* polarization, which in turn inhibits social cohesion.

This chapter specifically addresses whether authoritarian strategies have an effect on the level of polarization in society and the subsequent ability of different segments of society to coordinate. There are a number of regime types subsumed under the banner of authoritarianism. Differences between regimes lie in their institutions and the strategies they use to maintain power (i.e. cooptation, repression, or a combination of both). The differential effects of these strategies on polarization remain unclear, but understanding these effects will have implications for clarifying how authoritarianism works at the societal level. Importantly, it will also help to explain the erosion of effective opposition in particular authoritarian contexts.

I present a two-stage theory in this chapter, arguing that (1) particular authoritarian strategies generate polarization, and (2) polarization subsequently affects social cohesion and capacity for collective action. I provide evidence for this argument by utilizing lab-in-field experiments that uncover these connections. The experiments use survey analysis and behavioral measures to assess both the level of polarization in the sample, as well as the level of social cohesion. To elucidate causal mechanisms, I present a case study of Islamist groups since the creation of the PA, as well as analysis of interviews conducted with leftist party affiliates within the West Bank.

Results confirm the theory that authoritarianism exacerbates polarization and affects the ability and willingness of different groups to coordinate. These results shed light on the mechanisms of authoritarian control and provide pathways for future research on how regimes maintain power by neutralizing opposition over time. On a substantive level, these results also explain why Palestinians suffer from increasing polarization and a decreased capacity for collective action. By fostering polarization within society, authoritarian regimes have been able to both "produce and reproduce" themselves, entrenching their control further.[3]

What we know about polarization

The study of political polarization has emerged out of the study of democracies, particularly the United States. This literature defines public-level polarization as the dynamic in which a person's position is increasingly defined by their partisan affiliation. Scholars and polling experts equate this phenomenon with "ideological consistency."[4] Take, for example, the stance of the US Republican Party on reproductive health. Previously, Republicans did not necessarily have a clear stance on this issue, and it was not a part of the party's platform. Today, however, the creeping effect of partisan affiliation has created a dynamic in which being a Republican means having a particular stance on reproductive health. This dynamic is repeated across a wide variety of issues, wherein partisan affiliation entails increasing ideological consistency.[5]

Nevertheless, it is often difficult to assess polarization because it can be defined both at the party and the public level. Party polarization is defined as the increased divergence over time of party positions. For instance, to ascertain the increasing divergence of the Republican and Democratic Parties in the American system, researchers collect the voting records of members of Congress and map those records over a number of years.[6] In that way, we can trace the "process" of polarization temporally. However, this is only possible at the party level.

For that reason, when defining polarization at the public level, we focus on ideological consistency *within* each individual, assuming that increased ideological consistency at the individual level goes hand in hand with increased divergence between party positions in society.[7] The reason ideological consistency is taken as an indicator of political polarization is because, as the Pew Poll appendix notes, "there is no ex-ante reason for people's views on diverse issues such as the social safety net, homosexuality and military strength to correlate." But these views nevertheless "have a traditional 'left/right' association." Thus the more ideological consistency, the more evidence we have of a polarized view on the part of that respondent.

The causes of such polarization are also under constant debate. Some argue there is indeed increased polarization because party elites affect public opinion,[8] while others argue this elite–public feedback loop mostly affects those most politically active.[9] Outside of the United States, explanations in the comparative politics literature include the effect of elite opinion on the public,[10] pre-existing cleavages/historical trajectory,[11] or international involvement.[12] Although some of these explanations have explored polarization in the context of authoritarian states, most have focused on democratic contexts. Moreover, none have yet explored the link between the practice of authoritarianism itself with polarization in society.

There are reasons to believe authoritarianism may be linked to the phenomenon of polarization due to the strategies authoritarian regimes use.[13] The main objective of authoritarian regimes is to control their populations and prevent unauthorized mobilization by using combinations of repression and cooptation.[14] Repression is designed to raise the costs of collective action and make it less likely. It is often selective, targeting specific groups over others. Alternatively, cooptation is designed to *facilitate* certain mobilization, particularly that which is affiliated with the regime. This can include cooptation of segments of the population for votes during election times, for rallies in support of the regime, and other strategies.[15] Cooptation is often inclusive because the larger the pro-regime coalition, the more the regime benefits.[16] Therefore, certain regimes rely heavily on casting as wide a net as possible and coopting most broadly.[17]

However, if strategies target certain groups over others, then those strategies themselves may cause divisions and polarization. We have some reason to believe this is the case when reviewing work in political psychology. We know, for instance, that group identities are strengthened when groups in society have varying experiences—experiences that include targeted repression or exclusion from the regime's material benefits.[18] This is particularly the case when groups share *traumatic* experiences. Historically, there are a number of examples that fit this explanation, such as diaspora communities after particular traumas and victims of civil war.[19] Victimization and shared trauma can have profound effects on political identities generations down the line.[20] Thus if shared traumatic experiences help define identities in these many cases, then we can conclude that authoritarian practices, also intended to inflict trauma, have this effect as well.[21]

Such polarization may in turn be linked to less cooperative behavior. A number of reasons have been outlined to explain lack of cooperation generally. The political violence literature focuses on the effect of divisions on people's capacity to overcome collective action problems.[22] This is particularly the case in repressive contexts, such as within national liberation movements in colonial settings. Similarly, in the context of democratic transitions, polarized opposition forces are less likely to coordinate effectively against a ruling regime.[23] And, in the case of civil conflict, rebel groups achieve their goals less effectively when fragmentation is high.[24] We thus have reason to believe that divisions and polarization lead to less cooperative behavior.

All in all, the link between authoritarianism, polarization, and declining cooperation across groups is not an inconsequential one. Scholars have long recognized that the threat of mass mobilization is what keeps regimes accountable. As long as regimes can limit coordinated mobilization, they can maintain their power. To ensure coordinated mobilization never develops, authoritarian regimes foster divisions, secure in the fact that these divisions will create almost insurmountable costs to collective action. In that way, authoritarianism reproduces itself.[25]

The link between polarization and social cohesion

Informed by the abovementioned research, I outline a theory that links the practice of authoritarianism with polarization and declining social cohesion. First, authoritarian regimes create divisions within the societies they govern. Even if regimes attempt to build as large a base as possible, they will still try to limit cooperation between different groups. This sets up the regime itself as the main arbitrator between competing factions. Once stoked and exacerbated, these divisions can lead to increased polarization.

In authoritarian contexts, what is often a less relevant division is made salient through authoritarian strategies. Take, for instance, the salience of tribes in the Jordanian system. Even though not all Jordanians have strong ties to tribal institutions, people organize around these tribal identities in reaction to the regime's divide-and-conquer strategies.[26] This most clearly manifests itself in the electoral system, where the government often gerrymanders to increase tribal representation, which forces voters to coalesce around such divisions for the sake of electoral success. And in more homogenous populations, the main line of division becomes pro- and anti-regime.

But how do authoritarian strategies lead to division and polarization? I argue this has to do with the *type* of strategy, and specifically, whether it is *exclusionary* or *inclusionary*. Authoritarian strategies fall into two main camps: cooptation and repression. As commonly defined, cooptation entails giving certain segments of society a stake in the status quo by providing a variety of benefits. The most important aspect of this strategy is that it attempts to *include* certain segments of the population in the regime's institutions in a non-repressive manner. In this way, dissent is silenced and the regime can rely on a base of support.

Repression, on the other hand, is *exclusionary*. Strategies such as legal restrictions on opposition movements, limitations on the press, or outright violence target certain segments of the population but do not attempt to create a base of support. The opposite is in fact the case: the regime relies on repression when it regards challengers as outside the fold and unsusceptible to dissuasion from their opposition. This also creates divisions between those who are persecuted and those who are not.[27] Since group identities are often formed through shared trauma or grievance, we expect that authoritarian strategies generate polarization.

This theoretical expectation does not tell us *how* each strategy generates polarization, however. Both strategies engender costs to dissent, but in different ways. On the one hand, cooptation ties certain groups into the regime's fold in a material sense, and thus puts a discernable cost on opposing the regime. To dissent would mean facing material losses, which often seems unnecessary when cooptation entails access to power structures. Thus those facing cooptation become risk averse.[28] Dissenters that threaten the regime, and by association those who benefit from the regime, will be viewed with increasing distrust. Group identities begin to form around those "moderates" who work with the regime in power, and those "extremists" who threaten their material well-being. But since cooptation as a strategy is inclusionary, and brings a number of different groups to the table, this creates a shared identity across a spectrum of groups and an interest in cooperation and remaining "moderate."

Exclusionary strategies, on the other hand, limit options for targeted groups. They pose the extreme cost of bodily harm or death. In some instances, exclusionary strategies can spur regular citizens into open rebellion, because the alternative to active resistance is loss of life.[29] But not everyone in society is being repressed to this extreme level. Those who are repressed create an identity around shared trauma and develop grievances with those who do not share the same fate. One can argue that the cost of bodily harm, loss of life, or loss of freedom is a higher one to bear than the cost of losing a seat at the table and engenders a larger reaction from those under threat. For instance, after the coup in Egypt of 3 July 2013, the repression of the Muslim Brotherhood has provoked an even more polarized dynamic, in which Islamists have become increasingly radicalized and insular.[30] Therefore, we can expect that:

H1: *Inclusionary cooptation strategies will generate polarization to a smaller degree than exclusionary repression strategies due to the variation in imposed costs.*

The second stage of this theory involves the causal link between polarization and social cohesion. I build on Wendy Pearlman's definition, which disaggregates cohesion into three parts: leadership, institutional structure, and "sense of collective purpose."[31] I focus on that final aspect of social cohesion and define it as the capacity for collective action and cooperation between different segments of society, fueled by shared preferences.

Polarization directly limits this capacity through a number of mechanisms. Authoritarian strategies rely on stoking fear of regime crackdown, which generates "preference falsification."[32] In a repressive and polarized environment, people cannot be sure of whom to trust and where the interests of others actually lie. Therefore, they falsify their preferences in order to survive a possible crackdown. In this way, despite there being a high level of opposition to the regime, citizens remain acquiescent. Thus authoritarian strategies may obfuscate often natural alliances between different groups of people whose preferences align. In such a context, social cohesion declines and cooperation falters. And this is often a self-reinforcing situation.

Bahrain before and after the Arab Spring provides a useful example of this. Bahraini opposition figures note that polarization based on sect is a relatively new phenomenon.[33] Opposition groups representing both Sunni and Shia joined the protests in 2011.[34] In fact, experts agree that both the Bahraini uprising and general opposition were motivated in large part by economic grievances, not sectarian ones.[35] But, following brutal repression, this wide-ranging cohesion began to crumble. Sunnis involved in protests risked losing preferential treatment; Shias involved in protests found it risky to work with Sunnis who may not have been as committed to regime change. Bahrainis were polarized into different camps and their capacity for collective action against the regime declined significantly.[36] The uprising failed, and the regime continues to consolidate its power, all while different segments of the population struggle to achieve a semblance of a united front.

How is increased polarization linked to decreased social cohesion? Preference falsification under authoritarianism breeds distrust between possible allies and inhibits cooperation. This happens because authoritarian strategies have the effect of prompting grievances *between* different groups and an insularity *within* groups. Specifically, by targeting certain segments of the population, a regime is able to create a situation of haves and have nots.[37] Those within the targeted group will share in the trauma and lack of privilege associated with authoritarian crackdowns, producing an increasingly insular group whose members can only cooperate with one another. Moreover, those within the targeted group will look upon those of other groups with distrust and resentment and feel aggrieved due to their lack of privilege. Polarization thus leads to a decline in cooperation in the short term. And the inability to cooperate and mount serious challenges to the regime engenders a decline in social cohesion in the long term.

One particularly extreme example is the case of Syria. Those involved in the Syrian protests were initially inspired by the Arab Spring and called for reform rather than regime transition.[38] The protests became more vehement and widespread when the original calls for reform were met with a crackdown.[39] But this crackdown only targeted certain segments of the population: largely Sunni citizens in secondary urban centers. Moreover, the regime has historically treated minorities preferentially, giving them the clear message that their fates were intertwined with Assad remaining in power.[40] This generated grievances among certain segments of the population and insularity among others. What began as a non-sectarian, non-violent movement transformed into a highly polarized and fragmented rebellion.[41] The opposition fractured into a number of groups, and grievances between groups have exacerbated to the point of ethnic cleansing.[42] Today, the conflict has become existential for many groups within Syria, destroying the possibility for the emergence of a cohesive opposition against Assad's regime—now or in the foreseeable future.

Given these examples, we can expect that:

H2: *An increase in polarization between groups leads to a decline in cooperation and social cohesion.*

H3: *Groups most targeted by exclusionary strategies will be the most polarized and least willing to cooperate with others.*

H4: *Increased polarization will be characterized by insularity within groups and grievances between them.*

To sum up, I expect that the practice of authoritarianism generates polarization and declining social cohesion, but the severity of this dynamic depends on the type of authoritarian strategy. Exclusionary strategies will generate higher levels of polarization than inclusionary strategies. Such polarization leads to increased grievance between, and insularity within, groups, which in turn affects cooperation. In this way, authoritarianism generates declining social cohesion. In the absence of drastic changes to a regime's capacity, declining social cohesion makes challenges to the regime less likely.

How to study authoritarian strategies in Palestine, and what about the occupation?

The Palestinian territories are a unique case with two layers of governance: the Israeli occupation, and the PA, which behaves as a "subcontractor of repression" for the occupation.[43] Occupation is obviously very repressive, but in this scenario, Israel outsources much of its repression to the PA as an indigenous governing authority. This creates a dynamic in which the PA acts as a buffer between Palestinians and the Israeli occupation, and the relationship of Palestinians to their government more closely resembles that of a classic authoritarian regime. There is an inherent difference between an occupying power and an indigenous authoritarian regime in terms of their effect on political cohesion.[44] For our purposes, a focus on the conventional authoritarian regime, rather than just the occupation, is better suited to understanding the theory highlighted in this chapter.

The Palestinian territories provide evidence of both authoritarian strategies and increased polarization. First, in terms of authoritarian strategies, the PA relies heavily on the mechanism of cooptation by employing large numbers of Palestinians in its institutions.[45] As Tariq Dana notes, the PA's "patron–client" relationship between itself and its subjects is an effective tool of cooptation because it "secures loyalties," revives the "politics of tribalism" (and thus fragments Palestinian society into smaller parts), and "co-opts opposition."[46] The PA achieves this by acting as a source of income for many that rely on its continuation for their survival. And this safety-net role of the PA continues to expand, as leadership attempts to assuage the effects of the occupation and the stagnant Palestinian economy.[47]

Second, the PA also has the capacity to engage in repression with the help of the Israeli occupation. Many Palestinians have complained that the PA is increasingly operating as a "police state."[48] Not only is the police-to-citizen ratio incredibly high but the PA has also expanded its purview over online commentary, activism, and academia. Moreover, human rights organizations have documented that those who are imprisoned by the PA are subject to violent punishments,[49] often in coordination with the Israeli occupation. Coupled with the fact that almost every family relies on the PA in some way for their livelihood, this dynamic means dissent is effectively silenced.

There is also evidence that Palestinian society is becoming increasingly polarized. Polling data shows a clear bifurcation in Palestinian society. In the Palestine Survey Research Center's latest polls, respondents are almost evenly split on key contentious questions. For example, on a question related to whether or not the PA as an institution remained a worthwhile endeavor, respondents were almost evenly split (49 percent to 46 percent) on the issue.[50] This bifurcation is replicated across a number of issue areas and speaks to the polarization that exists in Palestine today.[51]

Given these dynamics, the PA provides a useful case study to examine the effects of authoritarianism on societies and how they function. Because of its unique status as a subcontractor of the Israeli occupation, the PA behaves in a similar fashion to many regimes in the Arab world. In the next section, I explain the utility of the laboratory experiment design and outline its use in this chapter.

Assessing polarization: laboratory experiments

The main independent variable of this study is authoritarian practices. I focus on how this variable affects two main dependent variables: polarization and social cohesion. This study utilizes a lab-in-field experiment, case study analysis, and interview analysis to explore these linkages. Specifically, I use the lab-in-field method because experiments are effective at isolating the causal effect of the variables of interest rather than relying on correlations. Moreover, the laboratory setting allows researchers to control the inputs for participants and minimizes random error. It is also useful because of the flexibility it provides in priming and targeting questions based on previous responses. That the experiments were done at the field site increases the external validity of the results.[52] The experiments uncover the relationship between authoritarian practices, polarization, and social cohesion. The case studies and interviews are used to make causal-process observations, in order to provide context and elucidate mechanisms more clearly.[53]

The experiments used for this chapter were conducted at Birzeit University, using a student sample. To my knowledge, this is the first social science experiment that has been conducted at Birzeit. Given conditions in the West Bank and the novelty of the design, there were some obstacles in data collection. This led to a less than ideal sample size (n=67).[54] The content also had to be highly tuned to the social and political conditions of Birzeit students, meaning that questions directly referenced relevant student groups, recent elections, and so on. Although this posed some challenges, it meant that the experiment had a greater level of internal validity, in contrast to the often highly theoretical laboratory experiments common in the discipline. This also increased ecological validity in the Palestinian context. The students' responses were kept entirely anonymous, with any response to questions remaining online in encrypted form on the Qualtrics platform. Behavioral measures were done on a physical piece of paper that was shredded at the end of the session during de-briefing.

The flow of the experiment was as follows. Students were first asked which political student group they most identified with. Birzeit University students are highly politicized, and student government is an important part of their daily affairs. The choices encompassed the three major parties (according to student election results): the Hamas-affiliated Islamist party, the Fatah-affiliated centrist party, and the Popular Front for the Liberation of Palestine-affiliated leftist party. Although these groups are theoretically independent of their affiliates, they often take positions similar to their namesakes. The group chosen by the respondent affected other questions later in the survey.

To assess the initial level of polarization, I asked students to place themselves on a scale (ranging from 1, Strongly Agree to 7, Strongly Disagree) in relation to three statements that encompass the positions of these political groups. Depending on the group they chose to affiliate with, I created an attitudinal polarization measure by averaging their ideological consistency score for the two other groups. For instance, if a student identified with Fatah, their polarization score would encompass their average level of agreement with the Islamists and the leftists on certain positions. This is similar to measures of polarization in the American context because it tests ideological consistency on the most prevalent issues to political groups in Palestinian society.

The students were then asked standard demographic questions. These were phrased in a similar way to national polls conducted by the Palestinian Center for Survey and Policy Research, which helped maintain a high level of external validity. The questions included age, income level in relation to society, residence (governorate), gender, and employment sector (PA or private).

Then, I presented the first experimental component: a survey experiment using a priming method to bring certain details to the forefront of respondents' minds. This component specifically tested variations of authoritarian strategies by priming for cooptation and repression. I also included a neutral condition. Respondents were assigned a treatment condition randomly in order to assess the independent effect of each treatment. The English translation can be found below:

> *Cooptation: The PA often funds the efforts of social activists on the basis that those activists will coordinate with the PA on their objectives and strategies.*

> *Repression: The PA often cracks down on the efforts of social activists, on the basis that those activists did not coordinate with the PA on their objectives and strategies.*

> *Neutral: The PA calls for the creation of a Palestinian state in the West Bank and Gaza, as well as a compromise with Israel on the basis of negotiations.*

After the priming, I gauged willingness to cooperate through two behavioral measures. The first behavioral measure included asking respondents how likely they were to sign a petition against corruption with members of the same affiliation as the ones they initially chose. If they said anything above "likely," they were provided a petition to sign ("Petition" measure). They were then asked how much time they would commit in the coming semester to a political campaign run by a different political affiliation ("Time Allocation" measure). In order to wash out any possible priming effects of these questions, respondents were then asked to do a counting exercise. Such an exercise is used so that respondents forget the wording of the previous question and can be asked new questions without a spurious priming effect. The behavioral measures were then repeated, but with flipped political affiliations.[55]

To assess whether the experimental conditions had an effect on the level of polarization, respondents answered the attitudinal measure from the beginning of the session again. This came after another counting exercise. The experiments concluded with a debriefing and explanation of the experimental method.

Experimental results

Testing hypothesis 1

To assess the effect of the different treatment conditions on the expressed attitudes of respondents, I ran a one-way ANOVA. This test was intended to see if there are differences in polarization scores across the experiment's treatment conditions for the entire sample. While results do not meet conventional levels of statistical significance, they are suggestive. Judging by the direction of coefficients, those who received the repression condition are more likely to express polarized views. And, when we assess how the treatment conditions differed from the neutral condition in aggregate, we find that priming for authoritarian strategies did generate more polarized responses. Those who received the neutral condition were less likely to express polarized views than those who received the treatments, given the difference in scores of the attitudinal measures. Although suggestive, this provides some evidence for hypothesis 1.

Table 6: One-way ANOVA results

Experimental condition	Means and standard deviations	N
Neutral	−0.159 (0.473)	22
Cooptation	−0.050 (0.394)	22
Repression	0.109 (0.499)	23
	F statistic: 0.1537	Total N: 67

Table 7: T-test of treatments vs control

	Treatment conditions	Control condition
Mean	0.035	−0.159
SD	0.455	0.473
SE	0.069	0.101
N	43	22
P value	0.114.	–

A comparison of t-tests between the treatment conditions, as well as each treatment versus the control condition, affirms these results. There are no statistically significant differences between groups that received the cooptation treatment versus the neutral condition. There is also no statistically significant difference between those who received the cooptation treatment versus the repression treatment. However, there are significant differences between those that received the neutral condition and the repression treatment.

Table 8: T-test combination results

	P value
Neutral vs Cooptation	0.424
Cooptation vs Repression	0.259
Neutral vs Repression	0.072*
	N= 67

Testing hypothesis 2 and hypothesis 3

To examine whether this suggestive polarization had an effect on willingness to cooperate, I also assessed the difference in scores between their willingness to sign a petition with those of the same versus different political affiliation. I did this for each political group as well as within each treatment group.

Table 9: T-test results of behavioral (petition) measure

	Islamist	Leftist	Fatah
Treatment	0.024**	0.100*	0.149
Cooptation	0.343	0.215	0.140
Repression	0.041**	0.374	0.520
N	18	10	17

Using this behavioral measure, we find results despite the small sample size. Whereas there were only suggestive results for the effect of authoritarianism on polarization, the treatments affected the willingness of respondents to cooperate with others. Authoritarian strategies decreased cooperation, as hypothesis 2 expected, but only under certain conditions: when repression was used, cooperation declined. The same was not the case for cooptation. This helps to provide evidence for the theoretical contention that exclusionary strategies have different effects from inclusionary ones.

As Table 9 shows, students affiliated with the Islamist political party and exposed to the authoritarianism treatment conditions were most affected, and their willingness to cooperate was lowest. As we can see from the difference in scores before and after the experimental treatment, Islamists were more likely to sign a petition if it was supported by other Islamists, and less likely to sign the same petition if it was supported by other political factions. Leftists, as a minority that is also embattled and targeted, had a similar reaction to the authoritarianism treatments. The treatment conditions, however, did not seem to have a significant effect on those from Fatah, the ruling political party. Only the most targeted groups were affected by authoritarian strategies and their polarizing effect, thus confirming hypothesis 3.

The same can be said of the time allocation measure: the treatment condition had an effect on Islamists, but not the other groups. The only difference between the two behavioral measures was the statistically significant results for the leftists in the petition measure, but no statistically significant results for them in the time allocation measure. This is due to the sample size issue rather than an inherent difference in measures or the effect of the treatments on respondent behavior. Results thus confirm hypotheses 2 and 3 on the effects of authoritarianism among the most targeted groups in society.

Table 10: T-test results of behavioral (time allocation) measure

	Islamist	*Leftist*	*Fatah*
Treatment	0.029**	0.347	0.187
Cooptation	0.168	0.391	0.172
Repression	0.100*	–	0.591
N	18	10	17

Authoritarian strategies and their impact on Palestinian groups: causal-process observations

Islamist groups

To demonstrate how repression-induced polarization leads to less cooperation, the following outlines a case study of Islamist groups and their reactions to the PA's strategies over time. I use this case study to test hypothesis 4, and breakdown polarization's effects by focusing on two main mechanisms: increased insularity within groups and increased grievances between groups.

Today's Islamist groups emerged in the first intifada, establishing themselves as an opposition to the political establishment's negotiations with Israel.[56] In the first years of the PA's existence, Islamists acted as opposition groups, often embarrassing the PA leadership in its ongoing attempts to build a state under Israeli scrutiny.[57] Arafat, president from 1994 to 2004, attempted both to repress and coopt these groups,[58] though they were still relatively free to build bases of support through charities, clinics, and other social services. These services "enhanced Hamas's credibility and expanded its social base."[59]

But these strategies had a toll on their operations. Islamist groups did not coordinate effectively and often conducted operations independently although other groups had shared objectives (such as the militant wings of Fatah, for example). And although these operations, particularly the suicide attacks, led to some concessions from the Israeli government,[60] they were largely ineffective in achieving a contiguous Palestinian state.

The second intifada further demonstrates this point. The eruption of Palestinian anger over a delayed Palestinian state led to resistance across the territories. Unlike the first intifada, this effort was uncoordinated, with many organizations across the political spectrum taking independent action.[61] This led to an increase in violence as a response, and an increase in violence between different Palestinian groups.[62] The PA's growing repression, backed by Israeli demands for an end to resistance groups, led to increased insularity within groups and grievances between them. Moreover, as a result of the increased fragmentation, the second intifada did not achieve its objectives as effectively as the first.[63]

Despite limited success, Islamist groups gained popularity in the territories, often as a direct response to disappointment in the PA's performance.[64] This was immediately recognized by Israel, international patrons such as the United States and the EU, and the Fatah leadership. In fact, British and US intelligence services suggested that the PA was best served if opposition movements were sidelined, and there were plans in effect to achieve that goal prior to the legislative elections.[65] In interviews with Fatah members, many admit that they recognized Hamas would win any election and blamed the United States for forcing them to hold elections that brought Islamists to power.[66] Hamas eventually won a plurality of the vote, upending Fatah's historic dominance.

The trajectory of Islamist politics in the Palestinian territories shows that the PA's authoritarian practices indeed had an effect on polarization, as demonstrated by Hamas's unwillingness to cooperate with other groups. However, Arafat's PA relied more heavily on cooptation, and Hamas was given some space to build support across the Palestinian territories. That Hamas was successful enough in mobilizing support, either through service provision or through electoral victories, shows that cooptation strategies were much less polarizing than repressive strategies.

Following Hamas's legislative victory, repressive exclusionary strategies increased polarization to the point of inhibiting cooperation altogether. Reaction included raids and arrests against Hamas sympathizers.[67] Protests by Hamas were attacked by the Fatah-dominated security apparatus. Moreover, Fatah members today fully admit they were given orders not to cooperate with the new government in their capacity as bureaucrats.[68] Members of the security forces also refused to cooperate, and certain branches mobilized to violently remove the new government.[69] Although Hamas attempted to fight back using its own security forces, it lost its control over the PA in the West Bank but retained control over Gaza. The PA in the West Bank continued to be the recognized government internationally, while the Hamas government in Gaza was promptly blockaded by Israel and the international community. Over 600 Palestinians died in the infighting.[70] In the West Bank, opposition groups were quickly driven underground as many of their members were arrested. Islamic charities and affiliated religious leaders were the next to go.[71] Finally, President Abbas swore in an unelected interim government.

This episode had profound effects on how Islamist opposition groups functioned in the West Bank. For one, their traditional strongholds in particular camps and rural communities were targeted, as were their methods for popular outreach. This disrupted their capacity to coordinate effectively, not only because the PA raised the cost of collective action but also because it helped foster insularity within their ranks.[72] Although the Israeli occupation posed a number of challenges to all segments of Palestinian society, there was little coordination between various groups. Instead, they squabbled among themselves, with increasingly violent results. Palestinian society became more polarized, and grievances between different groups increased. Fatah members began to allege that Hamas members were implants, implementing foreign agendas and disloyal to the Palestinian cause. Many are adamant that there were no differences between Hamas and ISIS, and that Hamas was singleminded in taking power only so that it could repress Palestinians.[73]

Concurrently, Islamists became the persecuted party and manifested their grievances in increasingly uncoordinated ways. Repression has been found to decentralize movements, which is precisely what happened here.[74] Hamas members today paint Fatah supporters as traitors and collaborators, with that loosely applied term used to legitimize repression.[75] They often cite security coordination between the PA and Israel as a main grievance. Despite continued talks of reconciliation, Hamas spokespersons claim Fatah is attempting to rig any coming elections in order to ensure victory.[76] Thus there is a palpable lack of trust and cooperation between two sizable segments of the population.[77]

Moreover, Islamist groups cannot mobilize effectively, and non-violent activities are no longer tolerated. For instance, participation in student elections under an Islamist banner often gets students arrested.[78] As a result, disconnected "lone wolf" attacks on Israelis have become the norm of Islamist mobilization.[79] In order to avoid repression, they increasingly rely on secrecy and function by word of mouth.[80] Coupled with Israeli and PA repression, Islamist operations in the West Bank have transformed from a political strategy to a military one, with increasingly violent results.[81] Such a strategy by definition relies on insularity and makes coordination with other groups on common challenges much less likely. All in all, it becomes clear that increased polarization did in fact inhibit cooperation between groups, and Islamists became more insular with increased repression over time.

Leftist parties

To further illustrate the dynamic of increased repression, polarization, and their effects on cooperation, I also conducted interviews with leftist organizers in the West Bank. Once again, I focused on whether polarization generates increased insularity within, and increased grievances between, groups. Although leftist parties represent a smaller segment of society, they have historically played an important role in political mobilization against the occupation. They were integral to social service provision and responsible for much of the grassroots organizing that exemplified the pre-PA era of Palestinian politics.[82] As I will demonstrate using these in-depth interviews, their marginalization was not an organic development but a calculated PA strategy, and a direct result of its authoritarian practices.

The Palestinian left has struggled in recent years to maintain its popular outreach efforts and stay relevant in an increasingly polarized political environment. Activists report that, following Oslo, it became difficult to coordinate with other groups, as some groups decided to work with the PA while others maintained their opposition to the state-building project. Most of their work is successful solely in rural contexts, whereas the urban areas are mostly dormant.[83] Second, Fatah's control over PLO funds has proven a tool to pressure and control leftist factions within the PLO.[84] Finally, there has also been a process of "NGO-ization," wherein grassroots political organizations were coopted into the state-building project and transformed into NGOs with single-issue objectives.[85] All of this has fostered the internal fragmentation of leftist opposition groups.[86] The little cooperation that exists between groups depends on personal ties between members, and not shared political objectives.[87] As a result, cooperation remains meager, and a polarizing divide has arisen between those who work with the PA and those who refuse "collaboration."

As for dynamics between leftist groups and other opposition groups (i.e. the Islamists or other third parties), the activists I interviewed said that such cooperation was now non-existent in the West Bank. Islamists refuse to cooperate with grassroots organizations, both in rural and urban contexts.[88] Ideological disagreements prevent Islamists and other leftists from coordinating their actions, even though both groups agree in their criticisms of the PA.[89] International involvement in many of these groups has also created a divide.[90] "We face not one occupation, but many," said one activist when asked about the effect of international aid on her work.[91] Overall, international involvement generally, and economic aid specifically, is seen as a divisive factor in Palestinian politics. Moreover, Islamist groups have historically been the least attached to foreign aid. This has caused a divergence in their objectives and strategies in relation to those who receive strings-attached assistance.[92] Finally, many leftist groups took a pro-Fatah or neutral position during the crackdown on Hamas, exacerbating the polarizing division even further.[93]

How did this dynamic of polarization and non-cooperation develop? Many activists pointed to their fear of repression as a reason why cooperation between groups no longer exists. According to these organizers, this fear works in two ways. First, Islamist groups are particularly targeted and wary of working with others. The threat of repression limits the ability of leftist activists and organizers to coordinate with Islamist counterparts, and Islamist counterparts concurrently fear exposing their activities to those outside their inner circle.[94] Second, the idea of cooperation among opposition groups poses a challenge to the PA, so such cooperation provokes repercussions from the security apparatus.[95] As a result, activists lead independent campaigns within their own groups and rarely reach out to other organizations, corroborating the dynamic of insularity described in the theory. And repression's effects are not isolated to the Islamists; leftist groups have also been targeted in recent years in many of the same ways (torture, arrest, or crackdown on protests). Activists I spoke with confirmed that they often deliberately work "off the radar" and publicize events only through word of mouth to trusted allies.[96] Such inhibitions have an effect on group insularity, as well as the efficacy of their collective action efforts.

Cooptation by the PA has also exacerbated grievances between different groups. For example, activists within the Palestinian Communist Party report that PA officials have attempted to direct the party's leadership by meeting with them regularly and offering them the illusion of influence. This has caused a rift between the leadership and party members.[97] Activists from grassroots rural organizations also reported similar trends. They claimed the PA often restricts their activities to certain areas, in exchange for PA attendance at the event as a form of legitimation. PA officials also regularly tried to censor their messaging during these actions.[98] Finally, activists involved with center-left political parties such as Al-Mubadara reported that PA officials often attempted to place themselves on the party's committees. In this way, they "forced their vision" on Mubadara actions.[99] Members thus keep their activities secret in order to avoid preemptive PA involvement, but doing so erodes their own ability to sustain a popular movement in the process.

Perhaps the most novel way that the PA coopts political opposition involves the *hay'a*, or committee, system. PA ministers have purview over specialized committees within their ministries. The president, however, has the ability to move committees using presidential decrees. Some *hay'as* are often strategically removed from their ministries and subsumed under the PLO, which the president also controls. This way, when it is convenient to control the reins himself, President Abbas will convert committees into PLO *hay'as*. This is especially the case when the jurisdiction of that *hay'a* is sensitive and has a broad appeal. The leadership of these committees then targets existing grassroots organizations and incorporates them into the PA's chain of command.[100]

Rural popular resistance groups fell under the purview of this system, such as the one in the village of Bil'in. Bil'in lies in Area B, under both PA and Israeli jurisdiction. As the separation wall expanded, Israeli forces seized land from the village for the wall's path. In response, villagers formed a committee to protest and bring the issue to international attention. This committee was dominated by members affiliated with Fatah, but not the PA.[101] In fact, when the Bil'in movement started in 2005, many villagers were critical of the PA's role and worked independently of its officials. Members affiliated with leftist groups also took part. Bil'in gained popularity for its innovative protest actions and attracted significant international awareness.[102]

A *hay'a* centered on opposition to the wall has existed within the PA since 2003. But in 2014, the president assigned jurisdiction of the committee to the PLO. This *hay'a* has since inserted itself into the activities of Bil'in's committee, supposedly to oversee a "coordinated effort" across the territories. Many members of the village committee now work within the *hay'a*, but the same members now report that the *hay'a* is ineffective and that there is distrust between the villagers and leadership. They complain that it is difficult to sustain protests and that international participants now outnumber the local population in weekly actions. Thus the PA's cooptation through the *hay'a* system was able to control Bil'in's committee, which threatened the PA's role as the prime negotiator between Israel and the Palestinian people. Many popular committees across the territories have shared the same fate. Today, activists both within and outside the Bil'in movement complain of tensions between local committees and the various *hay'as*.[103]

Finally, leftist activists also argue that middle-class activism has been coopted almost entirely. Many argue that a declining standard of living, as well as increased dependence on loans and investment models (particularly following Fayyad's reforms), has "distracted" the middle class. The only segment of society that mobilizes today is the working class, specifically the agricultural workers and those who engage in manual labor. But even the unions that represent some of these groups have been coopted to some degree by the PA. Activists point out that their biggest victories involving workers' rights campaigns succeed in areas where unions are independent of the PA. For instance, campaigns in support of workers' rights have produced recent victories in the Tulkarm area. Activists note that the PA is not as entrenched in Tulkarm's unions as it is elsewhere, but this is the exception, not the norm.[104]

Furthermore, the PA's focus on "economic development" has coopted the middle class while disenfranchising the working class. These economic development schemes often involve industries that are unsustainable, tied to the economic primacy of Israel and the occupation, and are detrimental to health and living standards.[105] For instance, activists involved in union campaigns pointed out how the PA itself played a role in expanded industrial zones in the Tulkarm area, using the excuse of generating jobs.[106] The population in Tulkarm once relied on agricultural work for their livelihood, and many cultivated their own lands.[107] However, in 2014 the Israeli authorities confiscated large swaths of land in the Tulkarm area.[108] In this way, they have attempted to push agricultural workers to work in the expanding factories. These factories, which specialize in fertilizer and chemical production, have had adverse effects on the workers as well as surrounding areas. The Environmental Justice Atlas project notes that the expansion of these factories has caused air pollution, biodiversity loss, food insecurity, and an increased rate of occupational diseases (such as cancer) related to radiation and pollution.[109] Moreover, land confiscation and rising unemployment created the condition of surplus labor in this area. Israeli management within these factories was able to take advantage of this dynamic to pay illegally low wages and demand long hours.[110] Overall, such "economic development" schemes caused an increase in unemployment and worsening living conditions for Tulkarm residents. Middle classes tied up with these "development" opportunities fear being penalized financially for any dissent. The increasingly marginalized agricultural and manual labor workers are the only ones who mobilize, but the efficacy of their opposition is limited in a situation where unions are sometimes controlled by the PA itself.

These interviews with leftist activists reveal similar trends in the PA's practices. Through a combination of repression and cooptation, the PA has been able to erode the capacity of opposition groups. It does this not only through the threat of force but by making it more difficult for groups to work with each other. In an authoritarian environment, insularity becomes key to protecting the group from the regime's repercussions. But grievances arise between those who work with the regime and those who do not. Insularity also makes it difficult to reach across party lines. Thus insularity and grievance generate pro- and anti-regime polarization and make the possibility of effective opposition much less likely.

Discussion and conclusion

Given these results, we can conclude that the authoritarian conditions in the Palestinian territories have generated polarization. Specifically, the experimental analysis shows that repression has the effect of generating polarization. As for the link between polarization and decreased coordination, the behavioral measures in the laboratory experiment shed light on this relationship. In particular, we find that targeted opposition groups, such as the leftists and Islamists, are more likely to be polarized and refuse coordination with other parties. The qualitative evidence on both the Islamists and leftist organizations also corroborates the connection between rising polarization and decreased coordination. In the experiment, Islamists in particular reacted most strongly to the authoritarian treatments. Although priming only momentarily increases awareness in the respondent, the experiment nevertheless found significant results.

What does this mean for the actual practice of authoritarianism? It stands to reason that full-fledged authoritarian practices have a much stronger effect than mere priming during an artificial experiment. Thus, we can expect the effect of authoritarianism to be much stronger outside the confines of this research. Targeted groups are much more polarized than even this experiment can reveal, and much less likely to coordinate with others.

The two-stage theory proposed in this chapter can be used as a starting point for understanding how the practice of authoritarianism can affect social cohesion, particularly in the case of Palestine, and provides empirical basis for the two-stage theory on authoritarianism, polarization, and social cohesion. Using this theory, we can begin to understand how past authoritarianism erodes effective opposition and inhibits collective action, even when there are political openings. In the case of Palestine, this explains why Palestinians seem unable to coordinate an effective response to increased challenges related to the Israeli occupation.

$$4$$

DE-MOBILIZING A MOBILIZED SOCIETY

The findings of the previous chapter have no better illustration than actual mobilization patterns from the late 1980s until today. In the late 1980s, Palestinians in the West Bank and Gaza erupted in protest to challenge twenty years of occupation.[1] Despite overwhelming military control of these territories, and a heavy price to pay for protesting, Palestinians were able to sustain a diffuse, mostly non-violent protest using the organizational capacity of their civil society institutions.[2] In contrast, flash forward to circumstances in the territories today. Direct military occupation continues. The PA controls some of the territories directly, but hardships remain as negotiations for statehood stall indefinitely. And even though circumstances are more or less the same for the daily lives of Palestinians, they have been unable to organize effectively as they did in the past. By most accounts, Palestinians are "fatigued," but is individual fatigue truly the culprit behind the demobilization of a once highly engaged citizenry, with a robust civil society and capacity for collective action?

Around 90 percent of the Palestinian population now resides in PA-controlled areas, with supposedly greater self-determination and freedom, under less direct military occupation.[3] At the same time, the PA has grown increasingly authoritarian and repressive.[4] Disengagement is rampant, as demonstrated by the lack of mobilization and declining efficacy of civil society organizations.[5] Thus, the following questions arise: How has the PA affected political mobilization? Do the dynamics of polarization borne out in the laboratory experiments translate to real life protest?

The literature on the determinants of successful social movements and civil societies has given us some understanding of the prerequisites for robust political mobilization. For example, scholars have outlined how civil society that builds "social capital" has a large impact on good governance outcomes in the form of institutional efficacy.[6] Strong communities and social networks have been highlighted specifically as being linked to an individual's decision to participate and have also been linked to the subsequent success of the entire movement. Little work has been done, however, to address how conditions with such "opportunities" can subsequently degenerate. The dynamic within the Palestinian territories, where institutions and strong communities once existed that made collective action possible and effective, can help provide a look at this alternative dynamic. I argue that the PA can help illuminate some general conditions under which political engagement, in the form of mobilization, may decline. This chapter also examines societal-level dynamics, rather than just individual-level costs, which can better explain political mobilization patterns.

In this chapter, I assess the independent effect of the PA on political mobilization. The Interim Agreements of 1995 gave the PA varying levels of control across the territories. The decisions about the borders of the PA's control had little to do with the Palestinian population, but rather were decided based on the density of Israeli settlements in each area. I use this variation to assess the causal effect of the PA itself. I will demonstrate how the level of grievances garnered through Israeli provocation is not greater in one area over another, and thus can be held constant. In sum, I find that political mobilization has declined systematically in places where the indigenous regime, the PA, has more direct control. Counterintuitively, although all three areas of the West Bank face Israeli repression, political mobilization today is actually more prevalent in areas under direct Israeli occupation. This finding suggests that the PA does in fact play a role in the decline of political mobilization and engagement.

To assess the manner in which the PA is achieving this effect, I analyze its development over time using qualitative data and vignettes of mobilization. Findings suggest that directly following the PA's creation, the regime developed patronage networks in order to "tie in" various segments of the population. This led to polarization within society that persists to this day. However, this strategy had limited success, particularly because external support remained conditional. Frustrations erupted in the form of a second uprising, as well as direct opposition to the PA's rule. The regime has since shifted to focusing on its coercive capacity and has increasingly relied on repression to control political mobilization across the Palestinian territories. This repression strategy has polarized and fragmented political groups to an even greater degree. Overall, the PA's authoritarian strategies have led to declining political mobilization across the territories.

How the PA affects mobilization: theoretical framework and hypotheses

Previous work has found that strong communities can facilitate engagement and mobilization through the use of "social sanctions." Social sanctions are defined as the manner in which a community enforces particular behaviors and social order through both positive and negative endorsements.[7] The impact of the community on individual decisions in support of mobilization, rather than free-riding, is crucial, especially under conditions of high risk. Literature on the Palestinian territories notes the impact of social networks on the success and cohesiveness of the first intifada.[8] Alternatively, the more sporadic and much more costly second intifada has been attributed to the weakening cohesion of Palestinian society.[9]

Thus it is reasonable to assume that in cases where the regime has an inhibiting effect on the cohesiveness of society, and the strength of those social networks, the potential for communities to serve these functions is weakened dramatically. As previously mentioned, one way to inhibit social cohesion is by causing polarization, or an increasing divergence between two "camps" in society. These two camps diverge in both their preferences and behaviors—in this particular case, this involves preferences and behaviors related to the Palestinian national liberation project.[10] More generally, as societies become more polarized, we can expect the capacity for effective mobilization to begin to decline.[11] Therefore, in a more polarized society, political mobilization will decline.

This is the case because in a cohesive society, with strong social networks, the overall interest of its members is more readily discernible. When action is deemed necessary, people will mobilize. In a non-cohesive society with weak social networks, although individuals may come from the same community and live under similar conditions, similar interests may not exist. Social structures necessary to "sanction" members into action are not available in a polarized society, because effective sanctions must involve the threat of being sanctioned by the community *at large*. If the community is divided on whether mobilization is necessary, sanctions will not be a credible threat. So in this scenario, if mobilizations are attempted, we will see the classic free-rider problem occur.

In the context of the Palestinian territories, however, the regime does not have an effect uniformly. The PA only has access to certain segments of the West Bank, meaning any possible divisive effect of the regime does not affect the entire population.[12] Area A, where most Palestinians live, is under direct PA control. Most of the mobilizations that occurred during the first and second uprisings were in Area A specifically, as the site of most urban centers. Area B comprises mostly rural areas, and Area C is a mix of both. Israeli repression and intrusion, however, affects all three areas, so the motivation for mobilization, in terms of grievances around the occupation, exists across the territory.[13] Thus, if the regime has no effect, then the "naturally occurring" level of mobilization in Area A would be higher than in Area B and Area C, simply as a result of the level of population in those areas as well as a higher capacity to organize. If the regime *does* in fact have an effect, however, then these naturally occurring differences should disappear as mobilization is inhibited in some areas over others.

In areas under direct PA control, not only can the regime coopt the population in this area by offering services and employment but it can also more readily repress any dissent. The population is therefore more polarized: part of the population truly supports the PA as a result of patronage, part of the population falsifies its own preferences over fear of losing patronage, and part of the population opposes the regime but cannot organize effectively because others will not join, or because of PA repression.[14] Specifically in Area A, "naturally occurring" mobilization levels should be high, given the large numbers of Palestinians in close proximity and the high level of Israeli provocations. However, if the PA has a deterrent effect on mobilization, then:

H1a: *Area A, directly under control of the regime, will feature inhibited levels of mobilization despite a larger population and capacity for mobilization.*

In areas of mixed control (i.e. Area B), there is greater independence from the PA. Palestinians living in these areas are not solely employed by the PA. Given Israel's unwillingness to allow PA forces to operate, those living in mixed-control areas also do not face consistent PA repression. Thus there is less preference falsification, and the regime has a less polarizing effect in Area B than it does in Area A. But these areas are also sparsely populated and capacity for organization is generally lower. During the first and second intifada, for example, this area was less mobilized. This was the result of low population numbers and a preexisting lack of organizational capacity. But today, if the PA has an effect on mobilization, we should find that:

H1b: *Area B, under mixed control, will feature greater levels of mobilization than is "naturally occurring."*

Finally, in areas where the PA has no presence (i.e. Area C and Jerusalem), its effect on the polarization of society within that area is much less pervasive. That is not to say that there are no pro-PA political factions at work in Area C, but the PA itself has almost no effect on the cohesiveness of the community in these areas, since Palestinians in Area C are somewhat insulated from Palestinian institutions in their day-to-day lives. Those living in Area C all face the same conditions brought on by Israeli occupation but are thus less divided in their response, as there is no confounding effect of PA patronage or repression. In terms of its characteristics, Area C has the least amount of Palestinians (only 10 to 15 percent of the Palestinian population) and is mixed in terms of its rural and urban make-up. Palestinians in this area face a similar number of raids and repressive measures as other areas overall. If the PA has no effect on mobilization capacity, we should expect the "naturally occurring" mobilization level to be low in this area. This is due simply to the small number of Palestinians in this area, as well as their insulation from Palestinian organizations (i.e. less organizational capacity). On the other hand, if the PA does have an effect on the other areas (i.e. Areas A and B), we can expect that:

H1c: *Area C, void of PA control, will feature greater levels of mobilization than is "naturally occurring."*

Simply put, if the PA has an effect, the areas where we would expect less mobilization as a result of lower population levels and less organizational capacity (Areas B and C) will feature higher levels of mobilization despite these characteristics. I argue that this comes as a result of the PA's effect specifically, which has generated polarization and affected collective action within Palestinian society under its direct control.

Assessing political mobilization

To assess political mobilization over time, I will trace the change in this variable using historical records and previous work on various periods of Palestinian history. Specifically, I will assess political mobilization in three different time periods: before the PA was created (beginning with the first intifada), at the onset of conflict after the PA was created (the second intifada), and finally the dynamic that exists today. These three time periods were chosen to highlight the effect of the PA specifically by focusing on variation over time in levels of PA control. It is crucial to assess all three time periods in order to establish that the differences between areas we see today are in fact tied to the creation of the PA, and are not just pre-existing characteristics of these different locations. It is also the most effective way of assessing the possible mechanisms through which these changes occurred. To achieve comparability on the cases examined temporally, as well as achieve variation on the dependent variable of political mobilization, I will capitalize on the within-case variation provided by this case to look at political mobilization over time in three specific contexts: Area A, Area B, and Area C.

Before the PA's creation, all three areas were under Israeli occupation, and Palestinians in all areas faced similar conditions in terms of restrictions on freedom of movement.[15] Some areas, which were more rural, faced greater impediments to collective action simply as a result of the lower population numbers in these areas and less civil society intrusion.[16] But other than the naturally occurring differences of population size and distance from urban areas, all three areas had indistinguishable starting points.[17]

Today, the effect of Israeli policies can be "held constant" for all three areas, as all three face similar levels of repression and Israeli intrusion—and most of all, grievance. For example, although Palestinians in Areas B and C have been subjected to a more aggressive land appropriation campaign, Palestinians in Area A also face a decline in living standards as a result of the occupation's chokehold. Palestinians living in city centers, with more access to education and thus greater expectations for their futures, often find that they are highly limited as a result of the occupation's practices.[18] Perhaps their homes are not immediately or as often in danger, but their livelihoods and future success certainly are. In a 2016 public opinion poll, 25.4 percent of Palestinians cited the spread of employment and poverty as the most severe threat facing Palestinian society, closely behind 29.7 percent of Palestinians who cited the direct threat of land appropriation and occupation.[19]

Moreover, even in terms of sheer repression, PA officials have gone on record to say that there really is "no difference" between Areas A, B, and C anymore.[20] The data show that Area A accounts for almost 22 percent of intrusions despite supposedly being an autonomous area under PA control, with little reason for Israeli intervention.[21] Thus we can argue that grievances can be considered "uniform" at least in intensity, if not in specific cause.

Examining patterns of political mobilization over time in these three areas can help us assess whether political mobilization has indeed declined since the creation of the PA. To determine the causal mechanisms behind this trend, I will assess the reported levels of polarization and cohesion in these three areas at the different points in time described above. I define polarization as the presence, and increasing divergence, of two "camps" in society that disagree about the goals and strategies they should use in terms of their mobilization. I will operationalize this concept through my qualitative assessment by looking both at levels of coordination between different factions and levels of coordination across different administrative areas (Areas A, B, C). I use reports from activists to assess the variation in polarization, and subsequently the ability to coordinate, over all three time periods.

In order to assess the observable implications of the theory in the present day and provide further evidence to support the qualitative assessment, I utilize an original dataset of mobilization in the West Bank. This dataset covers one period of time, from 2007 to 2016. I included all mobilization from 2007 onward in order to account for the PA's effect on mobilization while holding certain exogenous conditions constant. Prior to 2007, the PA was not as consolidated, and so was not in the form it is today. After 2007, and Prime Minister's Fayyad's internal reforms, the PA consolidated its control over the territory more effectively. Thus an examination of post-2007 mobilizations would be the most useful assessment. If political mobilization is uniform across the different areas during this time, despite differences in population and mobilization capacity, then we can confirm the hypotheses presented in this chapter.

Using the Institute for Palestine Studies Chronologies, UN OCHA "Protection of Civilians" weekly reports, as well as *Shabakat al-Quds al-Akhbariya* (a Palestinian news network), I created a dataset of political mobilization that covers the type of mobilization, the date in which it occurred, the location, and whether or not it was in a rural, urban, or refugee camp setting.[22] I also collected data on the density of settlements around each neighborhood/village, and whether or not Israeli incursions had occurred in that location around the time of mobilization.[23] Location here means the village or city neighborhood in which the protest occurred. Using this dataset, we can examine whether Areas A, B, and C exhibit different levels of political mobilization.

Results: hypothesis 1

Prior to the PA: patterns of mobilization

Before the creation of the PA, the entire West Bank and the Gaza Strip were under direct military occupation. This occupation began in 1967 and subse-

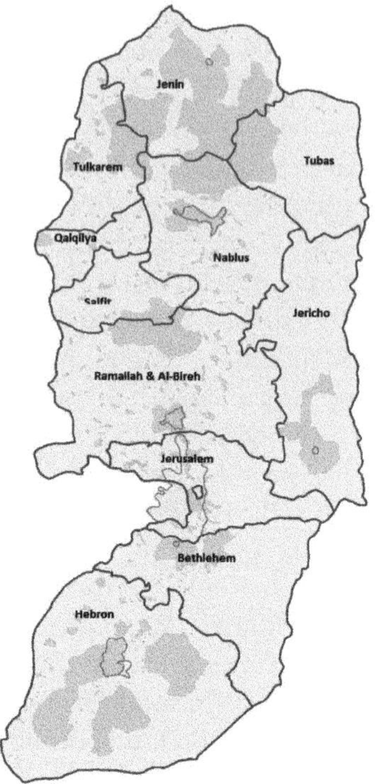

Figure 2. Map of the governorates of Palestine (map created by the author)

quently changed the dynamic of the conflict for the Palestinian population. Settlements were introduced into the West Bank and Gaza, renewing friction between Israelis and Palestinians since the 1948 forcible transfers. During this time, political engagement was severely repressed. During the intifada, for example, Defense Minister Yitzhak Rabin instituted an "Iron Fist" policy against any form of Palestinian nationalism and political activity.[24] If suspected of engaging in politics, a Palestinian could expect to be arrested, have their home demolished, and then subsequently be deported. Coupled with economic hardship, these repressive policies led to unprecedented levels of tension in the West Bank and Gaza.

These tensions erupted in the form of the first Palestinian intifada, or uprising. The precursor to the PA, the PLO (which at the time existed mostly outside the territories), had less to do with the emergence of the uprising and its initial organization. While the PLO forces coordinated on tactics with

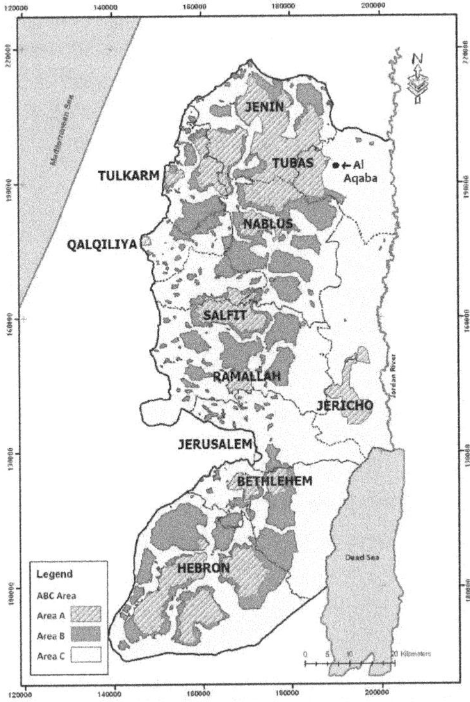

Figure 3. Map of areas A, B, C (map reproduced with permission from the Palestinian Hydrology Group)

forces on the ground, local organizers and institutions were more directly responsible first for organizing the uprising and its principles, and then facilitating its progress for the four years it lasted.[25] The intifada was decentralized and yet coordinated, which speaks to the high degree of coordination present in Palestinian civil society at that time. Moreover, during this time prior to the creation of the PA, urban centers accounted for much of the political mobilization against the Israeli occupation.[26] This can be explained both by the proximity of these urban centers to Israeli settlements and the fact that the Israeli military occupation focused primarily on Palestinian cities. Residents in many major cities across the West Bank, such as Jerusalem, Nablus, and Ramallah, were among the first to respond to the call of the Unified National Leadership.[27] Areas of the Palestinian territories where Fatah was most present were the areas with the most politicized citizens, and also the areas that suffered the greatest crackdown.[28] Jerusalem was a particular hotbed of activity during this time period as a stronghold of Fatah support and as the cosmopolitan capital of the Palestinian people.[29] Overall, Palestinians from the urban centers and adjacent refugee camps (i.e. high population areas) accounted for the bulk of intifada participants. Rural communities (those that would later become Area B) also took part, but to a lesser degree.[30]

Prior to the PA: levels of polarization

Before the intifada, clandestine political parties in the Palestinian territories focused on maintaining organizational capacity and some level of coordination with external forces (i.e. the PLO and sympathetic foreign governments). Polarization among Palestinian society was not a major factor in the coordination of political mobilization. Although some parts of the West Bank featured stronger support for one faction over the other, all major urban centers featured the presence of the entire Palestinian political spectrum. They also did not greatly disagree on the goals or strategies to be used in their popular struggle.

Subsequently, during the first intifada, Palestinian society was characterized by low levels of polarization and high levels of coordination among active political parties and across different areas. The UNLU emerged, for example, with the support and involvement of Fatah, the Popular Front, the Democratic Front, and the Palestinian Communist Party.[31] At the time, these were the major political parties at work in the territories, and it is significant that they were all represented within the UNLU. The high levels of cohesion meant that, for most of the intifada, those who took part in the uprising adhered to the principles set forth by UNLU. Fragmentation did not occur until after 1991, when the main thrust of the uprising was over. Islamist resistance groups (i.e. Islamic Jihad and Hamas) emerged but gained more traction after the PLO began talks with the Israeli government and preparation began for the creation of the PA.[32]

Before the creation of PA, patterns of mobilization did not differ greatly between parts of the territories. Rural communities were not as active as the urban centers due to their population levels and capacity, but otherwise there were no distinctions between what would later become Areas A, B, and C in the West Bank. Additionally, the level of polarization was low and was not an impediment to coordination among different parties/segments of the Palestinian population.

Following the creation of the PA: patterns of mobilization

Patterns of mobilization across the Palestinian territories changed drastically following the creation of the PA. Although the Palestinian population was indistinguishable between areas prior to the PA's creation, they were subjected to different administrative schemes following the denotation of Areas A, B, and C. The PA gained full control of Area A (18 percent of territory, 55 percent of the population), gained joint control of Area B (20 percent of territory, 41 percent of the population), but ceded full control to the Israeli occupation of Area C (62 percent of territory, 1 percent of the population, as it excludes East Jerusalem).[33] These allocations of control were decided based on the density of settlements in each vicinity rather than on any difference between Palestinians living in these areas. Rural areas, in Area B and some parts of Area C, were subsequently neglected politically as a result of the lower level of control in those areas.[34]

Under Arafat's leadership, the PA gained control of both land mass and significant portions of the population by employing large numbers of Palestinians within the PA itself. Pre-2000 staffing decisions were often political and served as a form of patronage to tie the population to the new state.[35] Patronage offered to certain segments of civil society also served to neutralize opposition in the form of organized groups. During this time, there were definite improvements in security without the use of excessive repression.[36] This dynamic can be attributed to the new patronage system, which served its function quite well. Nevertheless, patterns of mobilization differed greatly across these areas as a function of the PA's varying levels of intrusion.

The change in capacity for mobilization across the territories has no better illustration than in the events of the second intifada. When protests erupted in response to Israeli provocations, the manner in which the uprising spread differed dramatically from patterns of mobilization seen previously. For example, throughout the first intifada, there was a unified organization consisting of all relevant political parties. Protests emerged from major urban centers, as well as some rural communities. This is in contrast to what occurred in the second intifada.

Scholars and activists note that this uprising was characterized by polarization among Palestinians in both strategies and objectives.[37] Certain urban centers fell under the purview of Islamist resistant groups, while others remained Fatah strongholds but split off from the PA.[38] In some parts of Area A, for example, such as in the city of Ramallah, protests were inhibited despite

Israeli air strikes and incursions. On the other hand, in places such as Nablus and Jenin in northern West Bank (also part of Area A, and some parts of Area B), armed groups emerged. Rural communities took part only rarely. Palestinians in Area C and Jerusalem initially engaged in peaceful protests, but these protests were quickly repressed. Consequently, Palestinians in Jerusalem took part in periodic armed attacks against Israelis.[39] Unlike the first intifada in which Jerusalem played a key role, in the second intifada Jerusalemites were much more silent.[40] There were few large-scale mobilizations; instead, those who took part in the second intifada relied more readily on violent means. Mobilization declined in Area C as well to some degree, simply as a result of declining coordination across the territories.[41]

It is clear from the pattern of protest exhibited during the second intifada that mobilization was no longer uniform across the West Bank. Some places, such as Jerusalem, featured high levels of uncoordinated violence. Other areas, such as Ramallah in Area A, were less mobilized than past periods. Finally, rural areas in Area B remained largely unorganized.

Following the creation of the PA: polarization

In addition to the diminished level of mobilization in certain parts of the territories, the post-PA West Bank was also characterized by higher levels of polarization. Scholars have noted that the intrusion of the PA on civil society, for example, led to divisions among those involved and low levels of trust between them.[42] During the second intifada, this division manifested itself in the fragmentation of the uprising. Not only were participants polarized in terms of appropriate strategies and objectives but they also took up arms against each other. In fact, scholars point to the fragmentation and polarization of Palestinian society as the main explanation for the emergence of violent methods during the second intifada.[43] Even strongholds of Fatah support eventually split off from the PA during the uprising, thus creating conditions of lawlessness in significant portions of the West Bank.[44]

The PA held on to parts of Area A, such as Ramallah for example, and maintained control over the uprising in those areas. Citizens in these parts of the West Bank were the most reliant on the PA in terms of income and stability. This put them in contrast with Palestinian communities in other parts of the West Bank. Thus, as previously mentioned, parts of Area A exhibited less frequent mobilization and less coordination with other parts of the West Bank. However, in other areas, the PA quickly lost control to armed factions.

These groups took over so completely that all PA institutions were quickly disassembled. Citizens of these areas (parts of Area A and most of Area B) returned to traditional legal systems (i.e. clan and family rule) to regain some semblance of stability.[45] It took years after the uprising for the PA to regain control over these parts of the West Bank, and it is not entirely clear that they were able to accomplish this task fully in the rural areas. During the time of the second intifada, polarization became so severe in some parts of Area A and most of Area B (i.e. the rural areas) that not only were factions unable to work together but they also turned on each other.[46]

Finally, in Jerusalem and parts of Area C, divisions inhibited mobilization to a large degree. One major leader of the uprising working in Jerusalem, Marwan Barghouti, notes that despite attempts to initiate clashes with the Israeli occupation forces and thus start an uprising, the "differences in opinion" between the various political factions involved meant his attempts remained unsuccessful.[47] Despite some initial protests, factions in Jerusalem and other parts of Area C were too fragmented over their preferred strategies to cooperate with each other. Sustained protest efforts were non-existent, and much of the activity in Area C turned violent and sporadic as a result.

This dynamic is a far cry from the conditions of the first intifada, with the presence of an organization such as the UNLU. When comparing these two time periods, it becomes clear that not only did mobilization patterns differ following the creation of the PA but also that levels of polarization increased dramatically, thus further inhibiting the capacity of Palestinians to mobilize effectively. It is true that the presence of armed groups sustained the uprising for five years. But the fact that the uprising was much less coordinated and its participants much more polarized meant that the outcomes of five years of struggle amounted to very little political gain for the Palestinian population overall.

The West Bank today: patterns of mobilization

The failure of the second intifada, particularly with regard to the PA's ability to maintain order, led to a targeted campaign of revamping the security forces and regaining control over all parts of the West Bank.[48] The chaos brought on by militia-rule during the second intifada was slowly rectified by incorporating ex-fighters into the PA's salary base through a number of amnesty deals.[49] Following that, Fayyad was appointed prime minister after the 2006 legislative elections, tasked with implementing security sector reform in the name of "professionalization." In this way, the PA and its patrons wanted to guarantee that the fractionalization of security forces that took place during the second intifada could never occur again. To a large degree, these reforms succeeded. Fayyad limited corruption and the use of patronage, purged personnel, and consolidated control once more over the West Bank.[50] In addition, he increased coordination with the Israeli government.[51] In some parts of the West Bank, stability was gained through consensual means (primarily by coopting militia leaders and providing amnesty). In other parts of the West Bank, the PA regained control through repression. Political factions that did not reject the use of violence were targeted, particularly those of the Islamist persuasion.

These reforms and subsequent crackdown had the effect of further fragmenting mobilization across parts of the West Bank. Coupled with the failure of the second intifada to achieve political gains, these reforms made patterns of mobilization across the different areas highly divergent by increasing the polarization of society where the PA held power. Coordinated mobilization across the different areas is no longer the norm. Area A, including urban centers such as Ramallah, today feature very low levels of protest and other forms of political mobilization.

Scholars argue that in most areas, particularly Area A where most Palestinians live, mobilization is "elite-driven." These elites can be categorized into two main types: middle-class adherents of mostly defunct leftist organizations, and foreign-educated policy wonks who function through NGOs. Moreover, they are often prompted by economic issues. Even when participants take advantage of the opportunity to air other grievances, these protests are often "self-limiting."[52] Overall, the few protests that emerge are tied to particular personalities who have very little social backing. Thus they cannot mobilize or coordinate effectively across groups in Palestinian society.[53]

Attacks against the occupation persist in Area C, or in Jerusalem, where the PA has little or no control, but attacks are very sporadic and are often quickly repressed by the Israeli military.[54] A more notable development is the presence of large-scale mobilizations, which have occurred in these areas and actually been moderately effective. In Jerusalem, Palestinians have organized around religious and grassroots organizations, not the PA's institutions, on a number of occasions. The most recent example at the time of writing revolved around the issue of the Al-Aqsa compound and Israeli policies that restricted Palestinian access to the area. Palestinians mobilized in a sustained way and in large numbers. They maintained unity around their methods of protest and their demands. In a very short time, they effectively forced Israel to acquiesce. This was significant because such mobilizations within PA-controlled areas are unheard of. Even when people turn out in large numbers, it is rarely through a sustained campaign. Nevertheless, despite these short-term successes, collective action in marginalized communities of Area C or Jerusalem remains limited, given the absence of organizing vehicles.

Finally, in the rural areas of Area B, there has been an increased level of mobilization since the second intifada. This is an interesting dynamic given that this area was perhaps the most politically neglected following the creation of the PA and took part in the first uprising to a lesser degree than the other areas around the West Bank.[55] One explanation for this increase in mobilization in Area B, versus the inhibited levels of mobilization in Area A, can be traced to the increased Israeli settlement activity in these rural areas.[56] This dynamic has sparked a consistent and sustained mobilization effort across a number of key villages affected by the seizure of land for settlement purposes.[57] Most importantly, the PA only has limited control of the rural areas, and thus has less capacity to repress or coopt political activity in Area B.[58]

The West Bank today: levels of polarization

Nothing could have polarized Palestinian society further than the events following the second intifada. Hamas, an Islamist party, won a majority within the Palestinian national assembly, and then was quickly and forcibly removed from office. Hamas won specifically because it opposed the PA's position; thus the crackdown that has persisted against Hamas and its affiliates has exacerbated tensions between the two "camps" of Palestinian society.[59] Moreover, this crackdown began to target not only those affiliated with Hamas but also anyone who was vocal in their criticism of the PA.[60] Many complain that there is no effective civilian oversight of the security forces and that Fayyad and his successor Rami Hamdallah ruled solely by presidential decree.[61] This has led many activists to claim that Palestinian society has developed a "culture of fear," with the implicit understanding by all that the PA did not consider the current stage a "right time to protest" or mobilize.[62] Not only did the level of coordination between different factions severely diminish but levels of coordination across different administrative areas became almost non-existent.

These developments have significantly polarized Palestinian society between those who continue to support the PA as a representative of the

Palestinian people and those who claim that the PA lost all legitimacy following the crackdown on Hamas.[63] Those in Area A remain largely reliant on public sector salaries, which by many accounts is a key aspect of PA governance in maintaining its control over certain areas.[64] Those in Area B, the rural areas in particular, often have fewer ties to the PA through public sector positions or otherwise.[65] Many groups that operate within this area express criticisms of the PA (as well as Fatah, the main political party within the PA). Palestinians in Area C are mixed about their allegiances, with many political parties represented in this area without direct fear of crackdown. In fact, areas in Jerusalem under direct Israeli control have become "safe havens" for Hamas to continue its organizing illicitly.[66] This dynamic of division across the West Bank facilitates the lack of coordinated mobilization between areas. And *within* areas, it is still difficult to mobilize in a sustained manner similar to the first intifada as a direct result of this polarization. Table 11 below shows a summary of the qualitative findings on the levels of mobilization and polarization across areas and time periods.

As the table summarizes, before the PA all three areas exhibited high to middling levels of mobilization and low levels of fragmentation. This means that there was not only coordination between different factions but also coordination across different administrative areas. However, following the creation of the PA, this pattern begins to vary across areas. There is decreasing mobilization in areas with high levels of PA control (Area A) and increasing levels of polarization across the areas and across political factions. Finally, as a result of the PA's varying levels of control, and effect on polarization across areas, today we find that areas with lower levels of PA control have higher levels of mobilization. We also find that divisions across administrative areas and political factions today have made coordination between Areas A, B, and C almost non-existent. Ironically, despite lower numbers of people, Areas B and C exhibit more sustained levels of mobilization than Area A. Thus we can conclude that the PA's varying level of control has had a direct effect on levels of polarization, and subsequently levels of mobilization, across the West Bank.

Results: hypothesis 2

To test the hypotheses quantitatively, I assessed patterns of mobilization following the 2006 legislative elections using an original dataset. This not only provides further confirming evidence of the dynamics outlined in the qualitative assessment but it also serves as a rigorous test of my theory's observable implications in the present day. Most importantly, it allows us to quantify the differences between Areas A, B, and C, and assess whether they are indeed significant.

Table 11: Summary of qualitative findings

	Area A	*Area B*	*Area C*
Prior to PA	High levels of mobilization	Lower levels of mobilization	High levels of mobilization
	Low level of polarization	Low level of polarization	Low level of polarization
After PA and Onset of Second Intifada	Decreasing mobilization, not uniform	Low levels of mobilization	Decreasing mobilization, not uniform
	Increasing polarization	Low level of polarization	Increasing polarization
After Second Intifada	Low levels of mobilization	Higher levels of mobilization	Middling levels of mobilization
	High levels of polarization	Low levels of polarization	Lower levels of polarization

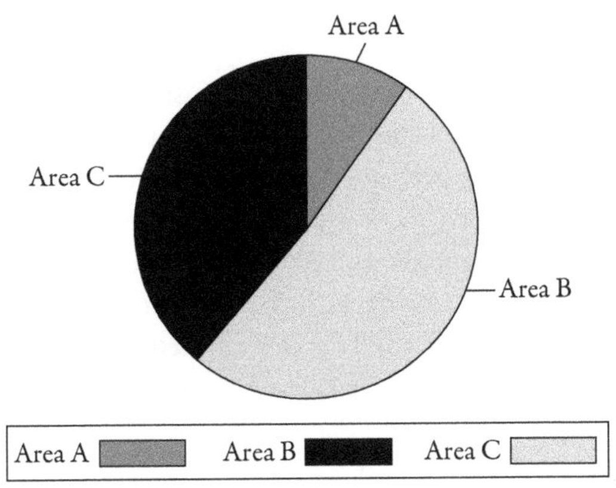

Figure 4. Number of protests by area

First, the sheer number of mobilizations across the three areas is very different. Figure 4 illustrates this most starkly: Area A, with the greatest population of Palestinians, features the *least* number of mobilizations by far. Area B and C hold the bulk of protests in the time period examined here (2007 to present). This is despite the fact that most Palestinians live in Area A and suffer limitations on mobility, the threat of Israeli incursions, and settler violence on a regular basis.

Of course, an examination by sheer number may not be the most accurate. Using a one-way ANOVA test, we can see whether the difference in number of protests across areas is truly statistically significant. A summary of these results can be found below.

Table 12: One-way ANOVA test results

Area	*Means and standard deviations*	*N*
A	0.045 (0.305)	11,025
B	0.071 (0.488)	20,071
C	0.058 (0.429)	19,342
	F statistic: 0.0000***	*Total N*: 50,438

As the F statistic in the table shows, the difference in number of protests across the three areas is indeed statistically significant (at the highest level of $p < 0.01$). Thus we can be confident that the difference in number of protests is not due to random variation.

Although the difference between areas is statistically significant, it stands to reason that some other variable is responsible for this difference rather than the PA itself. For example, perhaps settlement activity is just more severe in certain areas over others. In those areas, perhaps Palestinians protest more frequently due to their conditions. For that reason, we should explore the possibility that settlement activity explains the patterns of mobilization we see. In the database, I collected a full list of settlements within each Palestinian governorate. Then I ranked the governorates by the number of settlers within each. These results can be found in Figure 5 below.

With this figure in mind, we can assess the number of protests per governorate and get a general impression of whether settlement activity is solely

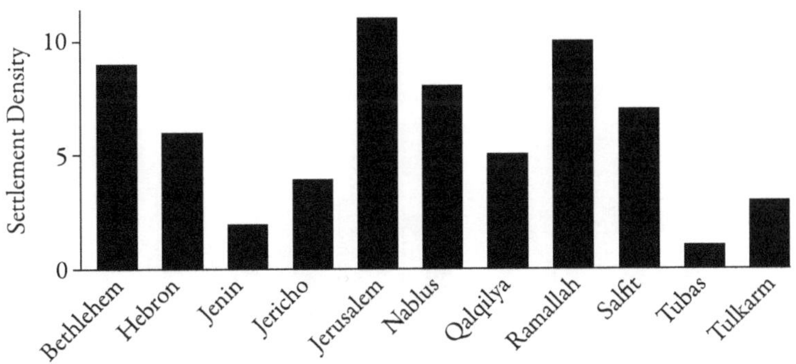

Figure 5. Settlement density by governorate

responsible for the number of protests in each governorate, or if there is some other factor at work. The average number of protests per governorate is in Figure 6 below.

A close look at this graph confirms that settlement activity is not in and of itself responsible for differences in protests across the governorates. For example, Nablus governorate has greater settlement density than Qalqilya, and yet Qalqilya has more protests. Settlement density in East Jerusalem is greater

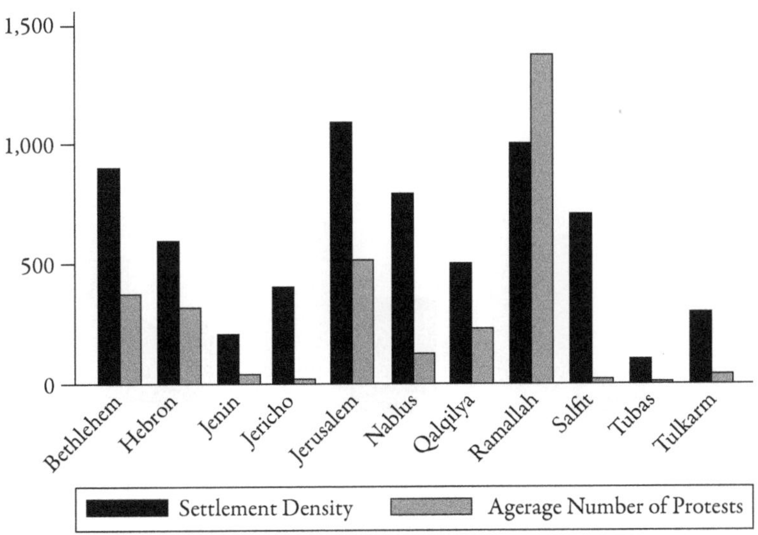

Figure 6. Settlement density by governorate compared with protests by governorate

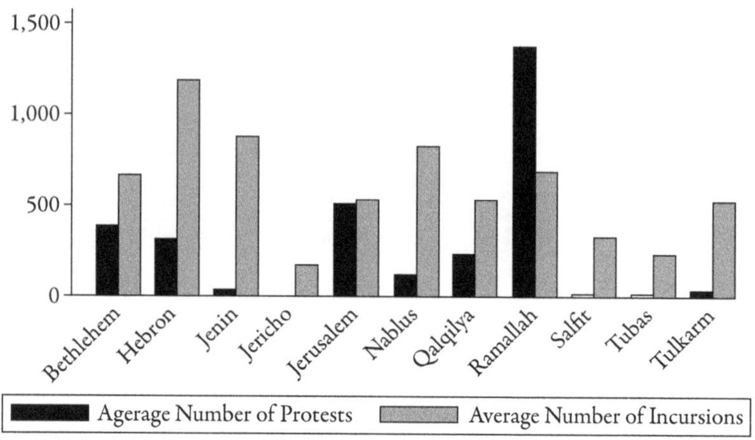

Figure 7. Average number of Israeli incursions compared with average number of protests by governorate

than in areas of Ramallah, but the average number of protests is much higher in Ramallah governorate. Moreover, a simple correlation test between settlement density and the occurrence of protest shows a very low correlation (at 0.11).[67] Thus it becomes clear that the effect of settlements, as an Israeli policy, cannot account for variations in mobilization across the West Bank.

Another possible explanation for the differential level of protest across areas is that Palestinians in Area A, under more direct PA jurisdiction, are merely much less aggrieved and have less to protest about. While the qualitative section shows that Palestinians certainly struggle in Area A as well, and that

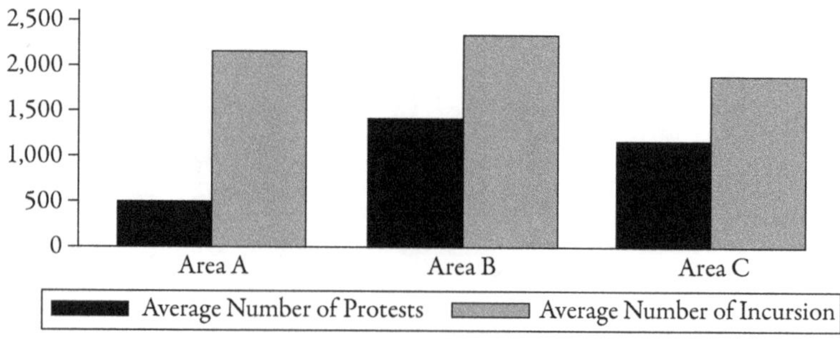

Figure 8. Average number of Israeli incursions compared with average number of protests by area

Israeli incursions are regularized across all three areas, such an explanation necessitates further inquiry. Therefore, I examine the average number of Israeli incursions per year as a proxy for grievance. I look at this variable across the various governorates (Fig. 7) as well as across the different areas (Fig. 8).

Once again, across areas and across governorates, the presence of Israeli incursions does not seem to predict the intensity of protests in any given place. For instance, Area A has a similar number of incursions to Area B and C, and yet Palestinians within Area A protest much less frequently. The alternative explanation of grievance, either due to IDF incursions or settler violence/activity, does not hold up in the data. The underlying cause of the differentiated nature of protests across the territories today also cannot be explained by an urban–rural divide, given that Area A (the most urban) is often the most acquiescent.

Finally, for the most rigorous test of the theory, I analyzed the data using a linear hurdle regression model.[68] This model is useful because it assumes that there are two processes at work: certain variables affect whether or not people mobilize, and then other variables affect how often they mobilize. A hurdle model is especially appropriate because there are many "zeroes" in the data (i.e. there are many instances of non-occurrence, or non-mobilization). To run such a model in this instance, one must identify the variables that motivate whether or not people mobilize, and then identify and include the variables that are responsible for the level of mobilization. In this case, given the theory outlined above, variables that motivate whether or not people mobilize include what area they live in and the population level in the area. Second, the variables that affect the intensity of mobilization include whether or not an Israeli raid/incursion has occurred in the location recently, and the number of settlements around that location. Both variables are proxies of grievance, given that the higher the number of Israeli raids or settlements, the more friction there is between Palestinians and the Israeli occupation. Presumably, this would lead to greater levels of protest. I also included a zero-inflated negative binomial regression for comparison.[69] This regression examines the effect of "Area" on the occurrence of political mobilization while controlling for relevant variables. The results of both models are in Table 13.

The model shows the statistical significance for both Area B and Area C across both models and in the same direction. This means, when we control for the effect of high population numbers, the occurrence of mobilization in Area A is very different from Area B and Area C. Mobilization is more likely in Area B, an area of rural communities and much lower population

Table 13: Regression results

	Model 1	Model 2
	Linear hurdle	*Zero-inflated neg. binomial*
Occurrence		
Area (categorical)		
Area B	2.535***	1.446 ***
	(0.304)	(0.091)
Area C	1.744***	0.809***
	(0.288)	(0.098)
Population	5.95e−06**	6.45e−06***
	(2.66e−06)	(1.09e−06)
Israel Raid	−	−0.016
		(0.076)
Settlement Density	−	0.139***
		(0.016)
_cons	−0.700**	−2.29***
	(0.339)	(0.197)
Selection		
Population	−	−0.0001***
		(6.42e−06)
Israeli Raid	0.796***	−1.295***
	(0.027)	(0.091)
Settlement Density	0.135***	−0.257***
	(0.005)	(0.018)
_cons	−3.091***	5.462***
	(0.044)	(0.189)
lnsigma/lnalpha	0.691***	0.097
	(0.039)	(0.211)
sigma/alpha	1.996	1.102
	(0.078)	(0.233)
N (total)	50,438	50,438
N(non-zero)	1,451	1,451
	LR chi2(3) = 1767.05	Wald chi2(5) = 436.58
	Prob>chi2 = 0.000	Prob>chi2 = 0.000

* p<0.05; ** p<0.01; *** p<0.001.

levels, than in Area A. And mobilization is also more likely in Area C to a lesser degree (i.e. smaller coefficient). When we account for the effect of high population numbers, settlement density, incursions, and increased capacity (in those high population areas), we still find that areas with *lower* population numbers and *less* capacity for coordination actually have higher levels of mobilization.

To predict cases of "certain zeroes" (i.e. cases that feature no occurrences of mobilization), we look at the second set of variables in the zero-inflated negative binomial model. The negative coefficients and statistical significance shows that Israeli raids and settlement density have a negative impact on the likelihood of a case being a "certain zero." This means that the increase of Israeli raids or settlement density increases the likelihood of protest.

Thus, when considering this data in combination with the qualitative assessment provided above, it becomes clear that the presence of the PA has a unique effect on collective action and has contributed directly to the patterns of mobilization (and de-mobilization) we see in Palestine today.

Protest vignettes

To illustrate this pattern more clearly, I will outline three protest movements that did not feature PA involvement, either initially or throughout the period of protest. These will be used to demonstrate how the lack of PA intrusion allowed the protest movements to succeed, relative to non-existent protests in areas under direct PA control, despite heavy Israeli repression. I will look at the examples of Bil'in, the 2017 Jerusalem protests around the Al-Aqsa mosque, and finally the Nabi Saleh protests.

Using Military Order 101, which states that no more than ten Palestinians can be allowed to congregate in the Palestinian territories, the Israeli military heavily repressed the protests that emerged in these villages, leading to high rates of injury and death. Nevertheless, as we shall see in the following vignettes, the protests were not only able to emerge but were even successful to some degree.[70]

Bil'in

Bil'in is a rural village of around 1,800 people in the governorate of Ramallah, located in Area B under dual PA and Israeli jurisdiction. In 2005, the Israeli government began work for what it called "the border wall" on the village's lands. This was a misleading term for two reasons. First, there is no internationally recognized border between Israel and Palestine: only the Green Line exists as a demarcation line, following the 1967 war. Moreover, Israel's wall is not being built along this Green Line; rather, the Israelis have used the "border wall" to confiscate large swaths of land from the West Bank in order to change facts on the ground and to maintain a defensive perimeter around the illegal Israeli settlements that proliferate in the area.

The Israeli government was confiscating a full 38 percent of the village's land.[71] This was unacceptable to the villagers, many of whom were dependent on the agricultural sector as a means of survival. In response, the villagers in Bil'in founded a local "Popular Committee against the Wall." This committee began organizing a series of weekly protests, conferences, and attempts at negotiation with the Israeli government. The committee's members pursued legal strategies, enlisting the assistance of Israeli activists, as well as direct action strategies such as protesting every Friday. Bil'in also became the site of international solidarity, with a large number of international activists taking part in the protests on a regular basis.[72]

The popular committee in Bil'in village was formed by Iyad Burnat and his family and friends, who became deeply involved in the movement. This popular committee was initiated outside the scope and oversight of the village's official council, which is a nine-member body appointed by the PA. This local council did not engage with the issue of the separation wall initially. Instead, the villagers organized the popular committee themselves, unprompted by official institutions. In fact, the villagers of Bil'in were often somewhat resistant to visits by PA officials. Attempts at coopting their movement, through official visits and photoshoots, were met unenthusiastically by the villagers.[73]

Because villagers did not rely on the PA initially, they were able to act against the occupation in creative ways, unencumbered by political considerations. They often relied on non-violent confrontations with the Israeli occupation to garner attention for their village's grievances. Bil'in villagers also did not shy away from engaging the international media and making connections with organizers and activists from abroad. Thus they incorporated a number of groups, including Anarchists against the Wall and the International Solidarity Movement, into their struggle. If the PA had been involved from the onset, it would have placed many more restrictions on some of these connections, in fear of political ramifications.[74]

As a result of their independence, the villagers of Bil'in were successful in pressuring the Israeli government to reroute the segregation wall in a way that allowed the village to regain some of its agricultural land.[75] And protests continued even after that, with the stated objective being an end to Israeli apartheid. In the closing statement of the Bil'in conference of 2013, the villagers reasserted their commitment to the Boycott, Divestment, and Sanctions (BDS) campaign, freedom for all political prisoners, and a unified national struggle.[76] In short, they committed themselves to the Palestinian national cause at its broadest level, even though their immediate demands had been met.

However, Bil'in's dynamism was eventually neutralized through the PA's previously mentioned *hay'a* system. The *hay'a's* attempt to control and direct the Bil'in popular committee ultimately reduced the efficacy of the whole movement. It reoriented village activities through formal channels and defused their organic energy and creative tactics. It also limited the political activities of Bil'in organizers to Areas B and C, making sure they never protested in Area A or demanded anything of PA officials directly. Activists involved with the popular committee insist that one of the biggest challenges facing their movement is having to coordinate with the PA leadership on their tactics and goals. This has made it more difficult to coordinate within the village and across villages with similar popular committees. While the villagers of Bil'in were able to obtain their initial demands from the Israeli government, their attempt to sustain the movement faced obstacles when the PA decided to get involved. The PA had a profound negative effect on collective action in Bil'in, similar to its role in a number of other areas across the West Bank.

Jerusalem

As previously mentioned, Jerusalem lies outside the control of the PA altogether, akin to Area C within the West Bank. Parts of Jerusalem lie under direct Israeli jurisdiction (J1), and others are essentially lawless enclaves that are not a part of the Israeli Jerusalem municipality but also have no PA presence (J2). Both the lack of PA involvement and the lack of Palestinian organizations in Jerusalem areas have had profound effects on the manner in which Jerusalemites organize and protest.

Palestinians in Jerusalem have faced a number of pressing issues since the creation of Israel in 1948 and the occupation of East Jerusalem in 1967. Following the 1967 invasion, institutions within Jerusalem that organized Palestinians in times of crisis were closed down, and new organizations were not allowed to emerge. Palestinians in East Jerusalem were not entitled to Israeli citizenship and were given "residency" IDs instead. These ideas created a precarious situation as Palestinians could be deported at any moment by the state. Palestinians in Jerusalem also boycotted municipal elections, for fear of granting legitimacy to the Israeli occupation of the city.[77] This tactic persists to this day, meaning Jerusalemites remain wholly unrepresented by authorities that have a direct impact on their lives. In sum, from 1967 to 1993, Palestinians in Jerusalem found themselves in growing isolation.

This pattern of isolation shifted slightly after 1993. Following the Oslo Accords, Israel tacitly ceded some ground to PA organizations in East Jerusalem so that they could service the Palestinian community in ways in which Israel itself was unwilling. They allowed for some level of PA involvement in East Jerusalem institutions, such as Al Quds University, as well as the existence of the "Orient House," the de-facto headquarters of the PLO within Jerusalem that housed a number of projects and initiatives.[78] The Israeli government also allowed, to some degree, PA "Preventive Security" officials to exercise a certain level of control over the Palestinian population, especially with regard to fighting crime and inter-Palestinian conflict.[79] Although the PA was involved more heavily in Jerusalem's politics during this time period, the scene was dominated by local leaders from the large families that make up the Jerusalem elite. These leaders, including, for example, Faisal al-Husaini, had enough charisma and local support to act as a "rival political center" to Arafat's Ramallah headquarters.[80] Thus despite greater PA intrusion during this time, Jerusalem political action remained somewhat autonomous in comparison with parts of the West Bank or Gaza. For some time after Oslo, Jerusalem was even described as the "center of gravity" of Palestinian politics—a far cry from what we see today.[81]

The Israeli stance on Palestinian organizing in Jerusalem changed, however, following the second intifada. Since then, Israel has taken an increasingly aggressive approach to Palestinian collective action and organizing, closing down the Orient House and leaving Jerusalemites ever more disconnected from their leadership. More importantly, the Israeli occupation has clamped down on Jerusalemites organizing even among themselves. The Israeli Security Agency, tasked with combatting "political subversion," included within this task anyone who opposed the Israeli occupation.[82] Therefore, Palestinians of all political persuasions became a target of Israeli forces in Jerusalem. Today, Palestinian political parties have become fragmented and almost non-existent in Jerusalem.[83] Even institutions such as the Chamber of Commerce, founded before the State of Israel existed, were closed down in the campaign of political repression that followed the second intifada.[84]

Given these restrictions, international donors have since neglected Palestinians of East Jerusalem in their aid, the PA has been unable to intervene and provide services, and the Israeli government has taken the political vacuum as a green light to pursue an aggressive settlement policy in the same areas. These settlements pose a continuous threat to Palestinians within Jerusalem, and political organizing often revolves around this problem. Moreover, Palestinians in Jerusalem are burdened with exorbitant taxes, called *arnona*, to the Israeli municipality even though they are provided with sub-par services. Around 90 percent of Jerusalem city's budget is directed toward Jewish Israeli neighborhoods despite the fact that Palestinians comprise at least 37 percent of the population. This all serves to economically marginalize these communities, in addition to their political disenfranchisement. In more recent years, the Israeli government has also pursued a policy of ethnic cleansing by way of the segregation/apartheid wall. This wall has been snaked around predominantly Arab neighborhoods of Jerusalem—such as Abu Dis, Bir Nabala, Hizma, among others—in order to cut them off from the center of the city. Inhabitants of these areas have also had their permanent residency revoked.[85] When looking at a map of Jerusalem, it becomes clear from the trajectory of the wall that the intention of the Israeli government is to excise the Arab neighborhoods from the Jerusalem municipality and maintain a majority Jewish presence in "official" Jerusalem. This disenfranchisement means that areas that were once considered part of Jerusalem are now cut off, and their inhabitants cannot access services or engage in the city's economy.

All these conditions compound to create an increasingly aggrieved population, with limited political institutions to direct their frustration. That alternative leadership has not been allowed to emerge has also increased the sense of despair and disenfranchisement in East Jerusalem.[86] Thus, when provocations in Jerusalem occur around key issues such as the Al-Aqsa mosque, a large-scale organized response seems unlikely. Nevertheless, the opposite has been the case: Palestinians in Jerusalem have been able to organize, at least in short bursts, in order to air their grievances and pressure the Israeli government into conceding on important topics. These efforts are often "highly localized," taking place almost "exclusively on the neighborhood level" and as a result of the "efforts of particular individuals," given the lack of centralized leadership.[87]

How do Jerusalemites organize themselves despite Israeli repression? Asef Bayat's concept of "non-movements" can help explain this phenomenon to some degree. Bayat defines non-movements as "the collective actions of non-collective actors." These movements "embody shared practices of large numbers of ordinary people whose fragmented but similar activities trigger much social change."[88] Thus, although there may not be a single unifying institution or organizing vehicle, Jerusalemites can channel their grievances at key moments to protest Israeli actions and demand change, in a sort of "non-movement" that flares up periodically.

Moreover, the lack of PA intrusion in the city has meant that Jerusalemites are relatively freer of the political limitations imposed by the Palestinian leadership. After 1993, the growth of the PA caused informal institutions that relied on family and social ties to recede.[89] Family networks had been responsible for organizing the first intifada's efforts; after Oslo, however, these family networks quickly lost "political weight."[90] Today, without PA intrusion, Jerusalemites are revitalizing some of these informal institutions, including the family networks. They have begun experimenting with forms of local organizing, including re-organizing the "popular committees" in particular neighborhoods, creating local security patrols, founding parent unions, and more.[91] At the very least, they are able to call for protests sure in the fact that a critical mass of other Jerusalemites will join them. This is unlike the situation in the West Bank, where turnout for collective action is often encumbered by individual political ties.

Activists note that the objective of these revitalized organizations is first and foremost to reconstruct social cohesion.[92] After the Oslo Accords, public, collective objectives were replaced with private, individual objectives: Palestinians in Jerusalem "ceded responsibility" to the PA's institutions and foreign aid, pursuing professional aspirations above the public good.[93] Thus, the informal institutions that have emerged today have attempted to undo this blow to social cohesion brought on by the creation of the PA, focusing on rebuilding a sense of community and responsibility. Although these informal institutions do not have the organizing capacity of a unifying organization like the UNLU, their existence proves that Palestinians can organize even in contexts of severe repression.

One such example is the July 2017 protests around the Israeli restrictions posed on the Al-Aqsa mosque. The Aqsa Compound, in the Old City of Jerusalem, has been the site of conflict since the mid-1990s.[94] In July 2017, Israeli soldiers outside the Old City were stabbed by a Palestinian assailant. Although the stabbings did not occur in the Aqsa Compound itself, the Israeli government used the occurrence as an opportunity to impose increased restrictions over the religious site. Fearing that this step was setting the precedent for even more restrictions, Palestinians began protesting to remove the specific restrictions that were imposed following the stabbings, as well as restrictions on access more generally.

As previously mentioned, PLO- and PA-affiliated institutions are not allowed to function in the city of Jerusalem due to the Israeli occupation's repressive policies. Thus, when the Israeli government imposed restrictions on the Aqsa Compound in this period, the PA was slow to react, as were the major Palestinian political parties. Instead, young people spread the call for protest through social media platforms.[95] As research shows, the social media campaign was locally organized and organically spread, rather than being imposed externally or by government entities.[96]

Many of those who took part in protests either came from the Old City or from the marginalized neighborhoods, such as Silwan and Ras al-Amud. They represented a variety of political parties, as these protest movements have in the past.[97] Participants relied on their social ties not only to spread the news about protests but also to agree on tactics. Many of the original participants had previously engaged in protesting settler incursions into the Aqsa Compound. These activists joined forces with religious organizations present in the Old City, such as the Islamic Waqf organizations, to unify efforts and provide a focal point for protests. They called for strategies that came naturally to participants, such as protesting at prayer time and engaging in mass prayer as a means of protest. They also unified the protest line, in the sense that everyone agreed to a boycott of praying within the Aqsa Compound until restrictions had been lifted, instead maximizing the disruption by praying in the streets and alleys outside. The PA did not take a position until a few days of intense activity had passed, and calls for protest from the political parties were also belated.

These July protests were not the first time protests have erupted in the suffocated neighborhoods of Jerusalem. Waves of dissent have been ongoing in recent years as economic and political policies of disenfranchisement have taken their toll. But what is interesting in the case of Jerusalem is that the Israeli occupation forbids groups with direct ties to the PLO or to the PA from functioning and, despite this prohibition, Palestinians in Jerusalem have been able to depend on their social ties to engage in mobilization campaigns when the need arises. In this case, protests were organized via independent calls for protest on social media. Unlike in cases such as Bil'in, the PA was unable to control or direct these protests, and so did not have the inhibiting effect on protests that it has on other areas of the territories.

Nabi Saleh

Nabi Saleh is a village lying between Ramallah and Nablus in the West Bank, on a main road that connects to Tel Aviv. Nabi Saleh's land is split between Area B and Area C; although all areas of the West Bank are supposed to transition to administration under the PA, Israel has taken liberties with Area C specifically for continued settlement expansion. Like Bil'in, Nabi Saleh found itself the victim of a land appropriation scheme as Israel began development on Halamish, a nearby illegal settlement. Nabi Saleh's villagers were suddenly unable to access their own lands and lived in constant fear of home demolition.[98]

Nabi Saleh is a smaller village than Bil'in, with around 550 people estimated to live in the village.[99] The village is defined by the Tamimi family, which is considered the main group/clan in Nabi Saleh.[100] Following the turmoil of the second intifada, Nabi Saleh, like many surrounding villages, reassessed previous resistance tactics. Many older villagers had participated in the first intifada and had been active in a number of political organizations. In an effort to rekindle the dynamism of those early years, the villagers in Nabi Saleh embarked on a protest movement in order to pressure Israel locally while garnering international attention. Their protest movement began in 2009, following in the footsteps of other village movements in Bil'in and Budrus. Initially, it was very successful at gaining attention at the global level.[101]

Villagers in Nabi Saleh capitalized on the strong ties between their families in order to mobilize the village. Members of the Tamimi clan quickly divvied up roles in the movement: some took over the website and social media posting, others filmed and photographed the protests, and yet others documented their activities in order to disseminate reports among supporters.[102] Many members of the Tamimi family were targeted by Israeli forces, and some lost their lives.[103] In a short period of time, Nabi Saleh's cause became synonymous with the plight of Palestinian villagers. The Tamimi children also became well-known icons of the Palestinian village resistance movement.[104] As a result, international activists and observers flocked to Nabi Saleh, with villagers estimating that at one point around a third of those demonstrating each week were from abroad.[105]

At first, villagers protested narrowly, focusing on the illegal Halamish settlement and its appropriation of the village's land. They specifically focused on the issue of the natural spring—the village's source of water—which was once on the village's land and had since become inaccessible. But, with increased global attention, the villagers ratchetted up their efforts and expanded their objectives. This came hand in hand with increased Israeli aggression—with the increase in injury and incidence of death, the villagers began demanding an end to the Israeli apartheid system altogether. They coordinated their protest movement with other villages and took part in actions across the West Bank. These included shutting down highways and demonstrating in front of other Israeli settlements and businesses.[106] Initially, there was a high degree of coordination between Nabi Saleh's villagers and the popular resistance committees in other villages facing land appropriation. Much of the leadership of these committees were personally acquainted with one another and often strategized over tactics and shared events.[107]

Like the other villages, many of the villagers in Nabi Saleh—at least two-thirds of the total, according to their own estimates—work within the PA.[108] Employment within the PA's institutions is often not substantive or demanding. Instead, these positions are intended to dispense salaries while keeping possible opposition in check. And villagers indeed corroborate this claim: Bassem Tamimi, one of the leaders of the Nabi Saleh movement, reported that PA officials had contacted him, making sure to point out that Nabi Saleh was allowed to demonstrate as long as the PA itself was not asked to take action. Protests were also to be limited to Area C and were not allowed to spill over to areas under PA jurisdiction.[109] Since many villagers depended on the PA for their livelihood, it became difficult to disregard such directives. This dynamic is of course not unique to Nabi Saleh, as a similar relationship exists between the Bil'in popular resistance committee and the PA, as the previous example outlined. In some instances, the PA has even intervened to stop protests from taking place in Israeli-controlled areas in order to avoid further clashes.[110] Coupled with the threat of losing their livelihoods, the PA's interventions have effectively neutralized the villagers and destroyed the efficacy of their protests.

Thus, in 2016, after seven years of weekly protests, the leadership in Nabi Saleh decided to end the protest movement.[111] They cited "fatigue" and an inability to mobilize the villagers effectively, particularly after a large-scale raid, unnoticed by the PA, ended with the arrest of many of the villagers. In a village of 600, over fifty had become physically disabled as a result of injuries incurred during protests, and more than half of the village suffered wider injuries at the hands of the Israeli occupation forces. In the context of increased PA control over the protest movements in the West Bank, activity in other villages had declined as well. This left less room for a coordinated effort, and the support of international participants remained tangential.[112] As a result, the Nabi Saleh protest movement withered away.

Conclusion

Using the qualitative assessment of different time periods, as well as the quantitative assessment of political mobilization patterns today, we can see that the PA has had an effect on how Palestinians protest. The within-case variation presented by this particular case gives us a unique opportunity to examine the effect of the PA specifically, holding other variables (such as differences in population or grievances) constant. On a theoretical level, this chapter—alongside the previous chapter—demonstrates the utility of examining the effect of authoritarian regime strategies over time, not only at the individual level but also at the societal level. Doing so helps provide a more accurate understanding of political mobilization (or lack thereof) in the non-democratic context of the PA. After all, it is becoming increasingly clear that individuals do not operate in a vacuum, and that the impact of their immediate society/community cannot be understated. Moreover, examining the effect of authoritarian strategies on societal cohesion can help us understand why some societies have a capacity for effective political mobilization and why others do not.

Moreover, this chapter helps prove the relationship borne out in the laboratory experiments of Chapter 3. It becomes clear from this analysis that the PA's increasing reliance on authoritarian strategies has affected the willingness and capacity of Palestinians to coordinate on common goals. Thus, when we look at the empirical record of protests across different time periods, we find that Palestinians are indeed more fragmented and less effective. Not only does this mean Palestinian society is unable to pressure its own leadership effectively but also that it is unable to face the main challenge of Israeli occupation overall.

5

THE EFFECT OF INTERNATIONAL INVOLVEMENT ACROSS THE STATE SOVEREIGNTY SPECTRUM

This book argues that externally backed repression demobilizes societies by strengthening authoritarianism, thus breeding polarization and a lack of social cohesion. But does this theory travel outside the bounds of the particular case of Palestine? After all, Palestine is a unique case as one of the last remaining countries under a complicated, multi-tiered occupation. Thus it is important to assess whether this theory can say anything about cases outside the condition of severely curtailed sovereignty.

Nevertheless, the Palestinian case is not as anomalous as one would assume at first glance. As Bassel Salloukh points out, the entire Middle East region is "a grand theater fought through proxy domestic and transnational actors and ideological competition in weak Arab states, including Lebanon, the West Bank and Gaza, post-war Iraq, Bahrain, and Yemen."[1] Thus, the entire region suffers from war, external intervention, and weakness in state capacity and sovereignty. The Palestinian case is therefore not removed from the general political experience in the Middle East.

In the next section, I will provide case study analysis of two cases across the state sovereignty spectrum: Iraqi Kurdistan and Bahrain. These two cases have different levels of autonomy, in contrast to each other and to the Palestine case. Unlike Palestine, the Kurdish Regional Government (KRG) has some degree of autonomy and sovereignty, and Bahrain is a full-fledged sovereign state. Nevertheless, as we shall see in coming sections, international involvement in both those cases has created many of the same dynamics highlighted in the analysis of the PA. By examining these cases, I will demonstrate the generalizability of the theoretical argument presented in this project.

I argue that the theory presented in this book is informed by the conditions of the PA specifically but is not limited in its scope to a single case. The dynamics of international intervention, authoritarianism, and changing state–society relationships are present in a number of cases across the Arab world.

The case of Bahrain

This case features heavy international involvement on the part of the United States and its allies, as well as rising authoritarianism and a fractured and polarized societal dynamic. Following the causal argument highlighted in Chapter 1, the causal chain is as follows: international involvement facilitated infrastructural power and insulated the regime from its public. As a result, the Bahraini regime was able to rely more heavily on authoritarian practices in order to maintain control rather than building a wide and more stable political coalition with all parts of its public. The public also became increasingly polarized into pro- and anti-regime camps, along sectarian/confessional lines. This division has led to declining social cohesion and an inability to mobilize effectively against the regime. Thus, over time, international involvement has helped to strengthen the authoritarian nature of the regime.

International involvement in Bahrain

Bahrain is an archetypical example of a state with an American military presence. Its location is highly valuable strategically, given its centrality in the Arabian/Persian Gulf, less than 400 miles away from the Strait of Hormuz. Its heavy American military presence comes with increased involvement across a number of dimensions—political, economic, and military. In this way, as this section will demonstrate, American involvement facilitated infrastructural power for the regime. Over time, this led the regime to become more authoritarian and allowed it to repress its opposition in order to maintain the strategic advantage of continued American military presence.

International involvement in Bahrain did not begin with the United States. Before the Second World War and the United States' ascendance as an international hegemon, Britain was the strongest international actor in the Arab Gulf generally, and in Bahrain's modern history specifically. The British backed the Al-Khalifa regime in its attempts to control the local population very early on, exacerbating the political conflict between Shia villagers and Sunni royalist factions (to its bloody conclusion).[2] Although these factions overlapped to a large degree with particular confessional communities in Bahrain, their struggle was not motivated by confessional identity. Rather, as Justin Gengler notes, "the divide … turned on a political question," mainly around the role of British intervention.[3] Thus, from the beginning of modern Bahrain's history, international involvement has exacerbated polarization around the role of international actors. In this case, the British also backed the Al-Khalifa faction's crackdown on its political opponents and helped consolidate the regime during that stage of its history.

The United States has since filled the role Britain once played in the Middle East. Specifically with Bahrain, the United States has maintained an interest in its internal domestic and foreign policies, especially with regard to Iranian influence after the 1979 Revolution. While the United States took over the British naval base in 1971, it did not establish the Fifth Fleet there until 1995. By both Bahraini and American accounts, however, this placement served American interests to a large degree by providing the United States with a strategic location from which to monitor Iran, as well as maintain regional stability. For the Bahraini regime, this has translated into support for its institutions and coercive capacity.

An American military presence has increased authoritarianism by facilitating infrastructural power on both political and economic fronts. Economically, the presence of US military installations accrues benefits to the local population through jobs.[4] The regime also dispenses these benefits selectively, as a form of segmented clientelism, or "political diversification."[5] This dynamic gives the regime options for cooptation, as well as creating a dependency between the US military presence and the regime's durability. Moreover, the United States provides the Bahraini military with arms sales that it has used to repress protest movements.[6]

Bahrain has always pursued policies that have disenfranchised large portions of the population based on sectarian motivations, and this has not posed an issue for American involvement or support. Indeed, the United States played a crucial role in providing political support to the Bahraini government during the uprising of 2011. For instance, President Obama released a statement "welcoming" the Bahraini government's attempts at reform, even as crackdowns ensued in the streets.[7] Then Defense Secretary Robert Gate's visit to the region and his meeting with Bahraini and Saudi officials prompted Saudi troops to move in as support for the Bahraini regime during its crackdown. And yet, throughout all this, the White House spokesperson claimed: "This is not an invasion."[8] In fact, the Saudi invasion was a calculated move agreed upon by the United States because it never had any real democracy promotion objectives in Bahrain. Instead, it has prioritized stability over democratic development because of the strategic necessity of the island. Thus, Saudi policy worked in line with US policy in the country, which was to maintain the status quo in a politically sensitive region considered "critical" to US interests.[9]

Overall, American decision-makers have made it clear that the success of the Bahraini opposition poses a risk to their own involvement in the country.[10] American military involvement, and its effect on political and economic dynamics, has thus provided the regime cover to ratchet up its use of repression. As a result, as demonstrated by qualitative data as well as measurements like the Polity score, Bahrain's level of authoritarianism has increased over time.[11]

American support shielded Bahrain from international action and reduced the likelihood of challenges to the regime. It did so by not only creating difficulties for the opposition in Bahrain to garner international sympathy or action but also by polarizing society internally. Historically, divisions have existed within Bahraini society, and the regime has attempted to capitalize on these divisions using divide-and-conquer strategies.[12] American involvement and its effect of increasing authoritarianism have exacerbated these divisions to a much larger degree in recent times.

Evidence of this polarization is not difficult to find, even prior to the Arab Spring and the ensuing Bahraini uprising. Public opinion data from Bahrain shows that Shia and Sunni citizens have very different relationships with their state.[13] Shia Bahrainis have a different conception of national identity from Sunni Bahrainis.[14] Material benefits and services also accrue disproportionately to Sunni citizens, with Shias being systematically excluded from employment in the public sector.[15] Finally, and most importantly, perceptions about the regime and its performance are drastically polarized along the sectarian divide. Sunni citizens report much less dissatisfaction than Shia citizens across a number of issue areas.[16]

Clearly, evidence for polarization exists. But what causes this polarization? It is easy to dismiss this sectarian divide as something primordial, dating back to the early days of Islam and the Yazid–Hussein rivalry. However, a closer examination of the historical record shows this is not the case. Beginning with the Al-Khalifa domination of the island, conflicts centered on political struggles and divides over the future of the Bahraini state. Confessional identity was not a motivating factor for mobilization. In fact, as late as the 1970s, Bahraini political activists note that the main divide was not sectarian, but rather leftist factions versus conservative royalist elements.[17] The sectarian divide did not become a salient one until very recently in Bahrain's history. And there is strong evidence to suggest that this divide was made salient and exacerbated purposely by the regime itself for the sake of maintaining control. As Gengler notes, the Bahraini monarchy chose short-term regime security over long-term political stability[18]—a dynamic that could not have existed without the external support and infrastructural power provided to the Bahraini regime by the United States, its international patron.

The Bahraini regime's authoritarian practices worked to polarize society and subsequently neutralize public pressures on the regime. First, cooptation mechanisms ensured that large swaths of the population became dependent on the regime not only for material benefits but also for protection from other segments of society. As the regime set itself up as the main arbiter of inter-group conflict, fear became the binding tool between state and citizen, rather than merely patronage.[19] As a result, polarization arose on the dividing line of haves and have nots, or "winners and losers."[20] Coupled with electoral gerry-mandering, which necessitates that Bahraini citizens organize around their sectarian identities, these forms of cooptation have *generated* group conflict.[21] Thus, when economic grievances arise that are relevant across the Sunni–Shia divide, the regime is quick to paint the issue as a form of sectarian conflict and direct groups against each other.[22] And since some groups are more beholden to the regime economically than others, this means they are increasingly "sensitive" to political positions that may irk the monarchy.[23] In this way, effective opposition to the regime is neutralized.

Where cooptation fails, the regime also uses repression as a tactic for increasing polarization and neutralizing opposition. This is best illustrated with the events of the 2011 Bahraini uprising. For the uprising to have been effective, it was not sufficient that Shia groups alone came out to protest. As Gengler notes, "so long as [the Shia] act alone, they lack the military prepon-derance necessary to physically overthrow the state."[24] Therefore, initially, the uprising focused on demands for democracy and accountability rather than sectarian-based demands from a Shia public to a Sunni regime. Indeed, the first groups involved in the uprising, such as the February 14th Youth Movement and Waad, were markedly secular with purely political demands.[25] Both groups have both Sunni and Shia members and have been credited with being the first movers in the Bahraini uprising. Moreover, Shias did not have grievances alone: Sunnis also reportedly had "pent-up political frustration" at having their loyalty "taken for granted."[26] But the regime recognized that Sunni–Shia coordination posed a real threat to its security. Thus, Sunni participants (particularly leadership) were quickly singled out, targeted for questioning, and jailed.[27]

Shia-dominated groups that followed cross-sectarian groups into the uprising were also targeted. The largest Shia opposition group, Al-Wefaq, has refused to engage in parliamentary elections due to the heavily gerrymandered districts and the government's refusal to reform. Other smaller groups that splintered off Al-Wefaq in the wake of the uprising have also been targeted heavily, with their political leadership arrested or driven to silence.[28] In some cases, these organizations have been dissolved entirely.[29] Finally, the regime expanded its repression to include even those who were not political as a means to discourage opposition in the future. This included attacking medical professionals who had provided services to protestors during the unrest.[30] In this way, the Bahraini regime completely decimated organizations and groups that were both interested in cross-sectarian mobilization and capable of mobilizing social groups effectively.

In the face of such repression, opposition in Bahrain became increasingly defined by sect, as individuals fell back on their "ascriptive ties" rather than politically motivated positions. Since the democratic opposition had been neutralized, these sectarian networks were all that remained to a majority of the population. These included "street movements" that engaged in violent action against security forces but otherwise did not articulate their demands or pressure the regime effectively.[31] As it became easier for the Bahraini government to be flagrantly sectarian, it also encouraged a similar reaction among the public. Thus, following the uprising, Bahrain's politics have become "even more entrenched along confessional lines"—an outcome that scholars note was a direct result of "the state's targeted persecution of groups and individuals who dared to advocate for cross-sectarian political cooperation."[32]

As such, it is clear that the Bahraini monarchy's authoritarian practices led to the polarization in Bahraini society that we see today (i.e. the two "camps" of increasingly radical Shia groups versus Sunni groups tied to the regime). This polarization degrades social cohesion and makes it difficult for those who oppose the regime to coordinate effectively in a manner that is supported by a critical mass of the population. To this day, this polarization makes it difficult for the opposition in Bahrain to achieve levels of mass support akin to the

2011 uprising. As a result, mass mobilization is not a credible threat to the regime, and authoritarianism is entrenched further.

Such a dynamic could not have been accomplished without the Bahraini regime's crackdown, which was facilitated and supported by external patrons. The Saudi invasion, greenlighted by the United States, came in the nick of time, as the uprising would have likely been able to pressure the regime to some degree, given its traction in both confessional communities, had the Saudi (and Emirati) forces not intervened in March 2011.[33] Thus it becomes clear that, as a result of international backing, the regime has been insulated from actually negotiating or compromising with the opposition, and has made the possibility of a viable opposition in the future more unlikely. The Bahraini regime was able to use polarization and division as a calculated tactic, comfortable in the knowledge that their major international patrons (the United States and Saudi Arabia) would not take action.

The case of Iraqi Kurdistan[34]

International involvement in Iraqi Kurdistan

The Kurdish national issue has been a source of contention in the Middle East since the end of the First World War. Just like many other national groups in the region, the Kurds had found themselves subjects of many passing empires over the years. Following the rise of the modern state in the Middle East, as a result of the Sykes–Picot Agreement (1916) and the European-imposed mandate system, the Kurds once again found themselves divided among a number of countries (Turkey, Syria, Iraq, and Iran). They were thus often tied up in regional politics, and intervention by regional powers in the Kurdish national movement and internal politics was the norm.

In Iraq, the Kurds were actually extended the greatest degree of autonomy by the central government. They were given the right to speak their language and exercise a level of self-governance over the northern region where they were most concentrated.[35] The Iraqi Kurdish leader at the time, Mullah Mustafa Barzani, in fact worked with Abd al-Karim Qasim, Iraq's first ruler after the monarchy had been overthrown, to eliminate shared political opponents. Rifts did not emerge between the Iraqi Kurds and the central government until Qasim attempted land reforms, which angered Kurdish landholders.[36]

It was at this time that the Iranian regime, under the American-allied shah, became involved in the first Kurdish rebellion on Iraqi soil. Even as the shah repressed Iranian Kurds, he supported Barzani in Iraq against the Qasim regime. Much of Iran's involvement stemmed from Qasim's shift toward the Soviet Union and the fact that he removed Iraq from the pro-Western Baghdad Pact. The shah was also wary of Qasim because of some territorial disputes over Arab-majority border regions in Iran.[37] This episode signified the first instance of international intervention generating polarization among Kurdish parties, specifically in this case the Kurdish Democratic Party (KDP) in Iraq versus the Kurdish Democratic Party in Iran. But, so far, this polarization existed between Kurds across country lines, and the Iraqi Kurdish political sphere remained firmly under the KDP's sole control.

In 1972, Iraq signed a treaty of "friendship and cooperation" with the Soviet Union, setting off alarm bells in Washington. It was at this point that the United States directly stepped in to Iraqi and Kurdish politics, rather than just supporting the shah's policies.[38] In this instance, Barzani appealed to American involvement by promising access to oil and pledging to fight Soviet "expansionism."[39] The Americans, under the Nixon administration and encouraged by Henry Kissinger specifically, decided to support a covert plan to funnel money and weapons to Iraqi Kurds in their uprising against the regime in Baghdad. Fueled by external backing, Barzani and the KDP became embroiled in intra-ethnic betrayals, including killing members of KDP Iran for the shah.[40] Moreover, Barzani himself began acting unilaterally and outwardly repressed his political opponents within the party, such as Jalal Talabani.[41] Barzani even had his son Massoud run the Parastin, an intelligence service, with the objective of weeding out disloyal members of the KDP.[42] The KDP thus angered its Iraqi Kurdish constituency, and divisions arose between different segments of the political leadership.

Opposition to Barzani within the KDP had been brewing for close to a decade, but the final straw was the behavior of Barzani and the KDP after 1972. As a result of his heavy-handed tactics, Barzani and the KDP failed in their revolt against the regime. This failure, and the opposition Barzani had engendered, manifested itself in the creation of the Patriotic Union of Kurdistan (PUK) in 1975, an organization intended to rival the KDP, the leadership of which consisted of ex-KDP members who had once struggled under Barzani's authoritarian conduct.[43] Talabani, who would later head the PUK, was one of these ex-members. In addition to ex-KDP members, the PUK encompassed many of the left-wing political groups in Kurdish politics opposed to Barzani's authoritarian decision-making and penchant for allying against other Kurds. Even though at this point in history US support for an independent Kurdistan was lukewarm at best, US involvement still polarized the Iraqi Kurdish leadership and led to authoritarian conditions.

Throughout the 1980s, the KDP and PUK competed for foreign backing and funding and internal support and recruits.[44] Polarization grew to such an extent that clashes broke out between the two groups on a number of occasions. It was only following Saddam Hussein's assault on the Kurdish region in the late 1980s during the Anfal campaign that the PUK and the KDP began coordinating together against a common enemy.[45] Saddam also made the mistake of invading Kuwait following the Anfal campaign. This opened up two fronts, which put pressure on his military capacity and provoked a military response from the United States and its allies.

The United States thus decided to launch the first Gulf war, intervening militarily and pushing a resolution through the UN to impose a no-fly zone on the Kurdish region. Scholars note that this measure "served as a vital pre-condition for the subsequent formation of the de facto state" we see today in Iraqi Kurdistan.[46] Indeed, elections were held in the Kurdish region and the Kurdistan Regional Government formed for the first time in 1992. Elections proved the polarization that existed not just at the level of political leadership but at the public level as well, as the Kurdish parliament had an almost equal number of delegates from the PUK and the KDP. Both parties had also won in two distinct geographic areas.[47]

The "penetration" of Iraq by foreign powers increased during this time period, especially in the Kurdish region.[48] As Gareth Stansfield notes, political elites learned to act autonomously, and different groups created "well-established links to patrons and supporters, many of whom are foreign."[49] Because of this excessive international involvement, the unprecedented political opportunity for the Kurds following the Gulf war was to some degree squandered. Civil war broke out in the 1990s between the KDP and the PUK. Both groups appealed to a number of external powers for support: the PUK appealed to Iran to attack the KDP, and the KDP appealed to Saddam Hussein himself to consolidate control over the PUK.[50] This resulted in thousands of deaths for both Peshmerga (the Kurdish militiamen) and civilians. The United States was often directly responsible for exacerbating polarization between the two forces: for instance, CIA operatives persuaded the PUK and the KDP to launch an attack on Saddam in 1995, but eventually relayed information that their plans had been compromised by Saddam's intelligence. The KDP decided to withdraw as a result of this information, but the PUK moved forward with the plan alone, resulting in deaths and subsequent crackdown by

Saddam.[51] This intervention is but one example of how American involvement, miscommunication, and hastily executed plots (which US forces did not end up supporting) bred a sense of betrayal and enmity between the two Kurdish groups.

Though the United States eventually intervened once again to end the civil war by mediating a peace treaty between the two parties, scholars today note that this did not resolve the underlying polarization that existed in Kurdish politics. In fact, the 1998 peace treaty between the PUK and KDP continued to institutionalize the split in Kurdish politics and reinforce dynamics of external intervention in domestic Kurdish affairs.[52] The treaty created a structure of two governments, two administrations, and two security forces, which persists to this day. And the motivation of the PUK and the KPD to sign such a treaty or show unity had little to do with integrating the two groups or agreeing on shared objectives; instead, it was intended to "secure access to power and related profits."[53] The United States provided revenue to Iraqi Kurdistan during this time using the Oil-for-Food Programme, with the UN's backing, which accounted for two-thirds of the total aid allocated to Iraq despite Iraqi Kurdistan accounting for only 15 to 20 percent of the population.[54] The United States also assured Kurdish parties that they would be protected from Saddam's regime during this time, thus providing externally backed infrastructural power.[55] Both parties "made a windfall" during this time, and the aid helped to consolidate their control over respective regions of Kurdistan.[56] Because of the large benefits they accrued, both parties felt compelled to utilize these resources by demonstrating unity on paper, without actually compromising on much of anything among themselves.[57] Much of their rivalry was channeled into a competition over American resources, further entrenching the polarization within Kurdish politics.[58]

With the 2003 US-led invasion of Iraq, the Kurdish parties were elevated to "king-maker" status within Iraqi politics as a major ally of the United States.[59] American involvement helped establish an unprecedented amount of autonomy for the Kurdish region and allowed the Kurds to play a key role in forming the Iraqi constitution. This gave the Kurds rights to a share of the Iraqi budget, a right to autonomous governance, and the possibility of resolving the issue of disputed territories (mixed Arab and Kurdish areas) in the future.[60] The United States was also involved in facilitating production-sharing agreements in disputed areas, tacitly approving Kurdish control of related oil fields.[61] Then Exxon Mobil executive and later Secretary of State Rex Tillerson approved these plans himself, which facilitated such agreements with other international actors, like the Turkish government.[62] This had the effect of generating infrastructural and extractive power for the KRG, as it increased its control over territory and resources.[63] Overall, although polarization between the political leadership persisted during this time, heavy American involvement was able to push the Kurdish statehood project further along.[64]

Public discontent, however, seemed to increase throughout this time period, particularly over the issue of dual, separate PUK and KDP administrations as well as economic conditions.[65] Accusations of corruption and nepotism became the norm in Kurdish politics, as did the repression of political dissidents, journalists, and ethnic minorities within the Kurdish region.[66] Both Kurdish parties relied heavily on patronage—in the form of employment, pensions, and transfer payments—in order to coopt a significant portion of the Kurdish population.[67] A full 24 percent of Kurds work either in the PUK or the KDP security forces. Kurdish leadership had tied wage security for common citizens to the fate of the party itself. This dynamic was sustained as a direct result of American policies in the Kurdish region, which scholars note "incentivized militarization and rent-seeking."[68]

Clearly, authoritarian conditions were worsening during this time period. This manifested itself in the creation of a third party, Gorran, which disrupted the two-party consensus to some degree initially. Although Gorran was not a major player, it spoke to the discontent of the Kurdish public that it was able to make gains in the Kurdish parliament. Attempts to work with the PUK and the KDP were not successful, and Gorran was expelled from the government over partisan conflicts and not allowed to fully engage in its role through the speaker of parliament position.[69] The KRG parliament, which was intended to bring together various political movements within Iraqi Kurdistan, no longer functions for that purpose.

Recent events in Iraqi politics also speak to the increased authoritarianism of the KRG, particularly under the auspices of Barzani. For instance, although Nouri Maliki, Iraq's prime minister from 2006 to 2014, was recognized as deeply authoritarian and divisive, the KRG coordinated with him on a number of occasions, even as Maliki repressed Sunni groups and re-militarized Iraqi politics.[70] The fight against ISIS took US support of Iraqi Kurdistan to the next level, as the United States and the KRG "concluded a military agreement in July 2016 which might establish long-term military and security cooperation," despite protests from the central government in Baghdad.[71] The Kurds used this alliance to advance sovereignty claims, especially as they gained territory from ISIS forces in disputed areas and reportedly did not allow Arab residents to return.[72] In the context of fighting the threat of terrorism, the United States had little patience for encouraging power-sharing between the KDP and the PUK, or for unifying state institutions.[73] Thus, the US alliance with KRG cemented the existing divisions within Kurdish politics yet again, and particularly exacerbated the KDP's growing power.[74] In fact, the polarizing effect of American policy in Iraqi Kurdistan has led to such deep divides between the PUK and the KDP that dehumanization of the other side has become not only common but ritualized.[75]

Another example is the issue of Kirkuk. As a disputed area between the Kurds and the government in Baghdad, the Kirkuk problem highlights the authoritarian manner in which the KRG conducted itself. The locals in Kirkuk, across every ethnic group, were marginalized in the process of negotiations between the KRG and the Iraqi government. Kurdish leadership did not bother consulting with Kirkuk residents.[76] The issue of Kirkuk became not only a struggle between Erbil and Baghdad but also a power struggle between the PUK and the KPD, given the pro-PUK sentiment prevalent within Kirkuk.[77] American involvement entrenched this dynamic further: the United States and its allies did not consider the opinions of the locals in Kirkuk and backed the existing Erbil–Baghdad negotiation setup. International patrons and the KRG did not consider public opinion in the Kurdish region generally either, which was more flexible on the issue of the disputed territory than much of the political leadership.[78] Thus, although the Iraqi constitution highlights the mechanisms by which to resolve territorial disputes, there is still no resolution to the issue of Kirkuk. Instead, residents of the Kurdish region found themselves increasingly marginalized.

The 2017 independence referendum episode in the Kurdish region is another example of both the increased polarization between political elites and the divergence between Kurdish leadership and the public. Barzani pushed the issue of the referendum despite the reservations expressed by Gorran and the PUK.[79] They argued that such a referendum could exacerbate the government in Baghdad as well as international opinion, which was more focused on the fight against ISIS than possible secession in Kurdistan. Despite this fact, Barzani acted unilaterally and the referendum was held anyway. It was particularly sensitive because the KRG decided to hold voting in areas considered disputed territory, where Kurds were not the majority of the population. Arab and Turkmen minorities reported intimidation during the voting process and complained that the voting booths were often placed in specific Kurdish areas to dissuade voting.[80] This was also not the first time ethnic minorities had complained of pressure and repression.[81]

Following the referendum, the Iraqi government took action to seize control of Kirkuk and the oil fields for which the KRG received 17 percent of the Iraqi budget. To avoid increased tension and bloodshed, Peshmerga under PUK control retreated from Kirkuk.[82] The KDP cried treason, whereas the PUK asserted it had been placed in an impossible situation over a referendum it had opposed. While still ongoing, events so far illustrate the manner in which division has become the norm of Kurdish politics, as has the leadership's lack of accountability to its public.

In sum, American involvement in the case of Iraqi Kurdistan was much more supportive of Kurdish aspirations than in the case of Palestine, in terms of their demands regarding sovereignty over specific territory. From providing a no-fly zone to supporting Kurdish demands in the Iraqi constitution, American foreign and military policy has supported Iraqi Kurds in every which way except the final step of secession. Despite this support, American involvement has had a similar effect—polarization between elites, an increasing lack of accountability to the public, and increased authoritarian conditions. This is because the American involvement was "autocratizing," facilitating the insulation of the Kurdish leadership from its public and prioritizing Kurdish territorial aspirations vis a vis the central government in Baghdad, rather than creating sustainable and responsive institutions in Iraqi Kurdistan.

Discussion

What do these findings suggest about the impact of American involvement? The case illustrates that American involvement in strategically sensitive areas has a particular effect on political development. Specifically, the United States has backed indigenous authoritarian regimes in cases across the Middle East—cases that the United States considers strategically important. This has led to polarization and a lack of social cohesion. American involvement in both cases facilitated authoritarian conditions through the causal mechanisms outlined above. And, as the cases show, this autocratizing impact of US involvement bears out across the state sovereignty spectrum. From a full state such as Bahrain, a semi-autonomous region like Iraqi Kurdistan, and an occupied territory like Palestine, when American interests have been defined by support for the status quo, US involvement has led to negative repercussions for state–society relations and levels of authoritarianism.

In the cases of Iraqi Kurdistan and Bahrain, we see a disintegration of democratic institutions that maintain accountability. In the Kurdish case, the

KRG parliament has been sidelined, and opposition forces are not allowed to engage in formal politics to the fullest extent. The president in the KRG also refuses to step down despite overstaying term limits. In Bahrain, attempts to challenge the authoritarian nature of the regime were neutralized by the Bahraini government and its patrons. Today, political opposition in Bahrain has been decimated.

If American involvement had remained indirect, or non-existent, in either case, I argue we would see a very different pattern of political development. Divisions may still have emerged among the Kurdish leadership over particular policies and strategies, but leadership on either side of the issue would have had to contend with a real opposition and come to some consensus or compromise, or risk facing public pressure and de-legitimization. Without the United States providing arms and security training, the Kurdish leadership would not have been able to rely on repression as a tool for silencing public opposition and would have had to make concessions to the public whenever policies were challenged. This is similar to the conditions in the Palestinian territories. Simply put, without the disrupting effect of American involvement, mechanisms of accountability would have continued to exist formally or informally. Instead, both countries have been put on a path of increased authoritarianism and demobilized societies.

CONCLUSION

This book has sought to answer two questions: (1) What demobilizes a once mobilized society? And (2) How does international involvement amplify or suppress these dynamics? The introduction outlined a theoretical argument that broke down these research questions into observable empirical implications. I argued specifically that in "penetrated" societies, international involvement creates a principal–agent problem between regimes and their publics. This facilitates an increase in authoritarian practices, which then polarizes society. These dynamics manifest themselves in declining social cohesion and mobilization.

We see this relationship borne out in Palestine. In the second chapter, I established a link between international involvement and a divergence in preferences between regime participants/elites and their public. I also presented evidence to show a polarizing effect of international involvement between different groups in society, based on their affiliation with the regime. While state–society relationships and the role of international involvement have been explored in the past, this chapter went further in presenting evidence for a clear divergence between regime participants and their public *as a result* of international involvement. It also added an important moderating variable to this relationship that had only been alluded to in the previous literature: regime affiliation. The preferences of citizens, and how they change in the context of international involvement, have a lot to do with their preexisting relationship, and proximity to, the regime. Some studies have recognized that economic ties to the state change political behavior, for example, but this study puts the salience of regime affiliation in full focus.

The role of international involvement in the PA and its state–society relations is of course just one case, but the dynamics of such involvement generalize to the entire region. As previously noted, international involvement (and particularly that of the United States) has a profound effect on regime strategies in the Arab world, as well as how publics react to them. However, in previous analysis, the public itself has not been disaggregated. In many circumstances, under authoritarian contexts, polarization within society creates different segments of the public with varying preferences and interests. This divide often exists between those affiliated with the ruling political regime and those who are not. It is imperative to include this important moderating variable if we are to understand the effect of international involvement on state–society relations in "penetrated" authoritarian states. The analysis in Chapter 2 is but one example, but the dynamics apply to many other cases.

In the third chapter, I examined the focus of this book's argument—specifically, I linked the effect of authoritarian strategies to polarization and declining social cohesion in a two-stage theory. I examined whether cooptation and repression had varying effects on levels of polarization. To test the second stage of the theory, I also examined whether polarized preferences had an effect on willingness to cooperate—particularly with regard to intergroup cooperation. The chapter argued that authoritarian practices can either be inclusionary or exclusionary. The results showed that repression, as an exclusionary strategy, generated more polarization than cooptation, an inclusionary strategy. Groups most targeted by repression were those least willing to cooperate with others across the political spectrum. In Palestine, this meant opposition groups, particularly Islamists, were unwilling to coordinate with others. By using experimental methods, the chapter was able to test the exact impact of authoritarian practices on political behavior, since most studies on this topic have not directly linked the practice of authoritarianism to long-term changes in societal dynamics. Chapter 3 also provides an example of the efficacy of laboratory experiments to test the causal relationships between variables of interest. Such methods can be used as a starting point for those interested in analyzing and testing the micro-foundations of particular relationships, especially in the context of the Middle East.

Finally, in the fourth chapter, I analyzed whether varying authoritarian strategies had an effect on mobilization patterns. The quantitative portion of this chapter focused on the time period since the "consolidation" of the PA following the second intifada, and the qualitative assessment compared across different time periods (before the PA, after the PA, and after consolidation). I presented evidence to show that the PA and its authoritarian practices did in fact have an effect on mobilization patterns in the Palestinian territories, with inhibited mobilization in the areas directly under PA control. I used the varying levels of PA control over the West Bank as a form of within-case variation in order to isolate the effect of the PA while holding relevant variables constant. The sub-unit level data used in this part of the book is in line with the trend in the literature that focuses on the smallest unit of analysis possible, as well as within-case variation, to explore causal relationships. Taken alongside the third chapter of this book, the analysis in Chapter 4 also helps to connect authoritarian practices to changes in political behavior; in this case, not only the frequency, but the nature and efficacy of mobilization.

All in all, this book joins a growing literature that examines the processes of demobilization and specifically links this process with the effect of international involvement on domestic outcomes. On that front, this project serves to build on the results of previous studies related to international patrons and their impact on citizen preferences or the behavior of regimes.[1] This project has developed this research further to provide a close look at demobilization processes, linking these processes to the entrenchment of authoritarianism in highly penetrated states. It has aimed to lengthen the causal chain by exploring both regime *and* societal outcomes, such as internationally backed authoritarian practices at one end, and decreasing social cohesion and mobilization at another. Although the book has primarily focused on the Palestinian territories, the theory presented is not exclusive to the case of the PA and can be applied to a number of cases across the Arab world in particular, where many of the same dynamics of international involvement and authoritarianism exist.

For that reason, Chapter 5 applied this theory to dynamics in other cases across the state sovereignty spectrum, particularly Bahrain and Iraqi Kurdistan. What that analysis found is that many of the same dynamics are borne out: American involvement in the national liberation project of Iraqi Kurdistan has insulated the political leadership and created dynamics of authoritarianism and increased polarization. In Bahrain, US-led support for the regime has exacerbated sectarian conflict and division. These dynamics have created certain legacies, suggesting that the issues of polarization and lack of social cohesion will continue to plague these societies for many years to come.

Future research

The findings of this book point to a number of possible avenues for future research. For researchers interested in Palestine specifically, the research points to the importance of understanding how new organizing mechanisms and institutions emerge and under what conditions. It would also be useful to engage in research seeking to explain the nature of formal and informal institutions in the Palestinian territories and how such institutions change under various configurations of repression.

Future studies examining the Palestine case can more thoroughly explore the complicating nature of the occupation on these dynamics. The PA is of course not the only regime in the region with high levels of international involvement, direct military intervention, or limited sovereignty. Thus the causal argument explored in this book generalizes to other cases, as the exploration of Iraqi Kurdistan and Bahrain demonstrated. However, it is impossible to deny that the PA is definitely unique in that it is one of the only cases where this intervention (military or otherwise) happens with such frequency. Accordingly, for scholars focused on the case of Palestine, it would be useful to assess the role of the Israeli occupation specifically and how it complicates the link between international involvement and authoritarianism. With the shifts in US foreign policy with regard to aid to the PA, now is also the time to conduct research on the impact of the decline of American intervention on Palestinian society. As I have argued, the legacy of externally backed repression may still continue to affect Palestinians and their political behavior; nevertheless, American withdrawal of aid and limited support constitutes a sizeable exogenous shift, which will surely have an impact on both the PA and its relationship to its constituency.

At the theoretical level, research on social cohesion and mobilization is also vital at this point in time. As previously mentioned, the strength of social ties can help determine whether or not collective action will emerge, as well as the efficacy of said collective action. It would thus be very useful to see how demobilization processes can be reversed, how social cohesion is "re-built" following repression, and under what conditions strong social cohesion exists in Palestine despite the dynamics described in this book.

Moreover, given the applicability of the book's theoretical argument to the broader Arab world, future research can use the findings of this project to examine social cohesion in other cases. In this way, scholars can outline more specifically the conditions under which the causal argument of this project applies and under what conditions outcomes may differ. This project's focus on polarization specifically, as a societal outcome of international involvement and rising authoritarianism, represents an opportunity for future studies. Subsequent research can examine the dynamics of polarization and how it is affected by authoritarianism in other cases, using similar experimental methods. In doing so, researchers will be able to examine this relationship across regime types, income levels, and changing salient variables (such as sectarian and non-sectarian dynamics and varying resource wealth). Laboratory experiments and surveys, particularly in the field, lend themselves to more precise replication.

Second, the concept of polarization merits greater assessment in the political science literature on the Middle East. This project has highlighted the link between rising authoritarianism and polarization and the importance of this link in understanding why political groups are unable to coordinate, even at times of political opening. But this project did not disentangle what *types* of polarization such a dynamic engenders. Is polarization working across groups, or also *within* groups? There is evidence to suggest both may be at work in the case of Palestine, but it is important to disaggregate which types of polarization work under which conditions. The effect of polarization on other important variables, such as institutional efficacy or tolerance at the societal level, would also be important to explore.

Third, on the topic of international involvement, future research can expand the theoretical argument of this book by examining aspects of the dynamic that this project did not cover. For instance, this project outlined a causal relationship that covered both regime and societal level outcomes, but many of the empirics focused on the societal end of that chain. Using secondary literature and qualitative data, I made the argument that international patrons provide infrastructural power to domestic regimes. However, there is a great deal left to explore regarding the issue of such infrastructural power, including exactly what it entails across cases and the *types* of infrastructural power with the biggest impact. Therefore, it would be useful to disaggregate that part of the causal chain in future studies and understand specifically which forms of infrastructural power are the driving factors behind increased authoritarianism. Finally, whereas international involvement in this particular case flows in one direction (i.e. all patrons involved are subordinate to the United States and share similar preferences), this is not the case for all instances of international involvement. In some cases, international patrons may be at odds with one another. It would be interesting to explore the dynamics of multiple patrons and provide context to existing formal models on the subject.[2]

In future studies, it would also be useful to address under what conditions the legacies of internationally backed authoritarianism—i.e. declining social cohesion and demobilization—may be reversed. If international involvement, through a number of mechanisms, can facilitate increased authoritarianism, polarization, and a lack of social cohesion, then what does it take for these self-reinforcing dynamics to be broken? Does the change have to emerge from shifts in the international patron's level or nature of involvement, through some sort of exogenous shock that affects the patron's capacity? Or is it possible that changes may be "bottom-up"? Cases in which there has been a high level of international penetration, and yet society has maintained a capacity for mobilization and low levels of polarization, would be useful for comparison. It would especially be useful to explore in order to understand what happens when the involvement of international patrons recedes.

What's next for the PA and the Palestinian cause?

At the time of this writing, the PA is facing unprecedented global and local challenges—challenges that the PA may not be able to weather intact. Coupled with the dynamics described in this book, these challenges may spell the beginning of the end for the PA, despite the fact that the PA has proven ever more capable of repression and cooptation with every passing year. Nevertheless, changing exogenous factors may be weakening the PA's consolidation.

First, the PA is facing increased local pressure from Israeli policies. For example, the Israeli government has increased its repressive measures against Palestinians, including the use of widespread arrest campaigns and draconian cybercrime laws.[3] Second, the PA is once again facing financial collapse, as Israel withholds the transfer of Palestinian tax revenue.[4] This means that PA employees—and their dependents—are facing months of partial salaries and eventually no salaries at all. Third, Israel has also dramatically increased its settlement activities across the West Bank, reaching levels of home demolition and new settlement approvals exceeding previous waves of expansion.[5] This is especially true of settlements in sensitive areas, such as East Jerusalem.[6] These provocations have caused tensions to erupt in protest and, inevitably, greater numbers of injuries or death. An unprecedented number of home demolitions took place in Jerusalem in 2016 and 2017 saw the rate of new settlement construction soar by 70 percent in the West Bank overall.[7] Indeed, at this point, Israeli politicians are speaking openly of West Bank annexation.[8] Given President Trump's announcement in 2019 that the United States would recognize Israeli sovereignty over the annexed region of the Golan Heights, one wonders whether this final step of annexing Palestinian territory officially, in contravention of international law, will only be met with American support rather than international condemnation.

As noted in previous chapters, the protests that have emerged as a result of these policies have increasingly worked outside the fold of formal institutions and politics. They are very much spontaneous eruptions of anger. Therefore, although they can be somewhat successful in the short term, they are less capable of developing long-lasting objectives or sustainability. Moreover, they often only emerge in areas where the PA does not have a direct effect. As a result, these protests remain fragmented. Nevertheless, with every wave of provocation and protest, the PA finds itself facing increasingly vehement criticism from wide swaths of the Palestinian public. Paradoxically, increasingly recalcitrant Israeli policies make it difficult for the PA to fulfill its policy objectives and engage in its role as a subcontractor for the occupation.

The PA is also facing unprecedented global challenges, especially with the advent of the Trump administration. While all American administrations have been supportive of Israel, especially via military aid and coordination, the Trump administration is the first to question the basis of the two-state solution altogether,[9] essentially questioning the role and viability of the PA itself. In response, the PA has attempted to express its dissent over these new American positions, but it remains to be seen how viable such a governing apparatus will be without the support of a major patron.

The Trump administration has also pursued a somewhat contradictory foreign policy in the Arab world, either deliberately or accidentally, which has left the PA even more isolated from regional support than it has been in the past. Trump's foreign policy has oscillated between a hands-off approach in the affairs of Arab regimes to an aggressive stance on a number of regional issues. This has empowered particularly belligerent actors in the Arab world to pursue unpopular and increasingly repressive policies, often risking American interests in the process.[10] But since the Trump administration has not staffed the State Department adequately and continues to contradict its own messaging, increasingly aggressive Arab regimes have taken advantage of this dynamic to pursue radical new policies.[11] This includes experimenting with normalization with Israel, gradually becoming more open about their coordination with the Israeli government on what they view as shared interests (especially the Iranian threat) and exporting Israeli tools of repression to their own countries.[12]

This increased coordination has inevitably come at the expense of the Palestinian question. To many Arab regimes, the biggest threat is not Israel;

rather, the biggest threat to regime durability, from their perspective, is homegrown opposition and, regionally, Iran. Additionally, these authoritarian regimes worry about a resurgence of democracy movements, particularly those that include Islamist groups. They remember the time of the Arab Spring as a time of deep crisis and have actively attempted to avoid such a reoccurrence in the future. As such, Arab regimes have become more open about the fact that the Palestinian issue is simply unimportant to their political goals. Under normal circumstances, such a position would be unimaginable, given fear over a public reaction. After all, a large proportion of those who live in the Arab world (88 percent, according to one poll) believe the Palestinian cause is personally important to them.[13] Nevertheless, Arab regimes today are relying on progressively repressive strategies to ensure acquiescence. They also know that the tide has turned on democracy rhetoric back in the United States. Thus Palestinians continue to lose out on traditional strongholds of support.

One example of this dynamic includes Trump's 2017 announcement on the recognition of Jerusalem as Israel's capital. The final status of Jerusalem has remained unresolved precisely because of its sensitive nature. Any issue deemed irreconcilable during the 1994 Oslo Accords was pushed off to final negotiations so as not to impede the process of the peace talks. The international community has therefore refrained from recognizing Jerusalem as any party's capital. Furthermore, the 1967 invasion of East Jerusalem as well as the settlement activity in that area has always been considered illegal under international law. Thus Trump's announcement and change in long-standing American policy sent shockwaves throughout the world, and across the Arab region specifically.

Protests erupted in a number of Arab countries, from Tunisia to Qatar. In many of those countries, anger over the Trump announcement spilled over into criticism of the regimes themselves.[14] These criticisms included accusing Arab regimes of not taking a stronger stance on the Palestinian issue. Many regimes put out statements of condemnation as a result and eventually also voted against the United States in a UN General Assembly resolution on the subject.[15] Nevertheless, criticism was muted from key constituencies, such as those in Saudi Arabia, where a wave of repression kept criticism of the Jerusalem issue, as well as the Saudi regime's response to it, at a minimum. There were even reports that Saudi Arabia had tacitly approved this chain of events and had floated the idea of giving Palestinians a suburb of East Jerusalem (Abu Dis) to serve as their capital.[16] A Bahraini official at one point referred to the crisis over Jerusalem as a "side issue" that should not deter

Bahrain and its allies from continued coordination with the United States over the important issue of battling Iran and Islamic "fundamentalism."[17] Finally, tapes emerged confirming that representatives of the Egyptian regime believed negotiations over Jerusalem to be useless. Egyptian officials were recorded saying that they would encourage Palestinians to accept Ramallah as their capital in order to avoid tension with the United States and Israel.[18]

Overall, it has become clear that Palestinians are increasingly on their own in their battle with the Trump administration's drastic new positions. The PA did indeed use strong language in condemning US policy and even refused to meet with Vice President Mike Pence during his visit to the region. But without traditional support from Arab allies, the PA has become even more ineffectual than before. That much is clear to its own constituency—the Palestinian people—who went out en masse to protest the announcement as well as the PA's role in allowing the situation to deteriorate to this degree.[19] Thus, now more than ever, the PA is facing a crisis of legitimacy.

So what's next for the PA? Although the PA may not cease to exist overnight, Israeli policies and other types of international pressure make it difficult for the PA leadership to continue its course as a "partner" in the peace process. Moreover, PA institutions (weak as they are) are being hollowed out even further.[20] Thus, if current exogenous pressures continue, we can expect the PA to dissolve gradually.

Nevertheless, despite the PA's unpopularity and ineffectiveness, we should not be quick to assume that Palestinians will be able to find a better alternative—at least in the medium term. This is because, coupled with increasing global and local challenges, the legacy of international involvement and repression in Palestine has created almost insurmountable conditions. These conditions include polarization, a lack of social cohesion, and ineffectual mobilization. This has created a situation in which Palestinians have a choice, in the medium term, of either retaining the PA or entering into a political vacuum. Such a vacuum has the potential for violent and explosive results, because many competing institutions to fill the void if/when the PA collapses are no longer relevant. The legacy of long-term international involvement and increased authoritarian strategies has neutralized Palestinian civil society and capacity for collective action to such a degree that, if or when the PA collapses, chaos would surely follow. And Palestinians would not be to blame in this instance for failing to articulate a coordinated response. Aside from the militia groups that would rise to the fore in such a situation, Palestinians have few remaining vehicles for organizing politically.

There are, nevertheless, a few hopeful trends despite the precarious situation created by the PA and its international patrons. First, many of the young people who engage in collective action and civil disobedience today are unconnected to existing institutions and power structures. They view the PA as part of the problem and are willing to consider alternative means to Palestinian resistance outside the Oslo paradigm.[21] Nevertheless, their lack of connection to institutions has meant that their protests and demands are not long-lasting. This is because, without an organizing structure, they are unable to sustain their social movements for very long. Despite this, that they are unconnected means that there is room for the development of new organizations capable of creative dissent and strategies to face the Israeli occupation, particularly in those areas where the PA does not function. In the future, we should expect these organizations to emerge in historically marginalized segments of society (i.e. among the working class and rural communities).[22] The international community should encourage the emergence of local organizing and community initiatives, both to combat the lack of political representation for Palestinians in places such as Jerusalem or Area C and to help Palestinians resist Israeli policies that are essentially intended to remove them altogether. Any activism that seeks to pressure the PA over its repressive policies should also be supported.

Moreover, activism within Israel among its Palestinian citizens has increased since the late 1980s, and particularly after the second intifada. There is a sense of awakening among Palestinian citizens of Israel, and a reconnection between them and the Palestinian cause. Starting with now-exiled Knesset member Azmi Bishara, the political leadership within the Palestinian community in Israel began articulating a different narrative in the early 1990s.[23] This narrative emphasized the connection between hardships within Israel and the occupation outside it. Palestinians would no longer ask for rights as some sort of external minority, Bishara argued. Rather, they were the indigenous peoples of the land and were entitled to full rights and liberties within it. Moreover, Bishara emphasized that Israel's animosity toward other Arab states was of no concern to its Palestinian citizens. He made a number of controversial visits to Arab states and expressed support for their efforts to combat Israeli occupation. Above all, he emphasized the Palestinian Arab identity (i.e. the natural kinship and shared roots) that existed between Palestinians within Israel and Palestinians and Arabs outside.[24] This narrative shift has since changed the political landscape within Israel, bringing to the fore Knesset members such as Jamal Zahalka and Haneen Zoabi, and making the "Joint List" (a political alliance of Arab parties) the third largest party in the Knesset at one point, despite the many attempts to repress the movement.[25]

Concurrently, some Palestinian citizens of Israel organized around the newly revitalized Islamist Movement in 48 Palestine. The Islamist Movement was created in 1971 and gained particular popularity in the 1980s and 1990s.[26] In particular, Palestinians within Israel coalesced around the leader of the northern branch of the movement, Sheikh Raed Salah. Salah was politically active and popular, winning local elections a number of times. He was also repeatedly targeted by the State of Israel for alleged ties to the Muslim Brotherhood, Hamas, and Iran, and served time in prison.[27] This did not dissuade Salah and his supporters, who continued to rally around him after his release. Salah took a special interest in organizing around the issue of Jerusalem and the economic and political marginalization of Jerusalemites. He was responsible for organizing trips from Palestinian communities within Israel to the Old City of Jerusalem in order to help revive the city's economy. The Islamist Movement, under his leadership, also took on a number of projects for Jerusalem's residents, including

> construction and rehabilitation of two large underground mosques, the Marwani and the Ancient Al-Aqsa ... house renovations in the Old City; the funding of alternative plans to the municipality's official ones (notably for the Abbasiya neighbourhood in the Old City and for the Bustan area in Silwan); activities for children in Silwan; and legal support and representation for residents of the Old City, Silwan and Sheikh Jarrah.[28]

Finally, Salah was also vocal and active in organizing demonstrations against Israeli policies against Arab Jerusalem, allying with Palestinian Christian organizations and figures like Archbishop Atallah Hanna.[29]

This shift has fueled a sense of shared grievance among Palestinian citizens of Israel and Palestinians within the occupied territories. It has also shifted the relationship of Palestinian citizens of Israel with the Israeli state: a growing majority of Palestinian citizens of Israel now see themselves as outsiders to the state and are no longer interested in assimilation. Activism among Palestinian citizens of Israel has thus increased, with a number of active civil society organizations emerging in the late 1990s and early 2000s. Such organizations included Adalah (a human rights organization and legal center),[30] Mada al-Carmel (an Arab research center),[31] the Arab Center for Alternative Planning (a civil society organization),[32] and the Mossawa Center (a civil society organization).[33] These organizations advocate for Palestinian rights, an end to the racialized settler-colonial character of Israel, and recognition of the Nakba. In sum, the increased political activity within Israel, particularly around the Palestinian issue, means that Palestinian citizens of Israel may emerge as leading voices of dissent in the future. This means that they may also present alternative institutions and strategies to the role of the PA, if or when it collapses.

Finally, some hopeful trends have emerged from the Palestinian community in the diaspora. Activism in the United States and Europe, especially around the BDS movement, has become increasingly successful over the last decade. The BDS movement has succeeded in both direct action and changes in legislation,[34] forcing the Israeli government to acknowledge the threat of such a grassroots movement on its overall legitimacy.[35] As a result, attempts by the Israeli government and its allies to repress the BDS movement have emerged in recent years, particularly in the United States.[36] Nevertheless, the BDS movement continues, gaining traction at a number of different levels. For Palestinians in the diaspora, the BDS movement has provided a shared framework upon which Palestinians anywhere can organize. To a large extent, such activism has overshadowed the background of participants or their political affiliations; instead, Palestinians everywhere can focus efforts on combatting groups and companies that facilitate the occupation. The narrow focus of the movement has thus been very effective.

Palestinians in the diaspora have also begun organizing transnationally and voicing serious challenges to the prevailing Oslo system. Organizations such as Al-Shabaka, for instance, have formed to conduct research, connect Palestinian academics and policymakers around the world, and coordinate on media engagement in order to facilitate awareness of the Palestinian narrative. Al-Shabaka was founded in 2008 by Palestinian academics and policymakers in the United States and has since expanded globally. The organization has policy fellows in the United States, Britain, and on the ground in Palestine, with over 200 members spread out over six continents. Importantly, it considers its main audience to be the Palestinian people and has embarked on research in order to facilitate institution-building within Palestinian society in the long term. At the time of this writing, Al-Shabaka has launched a number of key initiatives, including a study of how to revive the PLO and make it truly representative of the Palestinian community. The organization also works with key civil society actors on the ground in Palestine in order to develop sustainable projects and initiatives.[37]

Other initiatives have emerged along the same lines, intended to challenge the Oslo paradigm. One such initiative includes the Palestinians Abroad

Conference, held in Istanbul, Turkey, in February 2017, which brought together diaspora Palestinians from around the world. According to organizers, the conference was intended to "initiate a wide national movement to activate the role of the diaspora in defending the Palestinian right of return and the establishment of an independent Palestinian state with Jerusalem as its capital." That the organizers and participants vehemently disagreed with the Oslo paradigm, and called for a reevaluation of the PLO, irked the PA, which claimed that the conference was "suspicious" and provided a "free service to the Israeli occupation."[38]

Without delving too deeply into the history of the PLO, the fact remains that it is considered an exemplar of national liberation movements.[39] The PLO was able to sustain itself and evolve despite heavy Israeli violence, inter-Arab aggression, and a variety of new challenges. It is indeed for that reason that no other organization has ever emerged successfully to replace it. As Jamil Hilal notes, the PLO conferred on to Palestinians a "sense of unity" unparalleled by other institutions.[40] Thus some Palestinian voices—including this author—would argue that an attempt to supersede the PLO as an institution may be counterproductive and waste valuable resources.

As I have written previously, the PLO already contains within it the institutions by which Palestinians can hold their leadership accountable.[41] Bodies such as the Palestinian National Council (PNC; the legislative body intended to represent Palestinians both within historic Palestine and abroad) in theory act as a check on the power of the executive. Thus, to circumvent the centralization of power in the hands of Abbas and in the executive of the PA more generally, Palestinians should call for a reactivation of the PNC through new elections in the diaspora as well as in the territories. It should also incorporate all relevant political groups—including those of the Islamist persuasion—in order to be more broadly representative. In this way, the PLO can become a space of actual consensus-building.

Moreover, in today's environment of interconnectivity, it would not be too farfetched to call for elections both in the territories and abroad. Technological advancements, as well as past experiences around the world of "digital democracy" or "e-government," can help provide a starting point for Palestinians who are interested in reviving the PLO.[42] These previous experiences can be used to inform their efforts and initiate a registration campaign of Palestinians around the world as well as a subsequent election. As I have previously noted, "creating new institutions from the ground up in a fragmented and increasingly polarized environment might very well be impossible. It is therefore important to utilize the institutions Palestinians already have available and attempt to reform them rather than dispose of them altogether."[43]

All in all, these various movements and initiatives are hopeful trends for the future of the Palestinian cause in that they present alternatives and possible vehicles for organizing if/when the PA ceases to function. This is particularly the case with regard to Palestinian organizations within Israel, which are on the ground, closer to the issues at hand, and with long-standing relationships with Palestinians in the West Bank and Gaza. Thus, despite the political fragmentation facing Palestinians given the legacy of international involvement, we may yet see a resurgence of Palestinian activism in the future.

APPENDIX

Robustness tests

Table A1: Models 1 and 2 with staggered inclusion of control variables (see Chapter 2)

	Model 1	*Model 2*	*Model 3*	*Model 4*	*Model 5*	*Model 6*
	PA-affiliated	*Not PA-affiliated*	*PA-affiliated*	*Not PA-affiliated*	*PA-affiliated*	*Not PA-affiliated*
Democracy						
Autocratizing	−0.381	0.041	−0.340	0.039	−0.326	0.046
	(0.347)	(0.133)	(0.347)	(0.133)	(0.347)	(0.133)
Democratizing	−0.555*	−0.090	−0.584*	−0.097	−0.583*	−0.092
	(0.325)	(0.506)	(0.325)	(0.135)	(0.325)	(0.135)
Secularism	–	–	−0.363*	0.194**	−0.353*	0.188**
			(0.215)	(0.094)	(0.215)	(0.094)
Refugee	–	–	–	–	0.279	0.104
					(0.270)	(0.111)
N	182	1088	182	1088	182	1086

* p<0.05; ** p<0.01; *** p<0.001.

Table A2: Models 1 and 2 with staggered inclusion of control variables (continued)

	Model 1	*Model 2*	*Model 3*	*Model 4*	*Model 5*	*Model 6*
	PA-affiliated	*Not PA-affiliated*	*PA-affiliated*	*Not PA-affiliated*	*PA-affiliated*	*Not PA-affiliated*
Democracy						
Autocratizing	−0.293	0.031	−0.296	0.026	−0.304	0.025
	(0.348)	(0.133)	(0.348)	(0.133)	(0.349)	(0.134)

Democratizing	−0.483 (0.331)	−0.115 (0.136)	−0.512 (0.333)	−0.116 (0.135)	−0.517 (0.334)−0.114 (0.135)	
Secularism	−0.300 (0.218)	0.147 (0.095)	−0.287 (0.218)	0.127 (0.096)	−0.282* (0.219)	0.123 (0.095)
Refugee	0.331 (0.272)	0.087 (0.111)	0.296 (0.277)	0.114 (0.112)	0.295 (0.277)	0.094 (0.113)
Education	0.214* (0.110)	0.128*** (0.042)	0.224** (0.111)	0.122*** (0.042)	0.222** (0.111)	0.120*** (0.041)
Poverty Line			−0.107 (0.161)	0.067 (0.051)	−0.114 (0.163)	0.075 (0.056)
Political Affil.			0.009 (0.035)	−0.033** (0.013)		
N	182	1085	182	1085	182	1084

* p<0.05; ** p<0.01; *** p<0.001.

Table A3: Using political opposition variable[1] rather than political affiliation

	Model 1	Model 2
	PA-affiliated	Not PA-affiliated
Democracy		
Autocratizing	−0.249 (0.360)	0.014 (0.134)
Democratizing	−0.568* (0.343)	−0.115 (0.136)
Secularism	−0.437* (0.229)	0.121 (0.096)
Refugee	0.198 (0.296)	0.051 (0.118)
Education	0.209* (0.117)	0.135*** (0.043)
Employment	0.573 (0.627)	0.046 (0.114)
Poverty Line	−0.028 (0.172)	0.077 (0.052)
Political Opposition	−0.007 (0.312)	0.222* (0.123)
Location Type	0.100 (0.205)	0.104 (0.084)
Governorate	0.069** (0.034)	0.029** (0.015)

Peace Process	−0.474**	−0.252***
	(0.195)	(0.066)
N	182	1,084
LRchi2(11)	23.11	42.33
Prob>chi2	0.0171	0.000

* p<0.05; ** p<0.01; *** p<0.001.

Table A4: Inclusion of "education" and "democratizing" interaction term[2]

	Model 1	*Model 2*
	PA-affiliated	*Not PA-affiliated*
Democracy		
Autocratizing	−0.272	0.157
	(0.360)	(0.134)
Democratizing	−0.677	−0.462
	(1.195)	(0.379)
Secularism	−0.437*	0.136
	(0.229)	(0.096)
Refugee	0.192	0.042
	(0.294)	(0.119)
Education	0.197	0.104**
	(0.161)	(0.052)
Education Interaction	0.015	0.086
	(0.221)	(0.088)
Employment	0.559	0.046
	(0.635)	(0.113)
Poverty Line	−0.054	0.079
	(0.174)	(0.052)
Political Affiliation	0.053	−0.304**
	(0.038)	(0.013)
Location Type	0.057	0.114
	(0.205)	(0.084)
Governorate	0.081**	0.024
	(0.034)	(0.015)
Peace Process	−0.538**	−0.266***
	(0.181)	(0.065)
N	182	1,084
LRchi2(12)	25.05	45.16
Prob>chi2	0.0146	0.000

* p<0.05; ** p<0.01; *** p<0.001.

Demographic indicators

1. Indicator of refugee status:
   Are you a refugee?
   Yes or No

2. Highest educational attainment
   a. Illiterate
   b. Elementary
   c. Middle school
   d. High school
   e. Associate's degree
   f. Bachelor's degree
   g. Master's or higher

3. Employment
   a. Student
   b. Unskilled worker
   c. Housewife
   d. Skilled labor
   e. Small business owner
   f. Farmer
   g. Retired
   h. Unemployed

4. Income (two measures)
   "The poverty line in Palestine is 1800 shekel or lower per month. Tell us where your family lies."
   a. Much less than that
   b. Less than that
   c. Approximately that number
   d. More than that
   e. Much more than that
   f. Don't know/refuse to answer

   "What is your family's approximate monthly income?"
   a. Less than 600 shekel
   b. Between 600 and 1,200
   c. Between 1,201 and 1,800
   d. Between 1,801 and 2,400
   e. Between 2,401 and 3,000

f. Between 3,001 and 3,600
g. Between 3,601 and 4,200
h. Between 4,201 and 4,800
i. More than 4,801

Survey information

Student responses were kept entirely anonymous, with any response to questions remaining online in encrypted form on the Qualtrics platform. Any behavioral measures were done on a physical piece of paper that was shredded at the end of the session during de-briefing.

Survey (translated)

Political affiliation

1. Which of these political groups at Birzeit do you most agree with?
    a. Islamist group
    b. Fatah group
    c. Leftist group

Pre-treatment polarization

2. How much do you agree with the following statement:
    "Religion must be an important influence in society."
    a. Strongly Agree
    b. Agree
    c. Slightly Agree
    d. Neutral
    e. Slightly Disagree
    f. Disagree
    g. Strongly Disagree

3. How much do you agree with the following statement:
    "Income inequality is a very serious problem in Palestinian society."
    a. Strongly Agree
    b. Agree
    c. Slightly Agree
    d. Neutral
    e. Slightly Disagree

    f. Disagree
    g. Strongly Disagree

4. How much do you agree with the following statement:
    "The peace process that has led to PA control of the Palestinian territories is the best possible scenario for Palestinians at this time."
    a. Strongly Agree
    b. Agree
    c. Slightly Agree
    d. Neutral
    e. Slightly Disagree
    f. Disagree
    g. Strongly Disagree

Demographics

5. Gender
    a. Male
    b. Female
    c. Other

6. West Bank Governorate
    a. Nablus
    b. Jerusalem
    c. Ramallah and Al-Bireh
    d. Tulkarm
    e. Salfit
    f. Jericho
    g. Bethlehem
    h. Hebron
    i. Jenin
    j. Tubas
    k. Qalqilya
    l. Other/None of the above

7. Where do you or your parent/guardian work?
    a. The PA or an affiliated institution
    b. Private sector
    c. Other/None of the above

8. How would you describe your income level?
    a. Above average

b. Average

c. Below average

9. Age (input)

Treatments (one of three)

10. Cooptation: The PA often funds the efforts of social activists on the basis that those activists will coordinate with the PA on their objectives and strategies.

11. Repression: The PA often cracks down on the efforts of social activists, on the basis that those activists did not coordinate with the PA on their objectives and strategies.

12. Neutral: The PA calls for the creation of a Palestinian state in the West Bank and Gaza, as well as a compromise with Israel on the basis of negotiations.

Willingness to cooperate measures

13. [Selected political affiliation] is working on a petition against corruption in the PA's institutions. How likely are you to sign such a petition?
a. Very likely
b. Likely
c. Not very likely
d. Not at all likely

14. [Other political affiliations] are working on a campaign against corruption in the PA's institutions here on campus. How much time are you willing to dedicate to this effort on a weekly basis?
a. 0 hours
b. 1–2 hours
c. 3–4 hours
d. More than 5 hours

Counting exercise

15. How many dots are in this picture? (input)

Willingness to cooperate measures

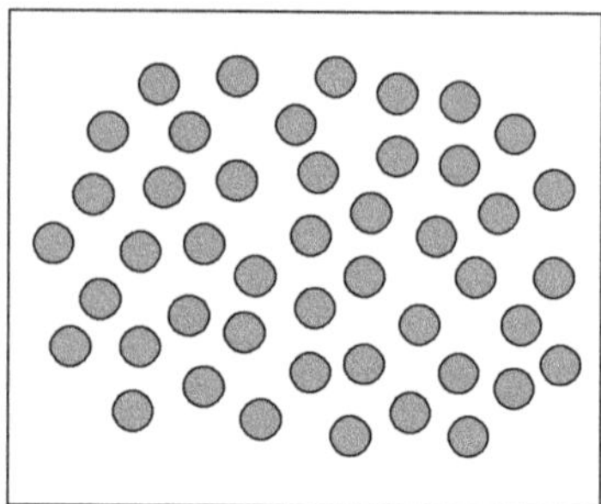

Image 1

16. [Other political affiliations] are working on a petition against corruption in the PA's institutions. How likely are you to sign such a petition?
    a. Very likely
    b. Likely
    c. Not very likely
    d. Not at all likely

17. [Selected political affiliations] are working on a campaign against corruption in the PA's institutions here on campus. How much time are you willing to dedicate to this effort on a weekly basis?
    a. 0 hours
    b. 1–2 hours
    c. 3–4 hours
    d. More than 5 hours

Counting exercise

18. How many dots are in this picture? (input)

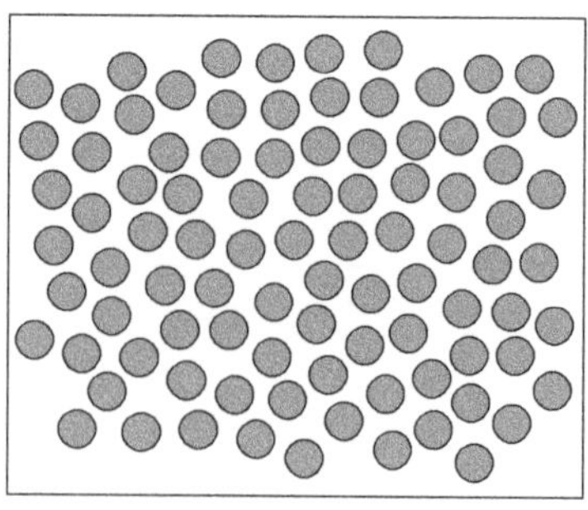

Image 2

Post-treatment polarization

19. How much do you agree with the following statement:
"Religion must be an important influence in society."
a. Strongly Agree
b. Agree
c. Slightly Agree
d. Neutral
e. Slightly Disagree
f. Disagree
g. Strongly Disagree

20. How much do you agree with the following statement:
"Income inequality is a very serious problem in Palestinian society."
a. Strongly Agree
b. Agree
c. Slightly Agree
d. Neutral
e. Slightly Disagree
f. Disagree
g. Strongly Disagree

21. How much do you agree with the following statement:
"The peace process that has led to PA control of the Palestinian territories
is the best possible scenario for Palestinians at this time."
a. Strongly Agree
b. Agree
c. Slightly Agree
d. Neutral
e. Slightly Disagree
f. Disagree
g. Strongly Disagree

Support of regime

22. How would you describe your support of the PA and its current
strategy?
a. Oppose
b. Neutral

c. Support

d. Don't know/Prefer not to answer

Power analysis

A post hoc power analysis revealed that an n of approximately 128 would be needed to obtain statistical power at the recommended 0.80 level. With the current sample size of 67, the probability of finding true significance is 0.523. A table is included for comparison.

Table A5: Power analysis

Alpha	Power	N	Delta	m0	ma	sd
0.5	0.523	67	0.25	0	0.1	0.4
0.5	0.697	100	0.25	0	0.1	0.4
0.5	0.802	128	0.25	0	0.1	0.4

Distribution of variables

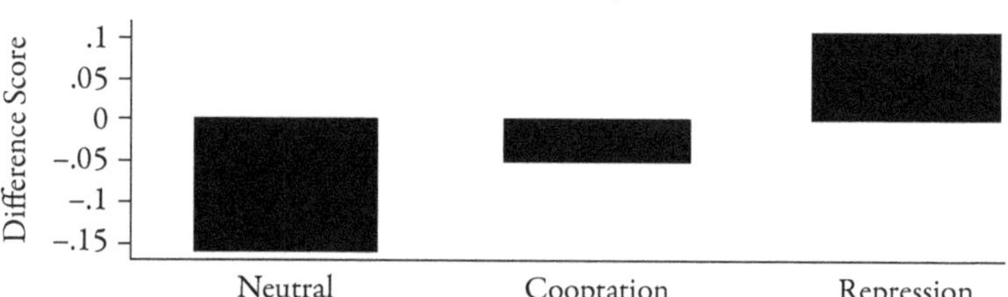

Figure A1: Polarization shift by treatment

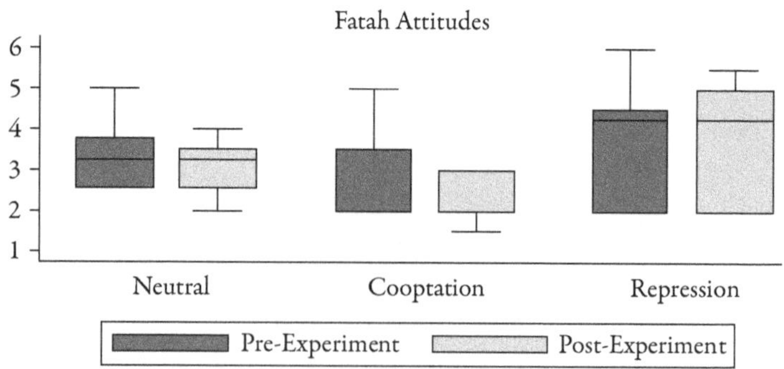

Figure A2. Fatah attitudes pre- and post-experiment

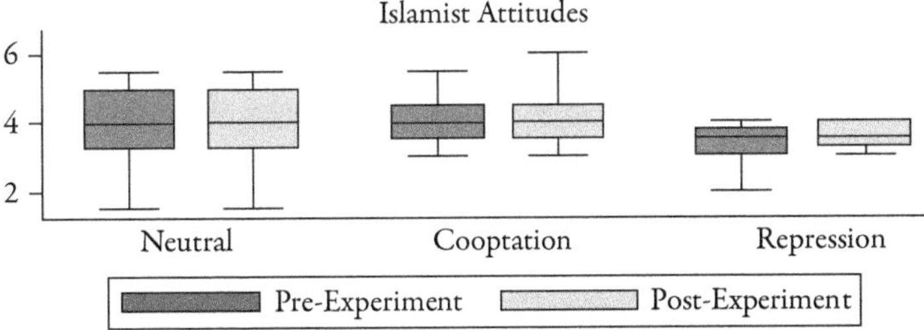

Figure A3. Islamist attitudes pre- and post-experiment

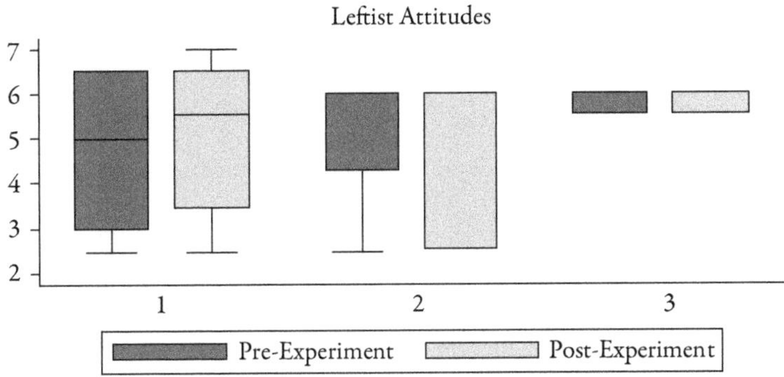

Figure A4. Leftist attitudes pre- and post-experiment

NOTES

INTRODUCTION

1. Interview with Palestinian activist, June 2015.
2. Palestinian society has one of the highest literacy rates in the world, and education has often been considered a tool of empowerment in Palestinian culture. "Education," UNDP Programme of Assistance to Palestinian People, 4 May 2015.
3. Amaney A. Jamal, *Barriers to Democracy: The Other Side of Social Capital in Palestine and the Arab World*, Princeton: Princeton University Press, 2007.
4. Spoilers meaning groups that attempt to derail negotiations in a period of conflict, based on Stephen John Stedman, "Spoiler Problems in Peace Processes," *International Security*, 22, 2 (Autumn 1997); doi:10.2307/2539366
5. The United States, in coordination with its allies, as outlined in the Palestine Papers WikiLeak release, as featured on "Palestine Papers," Al Jazeera English, 23 January 2011; http://www.aljazeera.com/palestinepapers/
6. Alexander George and Andrew Bennett, *Case Studies and Theory Development in the Social Sciences*, Cambridge, MA: MIT Press, 2007, p. 75.
7. To use Tom Najem's terminology from *Lebanon: The Politics of a Penetrated Society*, London: Routledge, 2012.
8. Jamal, *Barriers to Democracy*, p. 12.
9. This was the case particularly because there was a perception in the United States that some Arab states had drifted into the Soviet orbit. It was also at this time that both military and economic aid to Israel increased, making Israel the top recipient of US aid until 2004. See Jeremy Sharp, "US Foreign Aid to Israel," CRS Report no. RL33222 (retrieved from Congressional Research Service website: https://fas.org/sgp/crs/mideast/RL33222.pdf).
10. For instance, As-Saiqa (a member of the PLO) was funded by Syria, and the Arab Liberation Front (also a member) was funded by Iraq.
11. Avi Shlaim, *The Iron Wall: Israel and the Arab World*, New York: W.W. Norton, 2000, pp. 461–2.

12. Wendy Pearlman, "Precluding Nonviolence, Propelling Violence: The Effect of Internal Fragmentation on Movement Protest," *Studies in Comparative International Development*, 47 (2012), pp. 23–46.

13. Joe Stork, "The Significance of Stones: Notes from the Seventh Month," in Zachary Lockman and Joel Beinin (eds), *Intifada: The Palestinian Uprising against Israeli Occupation*, Boston, MA: South End Press, 1989, pp. 70–3.

14. Nasser Ishaq and Pekka Hakala, Area C: More than 60 % of the occupied West Bank threatened by Israeli annexation. Brussels: Directorate-General for External Policies of the Union Policy Department, European Parliament. Accessed June 2019. http://www.europarl.europa.eu/RegData/etudes/briefing_note/join/2013/491495/EXPO-AFET_SP(2013)491495_EN.pdf

15. Interview with PA official, June 2016. See also Mushtaq Husain Khan, "Introduction," in Inge Amundsen, George Giacaman, and Mushtaq Husain Khan (eds), *State Formation in Palestine: Viability and Governance during a Social Transformation*, New York: Routledge, 2004, pp. 1–12.

16. Jamal, *Barriers to Democracy*, pp. 1–14.

17. Karin Gerster and Helga Baumgarten, "Palestinian NGOs and Their Cultural, Economic and Political Impact in Palestinian Society," Rosa Luxemburg Foundation, December 2011.

18. On a number of occasions, Congress has threatened to end aid to the PA, citing Arafat's role in the PA specifically. For example, see "Congressional Record from October 25, 2000," 106th Congress, 2nd session, issue 146, no. 135: 24316–317.

19. Khan, "Introduction," p. 8.

20. Ibid., p. 6.

21. Anne Le More, *International Assistance to the Palestinians after Oslo: Political Guilt, Wasted Money*, London: Routledge, 2008, p. 82.

22. Khan, "Introduction," pp. 5–6, 8.

23. Abdelwahab El-Affendi, "Making Peace Gambles Work: The Oslo Accords, the Sudanese 'Comprehensive Peace Agreement' and Their 'Spirals of Insecurity,'" *Journal of Peace, Conflict, and Development*, 17 (2011), pp. 1–22.

24. Suzanne Goldenberg, "Rioting as Sharon Visits Islam Holy Site," *The Guardian*, 28 September 2000.

25. Pearlman, "Precluding Nonviolence, Propelling Violence."

26. Chris McGreal, "US Forces Israel to Lift Siege of Arafat," *The Guardian*, 30 September 2002.

27. Roger Cohen, "The Story of Palestinian Prime Minister Salam Fayyad," *The New York Times*, 14 February 2013.

28. Tariq Dana, "Social Movements in the Palestinian Territories," presentation, Arab Center for Research and Policy Studies Seminar Series, Doha, Qatar, 15 November 2017.

29. "Ruling Palestine II: The West Bank Model?," International Crisis Group, 17 July 2008, pp. 14–17.

30. Armin Rosen, "A Middle-Class Paradise in Palestine?," *The Atlantic*, 11 February 2013.

31. Maher Abukhater, "Palestinian Vulnerability Exposed as Israel Withholds Money," *Los Angeles Times*, 2 May 2011.

32. Tariq Dana, "Lost in Transition: The Palestinian National Movement after Oslo," in Mandy Turner (ed.), *From the River to the Sea*, London: Lexington Books, 2019, p. 73.

33. According to the Palestine Papers, addressed here by Ian Black and Seumas Milne, "Palestine Papers Reveal MI6 Drew Up Plan for Crackdown on Hamas," *The Guardian*, 25 January 2011.

34. Fred Abrahams, "Internal Fight: Palestinian Abuses in Gaza and the West Bank," Human Rights Watch Report, 2008.

35. Alaa Tartir, "The Palestinian Authority Security Forces: Whose Security?," Al-Shabaka, 16 May 2017.

36. John Koehler, *Stasi: The Untold Story of the East German Secret Police*, Boulder, CO: Westview Press, 1999, pp. 7–32.

37. Tartir, "Palestinian Authority Security Forces."

38. Interview with PA official, May 2016.

39. Interview with PA official, May 2016.

1. A THEORY OF INTERNATIONAL INVOLVEMENT AND ITS SOCIETAL EFFECTS

1. As outlined in Christian Davenport's definition in *How Social Movements Die*, New York: Cambridge University Press, 2015, p. 21.

2. Mancur Olson, *The Logic of Collective Action*, Cambridge, MA: Harvard University Press, 1965.

3. Ted Robert Gurr, *Why Men Rebel*, London: Routledge, 1970.

4. John McCarthy and Mayer Zald, "Resource Mobilization and Social Movements: A Partial Theory," *American Journal of Sociology*, 82, 6 (1977). See also Charles Tilly, *From Mobilization to Revolution*, New York: McGraw-Hill, 1978.

5. Alexander Lee, "Who Becomes a Terrorist? Poverty, Education, and the Origins of Political Violence," *World Politics*, 63, 2 (2011), pp. 203–45.

6. Benedict Andersen, *Imagined Communities*, London: Verso, 1983. Raymond Wolfinger and Steven J. Rosenstone, *Who Votes?*, New Haven: Yale University Press, 1980.

7. Jamal, *Barriers to Democracy*, pp. 1–14.

8. Gurr, *Why Men Rebel*. Charles Tilly, *From Mobilization to Revolution*, Reading, MA: Addison-Wesley, 1978.

9. An example of an exogenous shock is foreign-imposed regime change. For an example of structural conditions that weaken the ability of the regime to coopt,

see Kenneth Greene, *Why Dominant Parties Lose: Mexico's Democratization in Comparative Perspective*, Cambridge: Cambridge University Press, 2009, on the PRI's fall from power in Mexico as a result of neoliberal economic policies and retraction of party intrusion.

10. For instance, I am referring here to such examples as the Palestinian intifadas or 2011 Arab uprisings. The historical record is replete with the emergence of protest even under severely repressive environments.

11. Some scholars posit, for example, that repression pushes non-combatants into open rebellion and makes insurrection the only possible strategy. For example, Ted Gurr and R. Duvall, "Civil Conflict in the 1960s," *Comparative Political Studies*, 6 (1973), pp. 135–69; Elisabeth Wood, *Insurgent Collective Action and Civil War in El Salvador*, New York: Cambridge University Press, 2003.

12. Güneş Murat Tezcür, "Ordinary People, Extraordinary Risks: Participation in an Ethnic Rebellion," *American Political Science Review*, 110, 2 (May 2016), p. 248.

13. This is in line with Joel S. Migdal's idea of studying how the state may restructure society. See Joel S. Migdal (ed.), *Boundaries and Belonging: States and Societies in the Struggle to Shape Identities and Local Practices*, Cambridge: Cambridge University Press, 2004.

14. For examples, see the volume by Doug McAdam, Mayer Zald, and John McCarthy (eds), *Comparative Perspectives on Social Movements: Political Opportunities, Mobilizing Structures, and Cultural Framings*, Cambridge: Cambridge University Press, 1996. Paul Collier and Anke Hoeffler, "Greed and Grievance in Civil War," World Bank Policy Research Paper 2355, Washington, DC: World Bank, 2000.

15. Michael Taylor, "Rationality and Revolutionary Collective Action," in Michael Taylor (ed.), *Rationality and Revolution*, Cambridge: Cambridge University Press, 1988, pp. 63–91.

16. Hahrie Han, "The Organizational Roots of Political Activism: Field Experiments on Creating a Relational Context," *American Political Science Review*, 110, 2 (May 2016), p. 299. See also Tezcür, "Ordinary People, Extraordinary Risks," p. 247.

17. Pearlman, "Precluding Nonviolence, Propelling Violence," p. 28.

18. As cited in Davenport, *How Social Movements Die*, p. 21.

19. Ibid., pp. 23–36.

20. Ibid.

21. Ibid., p. 34.

22. Ibid., p. 34.

23. Joan-Maria Esteban and Debraj Ray, "On the Measurement of Polarization," *Econometrica*, 62, 4 (July 1994), pp. 819–51.

24. Wendy Pearlman, "Emotions and the Microfoundations of the Arab Uprisings," *Perspectives on Politics*, 11 (21 June 2013), p. 393.

25. Milan Svolik, *The Politics of Authoritarian Rule*, New York: Cambridge University Press, 2012, pp. 5–9.

26. See, for example, work on winning coalition sizes in authoritarian regimes, such

as Mark Peceny and Christopher K. Butler, "The Conflict Behavior of Authoritarian Regimes," *International Politics*, 41, 4 (2004), pp. 565–81; Natasha Ezrow and Erica Frantz, "State Institutions and the Survival of Dictatorships," *Journal of International Affairs*, 65, 1 (2011); and Jeffrey Pickering and Emizet F. Kisangani, "Diversionary Despots? Comparing Autocracies' Propensities to Use and to Benefit from Military Force," *American Journal of Political Science*, 54, 2 (2010), pp. 477–93.

27. Eva Bellin, "The Robustness of Authoritarianism," *Comparative Politics*, 36 (2004), pp. 144–5.

28. Christian Gobel, "Authoritarian Consolidation," *European Political Science*, 10 (2011), pp. 176–90, here p. 176.

29. Milan Svolik, "Authoritarian Reversals and Democratic Consolidation," *American Political Science Review*, 102 (May 2008), pp. 153–68.

30. Gobel, "Authoritarian Consolidation," pp. 176–7.

31. Thomas Ambrosio, "Beyond the Transition Paradigm: A Research Agenda for Authoritarian Consolidation," *Demokratizatsiya*, 22 (2014), pp. 471–95.

32. For example, establishing control over the military, which may incorporate a particular segment of the population or serve as a form of patronage for a large segment of the population.

33. Svolik, *Politics of Authoritarian Rule*.

34. Ibid.

35. David A. Lake and Robert Powell, "International Relations: A Strategic-Choice Approach," in David A. Lake and Robert Powell (eds), *Strategic Choice and International Relations*, Princeton: Princeton University Press, 1999, pp. 3–38. David Lake, "Legitimating Power: The Domestic Politics of US International Hierarchy," *International Security*, 38, 2 (2013), pp. 74–111.

36. David Lake, "The State and International Relations," in Christian Reus-Smit and Duncan Snidal (eds), *The Oxford Handbook of International Relations*, New York: Oxford University Press, 2008, pp. 41–61.

37. Peter Gourevitch, "The Second Image Reversed: The International Sources of Domestic Politics," *International Organization*, 32, 4 (Autumn 1978), pp. 881–912.

38. Lake, "State and International Relations."

39. Robert Putnam, "Diplomacy and Domestic Politics: The Logic of Two-Level Games," *International Organization*, 42 (1988), pp. 427–60.

40. Kristian Gleditsch and Michael D. Ward, "Diffusion and the International Context of Democratization," *International Organization*, 60, 4 (2006), pp. 911–33.

41. S. E. Finkel, A. Pérez-Liñán, and M. A. Seligson, "The Effects of US Foreign Assistance on Democracy Building, 1990–2003," *World Politics*, 59 (2007), pp. 404–39.

42. Emilie Hafner-Burton, "Trading Human Rights: How Preferential Trade Agreements Influence Government Repression," *International Organization*, 59

(July 2005), pp. 593–629. Michael Gilligan, "Is Enforcement Necessary for Effectiveness? A Model of the International Criminal Regime," *International Organization*, 60 (October 2006), pp. 935–67.

43. Amaney Jamal, *Of Empires and Citizens: Pro-American Democracy or No Democracy at All?*, Princeton: Princeton University Press, 2012.

44. Susan Hyde, "The Observer Effect in International Politics: Evidence from a Natural Experiment," *World Politics*, 60 (October 2007), pp. 37–63. Daniel Corstange and Nikolay Marinov, "Taking Sides in Other People's Elections: The Polarizing Effect of Foreign Intervention," *American Journal of Political Science*, 56 (2012), pp. 655–70.

45. Karam Karam, "An Analysis of Political Change in Lebanon in the Light of Recent Mobilization Cycles," in Laura Guazzone and Daniela Pioppi (eds), *The Arab State and Neo-Liberal Globalization*, Reading, UK: Ithaca Press, 2012, p. 12.

46. Ibid., p. 61.

47. To use Tom Najem's terminology from *Lebanon: The Politics of a Penetrated Society*, London: Routledge, 2012.

48. Sarah Bush, "Forms of International Pressure and the Middle East," Project on Middle East Political Science, 21 August 2015.

49. This definition is based on Lake, "Legitimating Power," and the definition of international hierarchy therein.

50. Andrew Stravers and Dana El Kurd, "Strategic Autocracy: American Military Forces and Regime Type," *Journal of Global Security Studies* (forthcoming).

51. Martha Finnemore, *National Interests in International Society*, Ithaca, NY: Cornell University Press, 1996.

52. Susan Hyde, "The Observer Effect in International Politics: Evidence from a Natural Experiment," *World Politics*, 60 (October 2007), pp. 37–63.

53. J. R. Vreeland. "Political Institutions and Human Rights: Why Dictatorships Enter into the United Nations Convention against Torture," *International Organization*, 62 (2008). B. A. Simmons and A. Danner, "Credible Commitments and the International Criminal Court," *International Organization*, 64 (2010), p. 225.

54. J. N. Druckman and A. Lupia, "Preference Formation," *Annual Review of Political Science*, 3 (2000), pp. 1–24.

55. Finkel, Pérez-Liñán, and Seligson, "Effects of U.S. Foreign Assistance on Democracy Building," pp. 404–39.

56. Jamal, *Of Empires and Citizens*, pp. 1–36.

57. Corstange and Marinov, "Taking Sides in Other People's Elections," pp. 655–70. Sarah Bush and Amaney Jamal, "Anti-Americanism, Authoritarian Politics, and Attitudes about Women's Representation: Evidence from a Survey Experiment in Jordan," *International Studies Quarterly*, 59 (2014), pp. 34–45.

58. Daniel Corstange, "Anti-American Behavior in the Middle East," *Journal of Politics*, 78 (2016), pp. 311–25.

59. William Wohlforth, "The Stability of a Unipolar World," *International Security*, 24 (Summer 1999), pp. 5–41. Daniel Nexon and Thomas Wright, "What's at Stake in the American Empire Debate," *American Political Science Review*, 101 (May 2007), pp. 253–71.

60. David Lake, "The New American Empire?," *International Studies Perspectives*, 9 (20 July 2008), pp. 281–9.

61. D. Vine, *Base Nation: How US Military Bases Abroad Harm America and the World*, New York: Metropolitan Books, Henry Holt & Co., 2015.

62. Micah Zenko, "US Military Policy in the Middle East: An Appraisal," Chatham House, 18 October 2018, p. 4; https://www.chathamhouse.org/publication/us-military-policy-middle-east-appraisal

63. Mark Lagon, "Promoting Democracy: The Whys and Hows for the United States and the International Community," Council on Foreign Relations, February 2011. Also see John Ikenberry, *After Victory*, Princeton: Princeton University Press, 2016.

64. Stravers and El Kurd, "Strategic Autocracy."

65. Joe Stork and Jim Paul, "Arms Sales and the Militarization of the Middle East," *MERIP Reports*, 112 (1983). T. C. Jones, "America, Oil, and War in the Middle East," *Journal of American History*, 99 (2012), pp. 208–18. Brynjar Lia, *Building Arafat's Police: The Politics of International Police Assistance in the Palestinian Territories after the Oslo Agreement*, Reading, UK: Garnet Publishing, 2007. Holger Albrecht, *Raging against the Machine: Political Opposition under Authoritarianism in Egypt*, Syracuse, NY: Syracuse University Press, 2013.

66. Ikenberry, *After Victory*.

67. Finkel, Pérez-Liñán, and Seligson, "The Effects of U.S. Foreign Assistance on Democracy Building."

68. Kristian Gleditsch and Michael D. Ward, "Diffusion and the International Context of Democratization," *International Organization*, 60, 4 (2006), pp. 911–33.

69. Steven Levitsky and Lucan Way, *Competitive Authoritarianism: Hybrid Regimes after the Cold War*, New York: Cambridge University Press, 2010.

70. Sean Yom, *From Resilience to Revolution: How Foreign Interventions Destabilize the Middle East*, New York: Columbia University Press, 2016.

71. Vickie Langohr, "Too Much Civil Society, Too Little Politics: Egypt and Liberalizing Arab Regimes," *Comparative Politics*, 36, 2 (2004), pp. 181–204. James Scott and Carie A. Steele, "Sponsoring Democracy: The United States and Democracy Aid to the Developing World, 1988–2011," *International Studies Quarterly*, 55 (2011), pp. 47–69. Joseph Wright, "How Foreign Aid Can Foster Democratization In Authoritarian Regimes," *American Journal of Political Science*, 53, 3 (2009), pp. 552–71.

72. Yom, *From Resilience to Revolution*. Jason Brownlee, *Democracy Prevention*, New York: Cambridge University Press, 2012. Some have noted the wholesale "export" of democracy is not always a successful venture, given the need to tailor programs

to specific local conditions. See the conclusion of the volume by Zoltan D. Barany and Robert G. Moser (eds), *Is Democracy Exportable?*, Cambridge: Cambridge University Press, 2009, for more details.

73. Rachel Vanderhill, *Promoting Authoritarianism Abroad*, Boulder, CO: Lynne Rienner, 2012. Thomas Ambrosio, "Beyond the Transition Paradigm: A Research Agenda for Authoritarian Consolidation," *Demokratizatsiya*, 22, 3 (2014), pp. 471–95. Kurt Weyland, "Autocratic Diffusion and Cooperation: The Impact of Interests vs. Ideology," *Democratization*, 24, 7 (2017), p. 1237.

74. William Easterly, Shanker Satyanath, and Daniel Berger, "Superpower Interventions and Their Consequences for Democracy: An Empirical Inquiry," National Bureau of Economic Research Working Paper, no. 13992 (May 2008). See also Jeffrey Pickering and Mark Peceny, "Forging Democracy at Gunpoint," *International Studies Quarterly*, 50, 3 (11 September 2006), pp. 539–60.

75. Eva Bellin, "The Robustness of Authoritarianism in the Middle East: Exceptionalism in Comparative Perspective," *Comparative Politics* 36 (2004), pp. 139–57. Sean Yom and Mohammad Al-Momani, "The International Dimensions of Authoritarian Regime Stability: Jordan in the Post-Cold War Era," *Arab Studies Quarterly*, 30 (2008), pp. 39–60.

76. Joel Beinin, "Neo-Liberal Structural Adjustment, Political Demobilization, Neo-Authoritarianism in Egypt," in Guazzone and Pioppi, *Arab State and Neo-Liberal Globalization*, p. 24. For an assessment of US involvement in the case of Egypt, specifically with regard to particular aid programs, see Brownlee, *Democracy Prevention*.

77. Erin Snider, "US Democracy Aid and the Authoritarian State: Evidence from Egypt and Morocco," *International Studies Quarterly*, 62, 4 (27 December 2018), pp. 795–808.

78. Jamal, *Of Empires and Citizens*, pp. 1–36.

79. Brownlee, *Democracy Prevention*.

80. Andrew Stravers and Dana El Kurd, "Importing Autocracy: Regime Type and US Military Bases," *Journal of Global Security Studies*, forthcoming.

81. Osamah Khalil, *America's Dream Palace: Middle East Expertise and the Rise of the National Security State*, Cambridge, MA: Harvard University Press, 2016.

82. Ibid.

83. Mushtaq Husain Khan, "Introduction," in Amundsen, Giacaman, and Khan, *State Formation in Palestine*, p. 5.

84. Jeremy Wildeman, "Neoliberalism as Aid for the Settler Colonization of the Occupied Palestinian Territories after Oslo," in Alaa Tartir and Timothy Seidel (eds), *Palestine and Rule of Power*, Basingstoke: Palgrave Macmillan, 2019, pp. 158, 166.

85. Ibid., p. 160.

86. Mandy Turner, "Peacebuilding as Counterinsurgency in the Occupied Palestinian Territory," *Review of International Studies*, 41, 1 (January 2015), p. 76.

87. Mandy Turner, "No 'Plan B' Because 'Plan A' Cannot Fail: The Oslo Framework and Western Donors in the OPT, 1993–2017," in Mandy Turner (ed.), *From the River to the Sea*, London: Lexington Books, 2019, p. 273.

88. Ibid., p. 275. For a detailed breakdown of the aid management structure in Palestine, see figure 10.1 on p. 277.

89. Ibid., p. 281.

90. Ibid., p. 286.

91. Ibid., p. 286.

92. Turner, "Peacebuilding as Counterinsurgency in the Occupied Palestinian Territory," p. 92.

93. Sabrien Amrov and Alaa Tartir, "Subcontracting Repression in the West Bank and Gaza," *The New York Times*, 26 November 2014. Alaa Tartir, "How US Security Aid to PA Sustains Israel's Occupation," Al Jazeera, 2 December 2016. See also Tartir, "The Evolution and Reform of Palestinian Security Forces 1993–2013," *Stability: International Journal of Security & Development*, 4 (10 September 2015).

94. Turner, "Peacebuilding as Counterinsurgency in the Occupied Palestinian Territory," p. 95.

95. This is in line with research on the US role in international organizations generally, particularly for "important countries" such as those of strategic relevance. See Randall Stone's "The Scope of IMF Conditionality" or *Controlling Institutions: International Organizations and the Global Economy*, Cambridge: Cambridge University Press, 2011, as an example.

96. Turner, "No 'Plan B,'" p. 278.

97. Ibid.

99. As outlined in Davenport's definition in *How Social Movements Die*, p. 21.

100. Stravers and El Kurd, "Importing Autocracy."

101. Some have argued, for example, that Islamists are incompatible with the democratic process (Daniel Brumberg, "Islam Is Not the Solution (or the Problem)," *The Washington Quarterly*, 29 (2005), pp. 97–116; M. Steven Fish, "Islam and Authoritarianism," *World Politics*, 55 (2002), pp. 4–37; Samuel Huntington, *The Clash of Civilizations and the Remaking of World Order*, New York: Simon & Schuster, 1996; Elie Kedourie, *Democracy and Arab Political Culture*, 2nd edn, London: Frank Cass, 1994; Bassam Tibi, "Why They Can't Be Democratic," *Journal of Democracy*, 19, 3 (2008), pp. 43–8). The extension of this argument within American foreign policy is that they cannot be allowed to come to power (e.g. Hamas in 2006, Algerian elections 1991, etc.).

102. Such involvement included support of coups in Guatemala (1954), in Brazil (1964), in Uruguay (1969), support of Hugo Banzer of Bolivia in the 1970s, support of General Pinochet of Chile against democratically elected President Allende (1973), support of Haitian dictator François Duvalier throughout his

reign, military engagement in Panama (1989), support of death squads in El Salvador during the civil war (1980–92), and bolstering the regime of Peru's President Fujimoro who was convicted of human rights abuses in 2009 (as narrated in William Blum, *Killing Hope: US Military and CIA Interventions since World War II*, London: Zed Books, 2014).

103. Finkel, Pérez-Liñán, and Seligson, "Effects of U.S. Foreign Assistance on Democracy Building," pp. 404–39.

104. Inderjeet Parmar, "The US-Led Liberal Order: Imperialism by Another Name?," *International Affairs*, 94, 1 (1 January 2018), pp. 151–72.

105. Jamal, *Of Empires and Citizens*, pp. 19–21.

106. Referring to the term from Robert Putnam, *Making Democracy Work: Civic Traditions in Modern Italy*, Princeton: Princeton University Press, 1993.

107. More explanation of the issues surrounding the principal–agent problem, including moral hazard and adverse selection, can be found in Chapter 2.

108. When I use the term "elite" here, I mean it in a narrow sense to include decision-makers within the PA.

109. Jamal, *Of Empires and Citizens*, pp. 103–37.

110. I am speaking here, for example, about the underrepresentation of Islamist factions in Algeria, the Palestinian territories, and Egypt despite their electoral success. The first two cases saw the election results overturned with international support, and the third case saw a belated coup overturning the results with international acquiescence.

111. Beinin, "Neo-Liberal Structural Adjustment," p. 23.

112. Sanctions were imposed by the United States and salaries were indeed withheld from those who worked for the PA's apparatus following the election of Hamas to the Palestinian Legislative Council in 2006.

113. Yom, *From Resilience to Revolution*.

114. Dan Slater and Sofia Fenner, "State Power and Staying Power: Infrastructural Mechanisms and Authoritarian Durability," *Journal of International Affairs*, 65 (2011), pp. 15–29. Michael Mann, *The Rise of Classes and Nation-States, 1760–1914*, Cambridge: Cambridge University Press, 1993.

115. As in Migdal, *Boundaries and Belonging*. This can also be considered a form of "fiscal rentierism," i.e. accruing resources from outside sources, which has been found to decrease the level of democracy (Carlos Gervasoni, "A Rentier Theory of Subnational Regimes: Fiscal Federalism, Democracy, and Authoritarianism in the Argentine Provinces," *World Politics*, 62, 2 (2010), pp. 302–40).

116. Two examples of this include the case of the Muslim Brotherhood in Egypt, where repression from the Sadat regime helped to fragment its membership and affect its capacity for collective action. Another example is the case of Lebanese union movements during the post-civil war reconstruction era, in which "cooptation and repression" helped create divisions between groups and thus greatly

affected their ability to achieve their objectives (Beinin, "Neo-Liberal Structural Adjustment," pp. 23–34; Karam, "Analysis of Political Change in Lebanon," p. 58).

117. This takes a wider look at the polarizing effect of international influence, highlighted by Corstange and Marinov, "Taking Sides in Other People's Elections." An international patron's involvement in the political process of the target state polarizes the citizens within these states. It also has the effect of weakening the citizenry's commitment to democracy (ibid.; Jamal, *Of Empires and Citizens*).

118. Sean Yom, "Jordan's Protests Are a Ritual, Not a Revolution," *Foreign Policy*, 11 June 2018; https://foreignpolicy.com/2018/06/11/jordans-protests-are-a-ritual-not-a-revolution/

119. "Gulf States Pledge $2.5 Billion Aid Package to Jordan," Reuters, 11 June 2018; https://www.reuters.com/article/us-jordan-protests-gulf/gulf-states-pledge-2–5-billion-aid-package-to-jordan-idUSKBN1J7026

120. Hussain Al-Qatari, "Kuwait Sentences Lawmakers to Prison Over 2011 Protest," US News & World Report, 8 July 2018; https://www.usnews.com/news/world/articles/2018–07–08/kuwaits-highest-court-sentences-lawmakers-to-prison

121. Taylor, "Rationality and Revolutionary Collective Action."

122. Davenport, *How Social Movements Die*, p. 51.

123. Ibid.

124. Silvia Pasquetti, "Legal Emotions: An Ethnography of Distrust and Fear in the Arab Districts of an Israeli City," *Law & Society Review*, 47, 3 (22 July 2013), doi:10.1111/lasr.12028. Pasquetti, "Negotiating Control," *City*, 19, 5 (3 October 2015), doi:10.1080/13604813.2015.1071121

125. See, for example, the 2018 "Jewish Nation-State Law," which was passed in the Israeli Knesset.

126. Jamal, *Barriers to Democracy*.

127. Stravers and El Kurd, "Importing Autocracy."

128. Ibid.

129. See the volume by Steven Levitsky et al. (eds), *Challenges of Party-Building in Latin America*, Cambridge: Cambridge University Press, 2017.

130. Greene, *Why Dominant Parties Lose*.

131. John Gerring, *Social Science Methodology: A Unified Framework*, Cambridge: Cambridge University Press, 2013, pp. 228–9. Mediating variables explain the how and why of a causal relationship. Such variables can also be described as the mechanisms by which X leads to Y. If, under certain scope conditions, the independent variable does not lead to particular mediating variables, then X would not cause Y in that circumstance. There is precedence for examining a long causal chain in the study of the Arab world in particular. As Bassel Salloukh, "Overlapping Contests and Middle East International Relations: The Return of the Weak Arab State," *PS: Political Science & Politics*, 50, 3 (12 June 2017), p. 661, points out,

the study of Arab politics must emphasize "the overlap among domestic, transnational, and geopolitical material and immaterial factors," which often entails examining variables at the macro-level as well as their micro-level outcomes.

132. Pearlman, "Precluding Nonviolence, Propelling Violence," p. 28.

133. Jacob Ricks and Amy H. Liu, "Process-Tracing Research Designs: A Practical Guide," *PS: Political Science & Politics*, 51, 4 (October 2018), pp. 2–3.

2. "AMERICANS HAVE TAUGHT US: THERE IS A DIFFERENCE BETWEEN DEMOCRACY AND CREATING PROBLEMS"

1. Turner, "No 'Plan B' Because 'Plan A' Cannot Fail," p. 284.

2. I include in this definition the constitutive components of "involvement" as a variable, since one type of involvement often follows the other. For instance, pressure on the PA is never confined only to rhetoric but also includes changes in foreign aid policy and material support. Even when the pressure begins in diplomatic statements, it is clear to actors on the ground that this implies a threat in material support if pressure is not heeded.

3. John Zaller, *The Nature and Origins of Mass Opinion*, New York: Cambridge University Press, 1992.

4. Ryan L. Claassen and Benjamin Highton, "Policy Polarization among Party Elites and the Significance of Political Awareness in the Mass Public," *Political Research Quarterly*, 62, 3 (9 September 2008).

5. Lisa Blaydes and Drew A. Linzer, "Elite Competition, Religiosity, and Anti-Americanism in the Islamic World," *American Political Science Review*, 106 (May 2012), pp. 225–43.

6. Jamal, *Of Empires and Citizens*, pp. 1–36. Sarah Bush and Amaney Jamal, "Anti-Americanism," *International Studies Quarterly*, 59 (2014), pp. 34–45.

7. Jennifer Gandhi and Ellen Lust-Okar, "Elections under Authoritarianism," *Annual Review of Political Science*, 12 (2009), pp. 403–22.

8. Jamal, *Of Empires and Citizens*, for example, assumes that because of international involvement, elites that may under normal conditions support democracy become *anti*-democratic for the sake of maintaining stable ties with international powers, a logic reflected at the public level as well.

9. Ibid., pp. 1–36.

10. Ibid.

11. This is in line with the general argument in research by Alexei Abrahams, "Not Dark Yet: The Israel–PA Principal–Agent relationship, 1993–2016," in David Lake and Eli Berman (eds), *Principal–Agent Relationships in Asymmetric Conflict* (forthcoming).

12. Lyne, Nielson, and Tierney, "Delegation under Anarchy," p. 58.

13. Ibid., p. 50.

14. Jamal, *Of Empires and Citizens*, pp. 1–36.

15. For more, see Lake, "Legitimating Power." There are a number of examples of this occurring, including the Palestinian legislative elections in 2006 and the Algerian legislative elections in 1991.

16. Stephen Zunes and Emily Schwartz Greco, "The Rise of Hamas," Foreign Policy in Focus, 22 June 2007.

17. For example, the public in the case of Palestine did in fact exert their pressure by bringing Hamas to power in a surprise outcome in the legislative elections of 2006.

18. Lyne, Nielson, and Tierney, "Delegation under Anarchy," p. 31. Darren Hawkins and Wade Jacoby, "How Agents Matter," in Darren Hawkins (ed,), *Delegation and Agency in International Organizations*, New York: Cambridge University Press, 2006.

19. Finkel, Pérez-Liñán, and Seligson, "Effects of US Foreign Assistance," pp. 50–82.

20. Jamal, *Of Empires and Citizens*, pp. 1–36.

21. Jack Holland, "Why Is Change So Hard?," in Jack Holland and Michelle Bentley (eds), *Obama's Foreign Policy: Ending the War on Terror*, New York: Routledge, 2014.

22. Jamal, *Of Empires and Citizens*, pp. 1–36.

23. Take, for example, the Arab Spring protests, particularly in sensitive places such as Bahrain. There was little international support for the protest movement, yet it emerged and continued until its suppression.

24. D. Canache, J. Mondak, and M. A. Seligson, "Meaning and Measurement in Cross-National Research on Satisfaction with Democracy," *Public Opinion Quarterly*, 65 (2001), pp. 506–28.

25. R. Dalton, "Political Support in Advanced Industrial Democracies," in Pippa Norris (ed.), *Critical Citizens: Global Support for Democratic Governance*, Oxford: Oxford University Press, 1999. D. Plotke, "Representation Is Democracy," *Constellations*, 4 (1997), pp. 19–34. N. Urbinati and M. E. Warren, "The Concept of Representation in Contemporary Democratic Theory," *Annual Review of Political Science*, 11 (2008), pp. 387–412. Matthew Rhodes-Purdy, "Beyond the Balance Sheet: Performance, Participation and Regime Support in Latin America," PhD diss., University of Texas at Austin, 2015.

26. Rhodes-Purdy, "Beyond the Balance Sheet: Performance," p. 70.

27. David Crow, "Citizen Disenchantment in New Democracies: The Case of Mexico," PhD diss., University of Texas at Austin, 2009, pp. 15–17.

28. Ibid.

29. Mohammed Daraghmeh, "Abbas' Government Sued over Alleged CIA-Backed Wiretapping," AP News, 6 February 2018.

30. For more information on how these indicators were measured, please refer to the appendix.

31. The decision to subgroup this analysis was made before the data collection or run-

ning of results. It was an integral part of the theoretical argument I proposed in a dissertation prospectus, May 2015.

32. For instance, Salam Fayyad, Hanan Ashrawi, and other figures who have worked for the PA's institutions but now represent splinter parties (with little legislative success).

33. Interview with PA official no. 1, 17 June 2015.

34. Interview with PA official no. 5, 5 June 2015.

35. Interview with PA official no. 1, 17 June 2015.

36. Interview with PA official no. 1, 17 June 2015.

37. Interview with PA official no. 3, 13 June 2015.

38. Interview with PA official no. 2, 17 June 2015.

39. Interview with PA official no. 4, 7 June 2015.

40. Interview with PA official no. 4, 7 June 2015.

41. Interview with PA official no. 4, 7 June 2015; interview with PA official no. 7, 5 June 2015.

42. Interview with PA official no. 4, 7 June 2015; interview with PA official no. 8, 3 June 2015.

43. Interview with PA official no. 7, 5 June 2015; interview with PA official no. 4, 7 June 2015.

44. Interview with PA official no. 3, 13 June 2015; interview with PA official no. 7, 5 June 2015.

45. Interview with PA official no. 3, 13 June 2015; interview with PA official no. 7, 5 June 2015.

46. Interview with PA official no. 3, 13 June 2015; interview with PA official no. 8, 3 June 2015.

47. Interview with PA official no. 7, 5 June 2015; interview with PA official no. 8, 3 June 2015; interview with PA official no. 3, 13 June 2015.

48. Interview with PA official no. 4, 7 June 2015.

49. Interview with PA official no. 9, 3 June 2015.

50. Interview with PA official no. 2, 17 June 2015.

51. Interview with PA official no. 3, 13 June 2015.

52. Interview with PA official no. 3, 13 June 2015.

53. Interview with PA official no. 3, 13 June 2015. Similar arguments are made across the region by authoritarian regimes in an attempt to dissuade opposition from pursuing action, "warning that the alternative to the regime was chaos or Islamic radicalism" (Wendy Pearlman, "From Palestine to Syria: Three Intifadas and Lessons for Popular Struggles," *Middle East Law and Governance*, 8, 1 (19 July 2016), p. 393).

54. Interview with PA official no. 4, 7 June 2015.

55. Interview with PA official no. 4, 7 June 2015.

56. Interview with PA official no. 10, 5 June 2015.
57. Interview with PA official no. 1, 17 June 2015.
58. Interview with PA official no. 1, 17 June 2015.
59. Interview with PA official no. 1, 17 June 2015.

3. THE LEGACY OF REPRESSION

1. Parts of this chapter were published in a special issue of *Middle East Law and Governance*, 10, 3 (October 2018), under the title "The Legacy of Authoritarian Strategies: Repression and Polarization in the Palestinian Territories."
2. President Mahmoud Abbas has overstayed his term limits although he has a four-year term. Moreover, legislative elections have been postponed indefinitely.
3. Pearlman, "Emotions and the Microfoundations of the Arab Uprisings," p. 393.
4. Pew Polls use ideological consistency as a measure of public polarization.
5. As demonstrated by increasing divergence between Republicans and Democrats in the Pew Polls as well as other measures (Shanto, Iyengar and Sean J. Westwood, "Fear and Loathing across Party Lines: New Evidence on Group Polarization," *American Journal of Political Science*, 59, 3 (July 2015), pp. 690–707; Alan I. Abramowitz, *The Polarized Public? Why American Government Is So Dysfunctional*, Upper Saddle River, NJ: Pearson, 2013).
6. Nolan Matthew McCarty, Keith Taylor Poole, and Howard Rosenthal, *Polarized America: The Dance of Ideology and Unequal Riches*, Cambridge, MA: MIT Press, 2006.
7. See Morris P. Fiorina et al., *Culture War? The Myth of a Polarized America*, Boston, MA: Longman, 2011, and Alan Abramowitz and Kyle Saunders, "Is Polarization a Myth?," *Journal of Politics*, 70, 2 (April 2008), pp. 542–55 for examples.
8. Seth J. Hill and Chris Tausanovitch, "A Disconnect in Representation? Comparison of Trends in Congressional and Public Polarization," *The Journal of Politics*, 77, 4 (October 2015). Claassen and Highton, "Policy Polarization among Party Elites."
9. Pew Polls suggest this, as well as Abramowitz and Saunders, "Is Polarization a Myth?" For more, see Marc J. Hetherington, "Review Article: Putting Polarization in Perspective," *British Journal of Political Science*, 39, 2 (April 2009), pp. 413–48.
10. Blaydes and Linzer, "Elite Competition, Religiosity, and Anti-Americanism," pp. 225–43.
11. Stathis Kalyvas and Matthew Adam Kocher, "How 'Free' Is Free Riding in Civil Wars? Violence, Insurgency, and the Collective Action Problem," *World Politics*, 59, 2 (January 2007), pp. 177–216. Paul Dower, Victor Ginsburgh, and Shlomo Weber, "Colonial Legacy, Polarization and Linguistic Disenfranchisement: The Case of the Sri Lankan War," *Journal of Development Economics* (2016). Rukhsana Siddiqui, "Failed Insurrections and Ethnic Cleavages: A Comparative Study of Zaire and Sri Lanka," *Peace Research*, 24, 1 (February 1992), pp. 37–56.

12. Corstange and Marinov, "Taking Sides in Other People's Elections," pp. 655–70. Bush and Jamal, "Anti-Americanism, Authoritarian Politics, and Attitudes about Women's Representation," pp. 34–45.

13. One example of this is the Muslim Brotherhood in Egypt, where repression from the Sadat era helped to divide its membership and limit its capacity for collective action. Another is the case of Lebanese union movements following the civil war, where "cooptation and repression" helped create divisions and impacted their effectiveness (Karam, "Analysis of Political Change in Lebanon," p. 58; Beinin, "Neo-Liberal Structural Adjustment," p. 34).

14. J. Fearon, "Self-Enforcing Democracy," *The Quarterly Journal of Economics* (2011), pp. 1661–708.

15. See Greene, *Why Dominant Parties Lose*, for an example of this in Mexico.

16. Maria Josua, "Cooptation as a Strategy of Authoritarian Legitimation: Success and Failure in the Arab World," paper presented at 6th ECPR General Conference, Reykjavik, August 2011.

17. Monarchs fashion themselves into "linchpins" in order to coopt more broadly (Russell E. Lucas, "Monarchical Authoritarianism: Survival and Political Liberalization in a Middle Eastern Regime Type," *International Journal of Middle East Studies*, 36, 1 (February 2004), pp. 103–19).

18. Arbitrary group membership during laboratory experiments created in-group and out-group distinctions, and helped curb shirking and free-rider problems (Catherine C. Eckel and Philip J. Grossman, "Managing Diversity by Creating Team Identity," *Journal of Economic Behavior & Organization*, 58, 3 (January 2005), pp. 371–92). In another experiment, a manufactured group identity fostered higher levels of intragroup cooperation (Lorenz Goette, David Huffman, and Stephan Meier, "The Impact of Group Membership on Cooperation and Norm Enforcement: Evidence Using Random Assignment to Real Social Groups," *American Economic Review*, 96, 2 (May 2006), pp. 212–16).

19. See Anthony D. Smith, *Myths and Memories of the Nation*, Oxford: Oxford University Press, 1999, pp. 203–24, on the creation of diaspora identities after trauma; Rashid Khalidi, *Palestinian Identity: The Construction of Modern National Consciousness*, New York: Columbia University Press, 1997, on the solidification of Palestinian identity during the conflict years before and after the Nakba, 1948; Laia Balcells, "The Consequences of Victimization on Political Identities," *Politics & Society*, 40, 3 (7 November 2011), pp. 311–47, on victimization and its effect on political identity following civil war. See also Murray Horwitz and Jacob Rabbie, "Individuality and Membership in the Intergroup System," in Henry Tajfel (ed.), *Social Identity and Intergroup Relations*, Cambridge, MA: Cambridge University Press, 1982, for more examples.

20. Noam Lupu and Leonid Peisakhin, "The Legacy of Political Violence across Generations," *American Journal of Political Science*, 61, 4 (October 2017), pp. 836–51.

21. Some work has been done on the effects of totalitarianism in particular, and its effect on structures of solidarity and political culture. See Aviezer Tucker, *The Legacies of Totalitarianism: A Theoretical Framework*, Cambridge: Cambridge University Press, 2015.

22. See, for example, Wendy Pearlman, *Fragmentation and Violence: Internal Influences on Tactics in the Case of the Palestinian National Movement, 1918–2006*, Cambridge, MA: Harvard University Press, 2007. Pearlman, "Precluding Nonviolence, Propelling Violence."

23. Guillermo O'Donnell and Philippe C. Schmitter, *Transitions from Authoritarian Rule*, Baltimore, MD: Johns Hopkins University Press, 1986.

24. Kathleen Cunningham, "Actor Fragmentation and Civil War Bargaining: How Internal Divisions Generate Civil Conflict," *American Journal of Political Science*, 57 (18 March 2013), pp. 659–72.

25. Pearlman, "Emotions and the Microfoundations of the Arab Uprisings," p. 393.

26. The differences between electoral rules of the legislative elections in 1989 versus 1993 led to weakening tribal impact in one election, and strengthening the role of tribes in the other. This goes to show that the salience of tribal identity is manipulated by political decisions. See Curtis R. Ryan, *Jordan in Transition: From Hussein to Abdullah*, Boulder, CO: Lynne Rienner, 2002.

27. One example is the case of Lebanese union movements after the civil war, which posed a threat to political leadership. The state pursued divisive tactics, severely repressing particular groups as a means of control, and isolating others (Karam, "Analysis of Political Change in Lebanon," pp. 58–9). Beinin, "Neo-Liberal Structural Adjustment," p. 25.

28. In line with existing work on prospect theory that argues people are more risk averse in their decision-making when anticipating gain (Kurt Weyland, "Risk Taking in Latin American Economic Restructuring: Lessons from Prospect Theory," *International Studies Quarterly*, 40, 2 (June 1996), pp. 185–207).

29. Gurr and Duvall, "Civil Conflict in the 1960s." Wood, *Insurgent Collective Action and Civil War in El Salvador*.

30. Emma Graham-Harrison, "How Sinai Became a Magnet for Terror," *The Observer*, 7 November 2015.

31. Pearlman, "Precluding Nonviolence, Propelling Violence," p. 28.

32. Timur Kuran, "Now out of Never: The Element of Surprise in the East European Revolution of 1989," *World Politics*, 44 (1991), pp. 7–48.

33. Justin Gengler, *Group Conflict and Political Mobilization in Bahrain and the Arab Gulf: Rethinking the Rentier State*, Bloomington, IN: Indiana University Press, 2015, p. 61.

34. Major opposition group Waad represents both Sunni and Shia members and considers itself a secular organization. The February 14th Youth Coalition also represents both groups, and was heavily involved in generating momentum for the

Bahraini uprising. Shia groups also participated alongside the secular and leftist ones, including Al Wefaq and the Shia-dominated Haq Movement.

35. Samyah Alfoory, "The 2011 Bahraini Uprising: Women's Agency, Dissent and Violence," Georgetown Institute for Women, Peace & Security Research Paper Series, 5th series, September 2014. "Half of Bahraini Citizens Are Suffering from Poverty and Poor Living Conditions" (24 September 2004). Asya El-Meehy, "Relative Deprivation and Politics in the Arab Uprisings," Social Justice & Development Policy in the Arab World Research Report (May 2014).

36. Gengler, *Group Conflict and Political Mobilization in Bahrain and the Arab Gulf,* pp. 24–33.

37. Corey Robin, *Fear: The History of a Political Idea,* New York: Oxford University Press, 2004.

38. Christopher Phillips, "After the Arab Spring: Power Shift in the Middle East?," LSE Ideas (May 2012).

39. "We've Never Seen Such Horror," Human Rights Watch, 29 April 2015.

40. Majid Rafizadeh, "For Syria's Minorities, Assad Is Security," Al Jazeera English, 16 September 2011.

41. Burhan Ghalyon, "Has the Syrian Revolution Ended?," Al-Araby Al-Jadeed, 10 January 2017. Pearlman ("From Palestine to Syria," p. 99) calls this "fragmented clientelism."

42. Adam Lichtenheld, "Beyond Ethno-sectarian 'Cleansing': The Assortative Logic of Forced Displacement in Syria," Project on Middle East Political Science, 29 March 2017. Zeina Khodr, "Syria Deal: 'Population Swap' or 'Sectarian Cleansing?,'" Al Jazeera, 15 August 2015. Martin Chulov, "Iran Repopulates Syria with Shia Muslims to Help Tighten Regime's Control," *The Guardian,* 13 January 2017.

43. Amrov and Tartir, "Subcontracting Repression in the West Bank and Gaza."

44. Pearlman, "From Palestine to Syria," 101.

45. "Who Governs the West Bank?," ICG Report, p. 10. Around 24 percent of the population works directly for the PA and are said to provide for a third of the population. Government spending to GDP ratio is at 44 percent, and a large portion of the Palestinian population relies on the PA for essential services (according to Shaker Sarsour, Reem Naser, and Mohammad Atallah, "The Economic and Social Effects of Foreign Aid in Palestine," Palestine Monetary Authority, Research and Monetary Policy Department, November 2011).

46. Dana, "Lost in Transition," p. 74.

47. "Hamdallah: Our Social Welfare Organization Is a National Success and We Commit to Funding It Fully," Palestinian News and Info Agency, 1 May 2017.

48. As revealed by the Palestine Papers, the PA pursued a policy of mass arrest of its political opponents. Turner, "No 'Plan B' Because 'Plan A' Cannot Fail," p. 286.

49. Amrov and Tartir, "Subcontracting Repression in the West Bank and Gaza."

50. "Poll #63," Palestinian Center for Policy and Survey Research, December 2016.

51. Survey analysis is not always generalizable, given that survey questions change over time, making the dynamic of polarization difficult to assess. Thus it is useful to assess the dynamic of polarization directly without relying on proxy survey questions (Hill and Tausanovitch, "Disconnect in Representation").

52. Judd Kessler and Lise Vesterlund, "The External Validity of Laboratory Experiments: The Misleading Emphasis on Quantitative Effects," in Guillaume R. Fréchette and Andrew Schotter (eds), *Handbook of Experimental Economic Methodology*, New York: Oxford University Press, 2015, pp. 391–406.

53. David Collier, Henry E. Brady, and Jason Seawright, "Sources of Leverage in Causal Inference: Toward an Alternative View of Methodology," in Henry Brady and David Collier (eds), *Rethinking Social Inquiry: Diverse Tool, Shared Standards*, Lanham: Rowman & Littlefield, 2004.

54. A post hoc power analysis revealed that an n of approximately 128 would be needed to obtain statistical power at the recommended 0.80 level. With the current sample size of 67, the probability of finding true significance is 0.523. More information can be found in the appendix.

55. This type of context-specific behavioral measure is often used in studies where the authoritarian context makes it difficult to ask respondents direct questions, but also in contexts where abstract social science experiments may not be fully understood by respondents or enumerators at the field site. For an example, see Sarah S. Bush et al., "The Effects of Authoritarian Iconography: An Experimental Test," *Comparative Political Studies*, 49, 13 (6 April 2016), pp. 1704–38.

56. Dana, "Lost in Transition," p. 80.

57. Hamas conducted attacks after Oslo to "spoil" the peace process. See more in Miriam Elman, "Spoilers of Peace and the Dilemmas of Conflict Resolution," in Nimrod Goren and Miriam Elman (eds), *Spoilers of Peace and the Dilemmas of Conflict Resolution*, Tel Aviv: Israeli Institute for Regional Foreign Policies, 2012.

58. While Arafat cracked down on Hamas occasionally, and cooperated with Israel on targeting certain leaders, he still allowed Hamas to function and expand its public outreach. See, for example, Stephen Franklin, "West Bank Islamic Groups Show Militant and Softer Faces," *Chicago Tribune*, 17 August 1997. Lee Hockstader, "Arafat Says Crackdown on Hamas Not Over," *The Washington Post*, 4 November 1998.

59. Dana, "Lost in Transition," p. 80.

60. Robert Pape, "The Strategic Logic of Suicide Terrorism," *American Political Science Review*, 97 (August 2003), pp. 343–61.

61. Pearlman, "Precluding Nonviolence, Propelling Violence," p. 28.

62. "Statistics on the Death Penalty in the PA and under Hamas Control in Gaza," B'Tselem, the Israeli Information Center for Human Rights in the Occupied Territories, 1 January 2011. Erika Waak, "Violence among the Palestinians," *The Humanist* (January–February 2003).

63. Pearlman, *Fragmentation and Violence*.

64. "PLO vs. Hamas: Battle for Minds and Hearts," Newsmax, 7 December 2001. "Hamas Has the People's Heart," *The Economist*, 29 November 2001. James Bennet, "A New Mideast Battle: Arafat vs. Hamas," *The New York Times*, 6 December 2001.

65. According to the Palestine Papers, addressed here by Black and Milne, "Palestine Papers Reveal MI6 Drew Up Plan for Crackdown on Hamas." "Palestinian Papers: UK's MI6 'Tried to Weaken Hamas,'" BBC News, 25 January 2011.

66. Interview with PA official, May 2015.

67. Khaled Abu Toameh, "Hamas Protests PA West Bank Crackdown," *The Jerusalem Post*, 15 November 2008.

68. Interview with PA official, May 2015.

69. Dan Murphy, "Israel, US, and Egypt Back Fatah's Fight against Hamas," *The Christian Science Monitor*, 25 May 2007. Yezid Sayigh, "Inducing a Failed State in Palestine," *Survival*, 49 (July 2007), pp. 19–21.

70. Fred Abrahams, "Internal Fight: Palestinian Abuses in Gaza and the West Bank," Human Rights Watch Report, (2008).

71. Westervelt, "President Abbas Shuts Islamist Charities in W. Bank."

72. As Tariq Dana notes, Hamas's infrastructure was severely damaged, yet its capacity to organize is difficult to assess given the necessary turn to insularity following the PA's repression campaign. See "Lost in Transition," p. 82.

73. Interviews with Fatah members, May and June 2015.

74. Jannis Grimm and Cilja Harders, "Unpacking the Effects of Repression," *Social Movement Studies* (June 2017).

75. "Statistics on the Death Penalty in the PA," B'Tselem, 1 January 2011. "PCHR Condemns Practicing Torture," Palestinian Center for Human Rights, 16 July 2007.

76. "Hamas Refuses the Government's Call for Local Elections," Ramallah News, 31 January 2017.

77. The most recent polls show that those affiliated with Fatah or Hamas are the two largest portions of the population ("Poll #63," PCPSR 2016).

78. Hassan Obeid, "Student Political Groups Face Crackdown in West Bank," Al-Monitor, 24 December 2014.

79. Many stabbing attacks in the "knife intifada" have been linked to Hamas and other Islamist groups. See Peter Beaumont, "Israel–Palestine: Outlook Bleak as Wave of Violence Passes Six-Month Mark," *The Guardian*, 31 March 2016.

80. "Hamas Seeks to Ignite the Security Situation in the West Bank," Al Jazeera Arabic, 19 January 2017.

81. Ibid.

82. Jamil Hilal, "The Palestinian Left and the Multi-Layered Challenges Ahead," Rosa Luxemburg Foundation, 19 August 2010.

83. Interview with leftist activist, June 2016.

84. Dana, "Lost in Transition," p. 85.

85. Tariq Dana, "Social Struggle and the Crisis of the Palestinian Left Parties," Rosa Luxemburg Foundation, March 2016.

86. Ibid.

87. Interview with leftist activist, June 2016.

88. Interview with leftist activist, June 2016.

89. Hilal, "The Palestinian Left."

90. Interview with Mubadara activist, June 2016.

91. Interview with Communist Party activist, May 2016.

92. Dana, "Social Movements in the Palestinian Territories."

93. Haidar Eid, "Withdrawal from Participation as a Palestinian Strategy?," Al-Shabaka, 9 December 2013.

94. Interview with Mubadara activist, June 2016.

95. Interview with Mubadara activist, June 2016.

96. Interview with Communist Party activist, June 2016.

97. Interview with Bilin activist, June 2016.

98. Interview with Bilin activist, June 2016.

99. Interview with Mubadara activist, June 2016.

100. "About the Hay'a," Colonization and Wall Resistance Commission, 21 August 2016.

101. Interview with hay'a employee, June 2016.

102. Bil'in has been the subject of a number of documentaries, including *Bil'in Habibti* and *5 Broken Cameras*.

103. Interview with Mubadara activist, June 2016.

104. Interview with labor union activist, June 2016.

105. "Israeli Settlement Industries Polluting Tulkarem, Palestine," Environmental Justice Atlas.

106. Interview with labor union activist, June 2016.

107. Palestinian Economic Policy Research Institute, "The Economics of Agriculture in the Qalqilya and Tulkarem Districts: Improving the Profitability of Farmers Affected by the Separation Wall," Jerusalem: MAS, 2005.

108. Scarlett Kutyla, "Tulkarem Chemical Factory Exploits Palestinian Labour and Health," Middle East Monitor, 19 September 2014.

109. "Israeli Settlement Industries Polluting Tulkarem, Palestine."

110. "Workers' Struggles in Tulkarem Settlement Factories," Palestinian Grassroots Anti-Apartheid Wall Campaign, 9 February 2017.

4. DE-MOBILIZING A MOBILIZED SOCIETY

1. Protests erupted after clashes with Israeli military forces, and only later did political organizations act to organize these protests and work together.

2. Pearlman, "Precluding Nonviolence, Propelling Violence," pp. 23–46.

3. "Squaring the Circle," International Crisis Group, 7 September 2010.
4. The Palestinian territories have consistently been scored "not free" by Freedom House, for example.
5. Levitsky and Way, *Competitive Authoritarianism*. Jamal, *Barriers to Democracy*, pp. 1–14.
6. Putnam, *Making Democracy Work*. See also Jamal, *Barriers to Democracy*, for how civil society functions in authoritarian contexts.
7. Taylor, "Rationality and Revolutionary Collective Action," pp. 63–91. Sarah Elizabeth Parkinson, "Organizing Rebellion: Rethinking High-Risk Mobilization and Social Networks in War," *American Political Science Review*, 107 (2013), pp. 418–32.
8. Pearlman, *Fragmentation and Violence*.
9. Pearlman, "Precluding Nonviolence, Propelling Violence," pp. 23–46.
10. For instance, polarization in the Palestinian territories exists along the lines of those who support an incremental state-building project versus a liberation movement.
11. This theory and overall project builds off of Jamal, *Barriers to Democracy*, with the insight being the effect of the regime on mobilization in this case rather than on trust levels at the individual level.
12. The PA gained full control of Area A (18 percent of territory, 55 percent of the population), gained joint control of Area B (20 percent of territory, 41 percent of the population), but ceded full control to the Israeli occupation of Area C (62 percent of territory, 1 percent of the population, as it excludes East Jerusalem).
13. "Squaring the Circle."
14. As a result of "pluralistic ignorance," highlighted in Kuran, "Now out of Never."
15. This is in line with a "most similar systems" design, given that the three cases started with the same conditions and yet show very different results today.
16. Amal Jamal, *The Palestinian National Movement: Politics of Contention, 1967–2005*, Bloomington, IN: Indiana University Press, 2005, pp. 73–102.
17. I say "indistinguishable starting points" because of the populations living in those areas, variations in demographic make-up, etc. Since they had indistinguishable starting points and yet developed differently, we can pinpoint the reason for this varied development in the changes that occurred after the PA's creation.
18. The classic "relative deprivation" explanation for increased grievances (Gurr, *Why Men Rebel*).
19. "Poll #59," Palestinian Center for Policy and Survey Research, March 2016.
20. This is a direct quote from a PA official, echoed by a number of interviews conducted by this author between May 2015 and May 2016. Israeli forces often operate even in areas supposedly under direct PA control, without prior coordination ("Squaring the Circle").
21. According to the original dataset on mobilization developed by this author.

22. UN Office for the Coordination of Humanitarian Affairs, Occupied Palestinian Territory (2013–15), Institute for Palestine Studies Chronologies (2013–15), Shabakat al-Quds al-Akhbariya (2013–15), and the Palestinian Central Bureau of Statistics for village-level data.

23. There are four types of political mobilization covered in the dataset: marches, sit-ins, clashes, and union protests. If the expectations of this theory are correct, then the organizational capacity of any group in society should be affected. I also did not discount an incident of protest if it turned violent. Such incidents can still be considered a form of political mobilization even if not peaceful. I did not code, however, incidents of violence that did not involve a significant number of participants (e.g. isolated surprise attacks on soldiers or armed settlers perpetrated by one or two people).

24. Shlaim, *Iron Wall*, pp. 461–2.

25. The Unified National Leadership of the Uprising decided on strategies of civil disobedience and non-violent resistance, which for the most part was maintained throughout the main time period of the uprising (1987–91). They did so in coordination with the Palestinian Liberation Organization outside of Palestine, through organizations such as the Orient House in Jerusalem. For more information on the emergence of grassroots within the territories versus the centralization of PLO institutions in the diaspora, see Jamil Hilal, "PLO Institutions: The Challenge Ahead," *Journal of Palestine Studies*, 23, 1 (1993), pp. 46–60.

26. Jamal, *Palestinian National Movement*, pp. 30–54.

27. Ken Stein, "The Intifada and the Palestinian Uprising of 1936–1939: A Comparison," in Robert Freedman (ed.), *The Intifada: Its Impact on Israel, the Arab World, and the Superpowers*, Gainesville, FL: University Press of Florida, 1991.

28. Ibid., pp. 93–4.

29. "Extreme Makeover (II): The Withering of Arab Jerusalem," International Crisis Group, 20 December 2012, p. 6.

30. Ibid.

31. Stork, "Significance of Stones," pp. 70–3.

32. Pearlman, "Precluding Nonviolence, Propelling Violence," pp. 23–46.

33. This should read instead: Nasser Ishaq and Pekka Hakala, Area C: More than 60% of the occupied West Bank threatened by Israeli annexation. Brussels: Directorate-General for External Policies of the Union Policy Department, European Parliament. Accessed June 2019. http://www.europarl.europa.eu/RegData/etudes/briefing_note/join/2013/491495/EXPO-AFET_SP(2013)491495_EN.pdf

34. Jamal, *Palestinian National Movement*, pp. 30–54.

35. "Who Governs the West Bank?," p. 10.

36. Barry Rubin, *The Transformation of Palestinian Politics: From Revolution to State-Building*, Cambridge, MA: Harvard University Press, 1999, p. 25.

37. Pearlman, "Precluding Nonviolence, Propelling Violence," pp. 23–46.

38. For more information on the disarmament, demobilization, and reintegration pro-

cess following the second intifada, see "Ruling Palestine II: The West Bank Model?," *International Crisis Group*, 17 July 2008.

39. As cited in "Extreme Makeover II," p. 1: "During the second intifada, from October 2000 until October 2005, 30 suicide bombings and other attacks killed 195 people and injured many more in Jerusalem. Of these, 186 casualties resulted from attacks perpetrated by Jerusalem residents."

40. Ibid., p. 9.

41. The process of isolating Area C and Jerusalem began following the PA's creation.

42. Jamal, *Barriers to Democracy*, pp. 1–14.

43. Pearlman, "Precluding Nonviolence, Propelling Violence," pp. 23–46.

44. Barry Rubin and Judith Rubin, *Yasir Arafat: A Political Biography*, New York: Oxford University Press, 2003, pp. 185–215.

45. "Ruling Palestine," p. 3.

46. Pearlman, "Precluding Nonviolence, Propelling Violence," pp. 36–41.

47. Rubin and Rubin, *Yasir Arafat*, p. 205.

48. I focus on the West Bank because PA control over the Gaza territories ended following Hamas's electoral victory and subsequent removal. Although today there is some coordination between the PA government in the West Bank and the Hamas government in Gaza, the same dynamic of PA control does not exist outside the West Bank. Thus it would not be a useful comparison.

49. "Ruling Palestine II," pp. 14–17.

50. "Squaring the Circle," pp. 6–10.

51. M. Dumper, "Policing Divided Cities: Stabilization and Law Enforcement in Palestinian East Jerusalem," *International Affairs*, 89 (2013), p. 1258.

52. "Buying Time? Money, Guns and Politics in the West Bank," International Crisis Group, May 2013, p. 13.

53. Dana, "Social Movements in the Palestinian Territories."

54. "Squaring the Circle," p. 21.

55. Jamal, *Palestinian National Movement*, pp. 81–90.

56. Daniella Cheslow, "Palestinian Nonviolence: Is the Budrus Model Still Viable?," *The Christian Science Monitor*, 10 December 2010.

57. For example, Bil'in, Nil'in, Kafr Qaddum, and Budrus are centers of rural activism against the settlements and have attracted international attention for their sustained non-violent protest movement.

58. First because PA security forces have limited access, and also because the populations living in the rural areas cannot easily work for PA institutions and thus do not receive the same level of targeted patronage.

59. "Squaring the Circle," p. 28.

60. "Ruling Palestine," pp. 28–33.

61. "Squaring the Circle," pp. 3–5.

62. Ibid., p. 30.

63. Feras Abu-Helal, "The Conflict over Palestinian Legitimacy," *Middle East Monitor*, 4 June 2013.

64. Around 24 percent of the population works directly for the PA and are said to provide for a third of the population. Government spending to GDP ratio is at 44 percent, and a large portion of the Palestinian population relies on the PA for essential services (according to Sarsour, Naser, and Atallah, "Economic and Social Effects of Foreign Aid").

65. Villagers in places like Nil'in, Kafr Qaddum, and Budrus rely on farming. Their protest movements were initiated as a result of farmland confiscation.

66. Certain mosques and organizations are affiliated with Hamas, for example. See "Extreme Makeover II," p. 7.

67. I also calculated the Spearman correlation coefficient, which is useful when comparing a continuous variable with an ordinal one. The coefficient was close to the original correlation coefficient at 0.12. It was statistically significant at this value, but still only weakly positive.

68. A hurdle model is a modified count model in which there are two processes, one generating the zeros and one generating the positive values. The two models are not constrained to be the same. The concept underlying the hurdle model is that a binomial probability model governs the binary outcome of whether a count variable has a zero or a positive value. If the value is positive, the "hurdle is crossed," and the conditional distribution of the positive values is governed by a zero-truncated count model.

69. Negative binomial regressions are used when your dependent variable is a count variable, but the variable does not follow a Poisson distribution. This model also presumes that different processes determine whether a data point is a "certain zero" and whether a data point has a low count or a high count. Therefore, to use this model, variables are specified to predict "certain zeroes," and then a second set of variables are included in a count model to predict changes in the main dependent variable. The variables I used in the count model are Area, population, Israeli raid, and settlement density. Certain zeroes were predicted using the same variables, minus Area, the main independent variable.

70. Natalie Tabar and Lauren Bari, "Repression and Nonviolent Protest in the Occupied Palestinian Territory: Case Study on the Village of al-Nabi Saleh," Ramallah: Al-Haq Institute, 2011, p. 11.

71. Applied Research Institute, Jerusalem, "Bil'in Village Profile," Bethlehem, 2012.

72. Shai Carmeli-Pollak (dir.), *Bil'in Habibti*, Tel Aviv: Claudius Films, 2006.

73. Iyad Burnat, "To End the Occupation, Dissolve the Palestinian Authority," *Electronic Intifada*, 11 December 2013.

74. Interview with Bil'in activist, May 2016.

75. Nigel Wilson, "Hundreds Mark 11th Year of Protests in Bilin," *Al Jazeera*, 19 February 2016.

76. "8th Bil'in Conference," Popular Struggle Coordination Committee, 2013; https://bilinconference.wordpress.com/

77. "Extreme Makeover (II)," pp. ii, 9.

78. Ibid., pp. 1–2.

79. Ibid., pp. 2.

80. Ibid., p. 3.

81. Ibid., p. 2.

82. Ibid., p. 1.

83. Ibid., p. 6.

84. Ibid., p. 3.

85. Ibid, p. 21. The report notes: "More than 7,000 Palestinians (out of 293,000) lost their Jerusalem residency rights between 2006 and 2011—as many as in the previous four decades combined."

86. Ibid., p. 4.

87. Ibid., p. 6.

88. Asef Bayat, *Life as Politics: How Ordinary People Change the Middle East*, Stanford: Stanford University Press, 2010, p. 14.

89. "Extreme Makeover (II)," p. 9.

90. Ibid.

91. Ibid., pp. 11–12, 24.

92. Ibid.

93. Ibid, p. 9.

94. Even after the Israeli occupation of East Jerusalem in 1967, Jewish religious leaders were united around the idea that Jews should not enter the Noble Sanctuary/Temple Mount as a matter of religious principle. Therefore, the Al-Aqsa mosque remained a non-issue for decades. Beginning in the 1990s, however, religious Zionists (comprising at least 10 percent of the Israeli public) began agitating for a takeover of the Noble Sanctuary in order to build a "Third Temple" on top of the Al-Aqsa site. The ultra-orthodox Israeli community continues to reject this notion, but religious Zionists have united with increasingly right-wing Israeli administrations to push for changes to the status quo ("The Status of the Status Quo at Jerusalem's Holy Esplanade," International Crisis Group, 30 June 2015, pp. 4–5,15).

95. Ibid., p. 16.

96. Akin Unver, "What Twitter Can Tell Us about the Jerusalem Protests," *The Washington Post*, 28 August 2017; https://www.washingtonpost.com/news/monkey-cage/wp/2017/08/26/what-twitter-can-tell-us-about-the-jerusalem-protests/?utm_term=.a82c61c84271. See also Sami Al-Shami, *Campaigns in Support of Protesters and Al-Aqsa Continue on Social Media, Al-Araby Al-Jadeed*, July 21, 2017.

97. Jerusalemites have increasingly organized around the issue of Al-Aqsa and the other holy sites, mounting strikes and calling for protests whenever the Israeli

government imposes restrictions on Muslim prayer and access. See "Status of the Status Quo at Jerusalem's Holy Esplanade," pp. 2–3, 17.

98. Applied Research Institute, Jerusalem, "An Nabi Salih Village Profile," Bethlehem, 2012.

99. Palestinian Census Bureau of Statistics, as cited in "An Nabi Salih Village Profile."

100. Ibid.

101. Ben Ehrenreich, "Is This Where the Third Intifada Will Start?," *The New York Times*, 15 March 2013; http://www.nytimes.com/2013/03/17/magazine/is-this-where-the-third-intifada-will-start.html

102. Ibid.

103. Haggai Matar, "Mustafa Tamimi: A Murder Captured on Camera," +972 Magazine, 11 December 2011.

104. The film *Radiance of Resistance* was made about Janna Jihad, one of the children in the village. Ahed Tamimi, another child, was given a "courage award" in Turkey for her stance against an Israeli soldier. Most recently, Ahed became famous once again for defying an Israeli soldier's attempt to arrest her younger brother (2015) and getting arrested and held without bail for refusing to let soldiers enter her home (2017). See Jaclynn Ashly, "Nabi Saleh: 'It's a silent ethnic cleansing,'" Al Jazeera, 4 September 2017.

105. Interview with activist, May 2016.

106. Ehrenreich, "Is This Where the Third Intifada Will Start?"

107. According to the Popular Struggle Coordination Committee website: "About the Popular Struggle Coordination Committee," Bil'in Conference, 1 October 2013.

108. Ehrenreich, "Is This Where the Third Intifada Will Start?"

109. Ibid.

110. Interview with Bil'in activist, June 2016.

111. Allison Deger, "After Building a Protest Movement, West Bank Village of Nabi Saleh Steps Back from Weekly Friday Protests," Mondoweiss, 9 September 2016.

112. Ibid.

5. THE EFFECT OF INTERNATIONAL INVOLVEMENT ACROSS THE STATE SOVEREIGNTY SPECTRUM

1. Salloukh, "Overlapping Contests and Middle East International Relations," p. 661.

2. Gengler, *Group Conflict*.

3. Ibid.

4. See cases in Amy Austin Holmes, *Social Unrest and American Military Bases in Turkey and Germany since 1945*, New York: Cambridge University Press, 2014, for more examples.

5. Gengler, *Group Conflict*, p. 30. The term "segmented clientelism" was first used in

Steffen Hertog, "Segmented Clientelism: The Politics of Economic Reform in Saudi Arabia," PhD diss., University of Oxford, 2006, and in his subsequent work.

6. The hold on repression-related weapons sales between the United States and Bahrain was lifted in 2015. Moreover, many argue that arms sales to the Bahraini Defense Forces have ended up in the hands of Bahraini police. For more information, see Katzman, "Bahrain: Reform, Security, and US Policy," p. 25. See also Joshua Stacher, "Fragmenting States, New Regimes: Militarized State Violence and Transition in the Middle East," *Democratization*, 22, 2 (23 March 2015), pp. 259–75.

7. "Statement by the President on Bahrain," 2011.

8. Caren Bohan, "US Says Saudi Forces in Bahrain 'not an invasion,'" Reuters, 14 March 2011.

9. Hassan Oz, "Undermining the Transatlantic Democracy Agenda? The Arab Spring and Saudi Arabia's Counteracting Democracy Strategy," *Democratization*, 22 (2015), pp. 479–95. Stravers and El Kurd, "Strategic Autocracy."

10. Richard McDaniel, "No 'Plan B': US Strategic Access in the Middle East and the Question of Bahrain," Foreign Policy at Brookings, 2013; https://www.brookings.edu/wp-content/uploads/2016/06/24-us-strategic-access-middle-east-bahrain-mcdaniel.pdf

11. In 2009, before the uprising, Bahrain scored −7 on the Polity Scale (−10 being strongest autocracy, 10 being strongest democracy). By 2011, that had dropped to −8. Latest scores show Bahrain at −10 (the lowest possible score). See more at the Polity Score website, systemicpeace.org

12. Omar Alshehabi, "Divide and Rule in Bahrain and the Elusive Pursuit for a United Front: The Experience of the Constitutive Committee and the 1972 Uprising," *Historical Materialism: Research in Critical Marxist Theory*, 21 (2013), pp. 94–127.

13. Gengler, *Group Conflict*, p. 116.

14. Laurence Louër, *Transnational Shia Politics: Religious and Political Networks in the Gulf*, New York: Columbia University Press, 2008, pp. 23–4.

15. Gengler, *Group Conflict*, p. 118.

16. Ibid., pp. 105–8.

17. Ibid., pp. 61–2.

18. Ibid., p. 26.

19. Ibid., p. 30.

20. Ibid., pp. 30–2.

21. Ibid., p. 33.

22. Ibid., pp. 133, 142

23. Ibid., p. 132.

24. Ibid., p. 143.

25. El-Meehy, "Relative Deprivation and Politics in the Arab Uprisings," p. 15.

26. Gengler, *Group Conflict*, pp. 134–8.

27. Ibid., pp. 23, 82, 143. Also see Justin Gengler, "Bahrain's Sunni Awakening," Middle East Research and Information Project, 17 January 2012.

28. The leaders of the Haq Movement, a mostly Shia-dominated splinter group, were tried and given life sentences. See Americans for Democracy and Human Rights in Bahrain, "Champions for Justice: #BahrainPrisoners of Conscience," November 2013; http://www.adhrb.org/wp-content/uploads/2013/11/Champion-of-Justice-Abduljalil-al-Singace.pdf

29. Gengler, *Group Conflict*, p. 23.

30. Mary Ann Tétreault, "The Winter of the Arab Spring in the Gulf Monarchies," *Globalizations*, 8 (2011), pp. 629–37.

31. Gengler, *Group Conflict*, p. 23.

32. Ibid.

33. Ethan Bronner and Michael Slackman, "Saudi Troops Enter Bahrain to Help Put Down Unrest," *The New York Times*, 14 March 2011. See also Sean Yom and F. Gregory Gause, "Resilient Royals: How Arab Monarchies Hang On," *Journal of Democracy*, 23 (October 2012), pp. 74–88.

34. This section has previously been published in *Middle East Law and Governance* under the title "The Impact of American Involvement on National Liberation: Polarization and Repression in Palestine and Iraqi Kurdistan."

35. Kirstin Brathwaite, "Repression and the Spread of Ethnic Conflict in Kurdistan," *Studies in Conflict & Terrorism*, 37, 6 (June 2014), pp. 479–80.

36. Ibid.

37. Ibid., pp. 480–2.

38. Ayşegül Sever, "'Power Led' Outside Intervention in Kurdish Politics in Iraq and Turkey in the Early 1970s," *Middle Eastern Studies*, 49, 2 (March 2013), pp. 263–6.

39. Ibid., p. 266.

40. Brathwaite, "Repression and the Spread of Ethnic Conflict in Kurdistan," pp. 480–1.

41. Theodore Mclauchlin and Wendy Pearlman, "Out-Group Conflict, In-Group Unity?," *Journal of Conflict Resolution*, 56, 1 (December 2011), pp. 42–7.

42. Ibid., p. 48.

43. Ibid., pp. 49–50.

44. Ibid.

45. Ibid., p. 51.

46. Johannes Jüde, "Contesting Borders? The Formation of Iraqi Kurdistan's De facto State," *International Affairs*, 93, 4 (July 2017), p. 849.

47. David Romano, "Iraqi Kurdistan: Challenges of Autonomy in the Wake of US Withdrawal," *International Affairs*, 86, 6 (November 2010), pp. 1347–8.

48. Gareth Stansfield, "The Reformation of Iraq's Foreign Relations: New Elites and Enduring Legacies," *International Affairs*, 86, 6 (November 2010), pp. 1395–409.

49. Ibid., p. 1403.

50. Jüde, "Contesting Borders?," p. 859.

51. Mohammed Shareef, *The United States, Iraq and the Kurds: Shock, Awe and Aftermath*, Abingdon: Routledge, 2014, pp. 13–15.

52. Jüde, "Contesting Borders?," pp. 849–50. See also Hawre Hama and Megan Connelly, "Kurdistan's Struggle for Sovereignty: State, Societal, and Human Security," Case Analysis, Doha: Arab Center for Research and Policy Studies, September 2017.

53. Jüde, "Contesting Borders?," p. 849.

54. Denise Natali, "The Spoils of Peace in Iraqi Kurdistan," *Third World Quarterly*, 28, 6 (September 2007), p. 1113.

55. Ibid., p. 853. See also Natali, "Spoils of Peace in Iraqi Kurdistan," pp. 1116–17; Raad Alkadiri, "Oil and the Question of Federalism in Iraq," *International Affairs*, 86, 6 (November 2010), pp. 1318–20.

56. Natali, "Spoils of Peace in Iraqi Kurdistan," p. 1115.

57. Hama and Connelly, *Kurdistan's Struggle for Sovereignty*, pp. 3–4.

58. Ibid.

59. Yaniv Voller, "Kurdish Oil Politics in Iraq: Contested Sovereignty and Unilateralism," *Middle East Policy*, 20, 1 (Spring 2013), p. 70.

60. Natali, "Spoils of Peace in Iraqi Kurdistan," pp. 1120–1.

61. Alkadiri, "Oil and the Question of Federalism in Iraq," p. 1323.

62. Gareth Stansfield, "The Unravelling of the Post-First World War State System? The Kurdistan Region of Iraq and the Transformation of the Middle East," *International Affairs*, 89, 2 (March 2013), pp. 273–4.

63. Voller, "Kurdish Oil Politics in Iraq," pp. 72–3.

64. Ibid., pp. 1116–17.

65. Jüde, "Contesting Borders?," pp. 854–57.

66. Romano, "Iraqi Kurdistan," pp. 1353–6. See also Jack Healy and Namo Abdulla, "Iraqi Kurdistan, Known as Haven, Faces Unrest," *The New York Times*, 23 February 2011.

67. Hama and Connelly, *Kurdistan's Struggle for Sovereignty*, pp. 9–12.

68. Ibid.

69. Ibid., pp. 11–12.

70. Toby Dodge, "State and Society in Iraq Ten Years after Regime Change: The Rise of a New Authoritarianism," *International Affairs*, 89, 2 (March 2013), p. 247.

71. Jüde, "Contesting Borders?," p. 859.

72. "Kurds Deny Forcing Arabs from Iraq's Kirkuk," Al Jazeera, 7 November 2016. See also Hama and Connelly, *Kurdistan's Struggle for Sovereignty*, p. 3.

73. Hama and Connelly, *Kurdistan's Struggle for Sovereignty*, p. 862.

74. Ibid., pp. 5–6.

75. Ibid., pp. 8–9.

76. Stefan Wolff, "Governing (in) Kirkuk: Resolving the Status of a Disputed Territory in Post-American Iraq," *International Affairs*, 86, 6 (November 2010), pp. 1363, 1372–3.

77. Ibid., p. 1371.

78. Ibid.

79. "Gorran Believes in Kurdish Independence, But Deems Referendum 'illegal,'" Rudaw, 6 October 2017.

80. Christine McCaffray van den Toorn, "Internal Divides Behind the Kurdistan Referendum," Carnegie Endowment for International Peace, 11 October 2017. See also Hamdi Malik, "Turkmens Unite against Kurdish Designs on Kirkuk," Al-Monitor, 13 October 2017.

81. In previous elections, Arab tribesmen accused Kurdish parties of intimidation and even assassination, as did the Turkmen. See also Peter Bartu, "Wrestling with the Integrity of a Nation: The Disputed Internal Boundaries in Iraq," *International Affairs*, 86, 6 (November 2010), pp. 1337–40.

82. "Bafel Talabani: PUK Chose 'Tactical Withdrawal' from Kirkuk after Casualties," Rudaw, 21 October 2017.

CONCLUSION

1. Daniel Corstange, "Anti-American Behavior in the Middle East," *Journal of Politics*, 78, 1 (2016), pp. 311–25. Corstange and Marinov, "Taking Sides in Other People's Elections." Jamal, *Of Empires and Citizens*. Yom, *From Resilience to Revolution*.

2. See, for instance, Robert Powell, "Taking Sides in Wars of Attrition," *American Political Science Review*, 111, 2 (14 May 2017).

3. Nadim Nashif, "Surveillance of Palestinians and the Fight for Digital Rights," Al-Shabaka, 23 October 2017. Tamara Nassar, "Israel Arrests Community Leaders in Attempt to Quell Protests over Jerusalem," Electronic Intifada, 18 December 2017.

4. Jack Khoury, Amir Tibon, and Noa Landau, "Palestinians Say No Compromise on Tax Funds, Even in Face of Economic Collapse," Haaretz.com, 30 April 2019.

5. Megan O'Toole and Nigel Wilson, "A Record Year of Home Demolitions in East Jerusalem," Al Jazeera, 2017; https://interactive.aljazeera.com/aje/2017/jerusalem-2016-home-demolitions/index.html

6. "Israeli Settlement Building Soars in West Bank," Al Jazeera, 19 June 2017.

7. Jennifer Williams and Javier Zarracina, "The Growth of Israeli Settlements, Explained in 5 Charts," Vox, 30 December 2016.

8. Richard Pérez-peña, "Netanyahu's Talk of West Bank Annexations Is a Blow to Peace But No Surprise, Palestinians Say," *The New York Times*, 8 April 2019.

9. Nur Arafeh et al., "Trump, Jerusalem, and the Future of Palestine," Al-Shabaka, 18 December 2017.

10. One example is the blockade of Qatar by Saudi Arabia, Bahrain, the UAE, and

Egypt. All countries involved are American allies, and Qatar hosts the largest US military base in the region. The blockade has clearly impeded diplomatic relationships and shared military efforts between US allies. Yet, because of the Trump administration's contradictory positions, blockading countries have been able to maintain the blockade despite the challenges it poses to US foreign policy.

11. Antony J. Blinken, "How Rex Tillerson Did So Much Damage in So Little Time," *The New York Times*, 30 November 2017.

12. Ibrahim Fraihat, "Why Saudi–Israeli Normalization Could Be Dangerous," Huffington Post, 22 November 2017. Bill Marczak et al., "Hide and Seek: Tracking NSO Group's Pegasus Spyware to Operations in 45 Countries," Citizen Lab, 5 November 2018; https://citizenlab.ca/2018/09/hide-and-seek-tracking-nso-groups-pegasus-spyware-to-operations-in-45-countries/

13. "Arab Attitudes toward President Trump and his Middle East Policies and Positions," Arab Center, Washington, DC, 27 October 2017.

14. Activism around the Palestinian cause is often seen as a gateway to criticisms of Arab regimes and their lack of action on the issue of Palestine. For example, one report quotes a Jordanian palace official noting that: "instability at Al-Aqsa harms internal Jordanian security and King Abdullah's standing. We managed the Arab Spring with barely any protests of more than 800 participants. But an escalation at Al-Aqsa could bring out 80,000" ("The Status of the Status Quo at Jerusalem's Holy Esplanade," p. 19). And indeed, when the Trump administration made its announcement about Jerusalem, Jordan was rocked by large protests in a number of cities (Ali Younes, "Jordanians Demand Closure of US Embassy in Amman," Al Jazeera, 8 December 2017).

15. Peter Beaumont, "UN Votes Resoundingly to Reject Trump's Recognition of Jerusalem as Capital," *The Guardian*, 21 December 2017.

16. Anne Barnard, David Halbfinger, and Peter Baker, "Talk of a Peace Plan That Snubs Palestinians Roils Middle East," *The New York Times*, 3 December 2017.

17. "Jerusalem Is a 'Side Issue,' Says Bahrain FM," Middle East Monitor, 22 December 2017.

18. David Kirkpatrick, "Tapes Reveal Egyptian Leaders' Tacit Acceptance of Jerusalem Move," *The New York Times*, 8 January 2018.

19. Henriette Chacar, "Trump's Jerusalem Announcement Sparked Deadly Violence: From Israel," The Intercept, 18 December 2017.

20. "Buying Time? Money, Guns and Politics in the West Bank," pp. 1–3.

21. Ibid., p. 5

22. Dana El Kurd, "Mobilization across Class in the Palestinian Territories," in Alaa Tartir and Timothy Seidel (eds), *Palestine and Rule of Power: Local Dissent vs. International Governance*, New York: Palgrave Macmillan, 2019.

23. Azmi Bishara et al., "On Palestinians in the Israeli Knesset: Interview with Azmi Bishara," Middle East Report, 201 (October–November 1996), pp. 27–30.

Bishara, "'A Double Responsibility': Palestinian Citizens of Israel and the Intifada," *Middle East Report*, 217 (Winter 2000), pp. 26–9.

24. See Chapters 5 and 6 in Ilan Pappe, *Forgotten Palestinians: A History of the Palestinians in Israel*, New Haven: Yale University Press, 2014.

25. "Israel's Third Largest Bloc Is the Arab-Led Joint List," Middle East Eye, 18 March 2015.

26. Jack Khoury, "Founder of Islamic Movement in Israel, Abdallah Nimr Darwish, Dies at 69," *Haaretz*, 14 May 2017.

27. Ilene Prusher, "Israeli Arab's Rising Voice of Opposition," *The Christian Science Monitor*, 26 October 2006.

28. "Extreme Makeover (II)," pp. 17–19.

29. Ibid., p. 19.

30. "About," Adalah; https://www.adalah.org/en/content/view/7189

31. "About Mada al-Carmel"; http://mada-research.org/en/about/

32. "About ACAP," Arab Center for Alternative Planning; http://www.ac-ap.org/eng/?mod=articles&ID=13#.Wl0IXlWWbIU

33. "Mission Statement," Mossawa Center; http://www.mossawa.org/site/pageContent/id/1

34. Ben Jamal, "This Ruling Allows Councils to Boycott Israel: It's a Crucial Victory," *The Guardian*, 26 June 2017.

35. Tia Goldenberg, "Growing BDS Movement Raises Alarm among Israeli Leaders," *Haaretz*, 7 July 2015.

36. Patrick Strickland, "Wisconsin Governor Signs Anti-Boycott Israel Order," Al Jazeera, 28 October 2017. Ryan Grim and Glenn Greenwald, "US Senate's First Bill, in the Midst of the Shutdown, Is a Bipartisan Defense of the Israeli Government from Boycotts," Intercept, 5 January 2019.

37. Interview Nadia Hijab, Al-Shabaka founder, 29 January 2017.

38. "Palestinians Abroad Conference Kicks Off in Istanbul," Maan News Agency, 25 February 2017.

39. Azmi Bishara, "Interview with Azmi Bishara: The Future of the Palestinian Cause and Normalization with Israel, Part 3," interview by Wael Tamimi. Al-Araby TV, 1 April 2019.

40. Hilal, "PLO Institutions," p. 47.

41. Ines Abdel Razek et al., "Palestinian Leadership: What a New Model Might Look Like," Al-Shabaka, 7 June 2018.

42. See, for instance, the example of crowdsourcing the Icelandic Constitution in Alexander Hudson, "When Does Public Participation Make a Difference? Evidence from Iceland's Crowdsourced Constitution," *Policy & Internet*, 10, 2 (18 December 2017), pp. 185–217.

43. Razek et al., "Palestinian Leadership."

APPENDIX

1. A variable defined by whether respondents affiliated with Fatah, the ruling party, or not.
2. To assess whether a certain level of education affects preferences for democracy.

BIBLIOGRAPHY

Abdel Razek, Inès, Ali Abdel-Wahab, Tareq Baconi, Marwa Fatafta, and Dana El Kurd, "Palestinian Leadership: What a New Model Might Look Like; Al-Shabaka," Al-Shabaka, 7 June 2018; https://al-shabaka.org/circles/palestinian-leadership-what-a-new-model-might-look-like/ (accessed 12 May 2019).

Abrahams, Alexei, "Not Dark Yet: The Israel–PA Principal–Agent Relationship, 1993–2016," in David Lake and Eli Berman (eds), *Principal–Agent Relationships in Asymmetric Conflict*, forthcoming.

Abrahams, Fred, "Internal Fight: Palestinian Abuses in Gaza and the West Bank," Human Rights Watch Report, 2008; https://www.hrw.org/sites/default/files/reports/iopt0708webwcover.pdf

Abramowitz, Alan I., *The Polarized Public? Why American Government Is So Dysfunctional*, Upper Saddle River, NJ: Pearson, 2013.

Abramowitz, Alan I., and Kyle Saunders, "Is Polarization a Myth?," *Journal of Politics*, 70, 2 (April 2008), pp. 542–55.

Abu Toameh, Khaled, "Hamas Protests PA West Bank Crackdown," *The Jerusalem Post*, 15 November 2008; http://www.jpost.com/Middle-East/Hamas-protests-PA-West-Bank-crackdown (accessed 12 May 2017).

Abu-Helal, Feras, "The Conflict over Palestinian Legitimacy," Middle East Monitor, 4 June 2013; https://www.middleeastmonitor.com/20140124-the-conflict-over-palestinian-legitimacy/ (accessed 20 May 2015).

Abukhater, Maher, "Palestinian Vulnerability Exposed as Israel Withholds Money," *Los Angeles Times*, 2 May 2011.

Albrecht, Holger, *Raging against the Machine: Political Opposition under Authoritarianism in Egypt*, Syracuse, NY: Syracuse University Press, 2013.

Alfoory, Samyah, "The 2011 Bahraini Uprising: Women's Agency, Dissent and Violence," Georgetown Institute for Women, Peace & Security Research Paper Series, 5th series (September 2014), pp. 1–17; https://giwps.georgetown.edu/sites/giwps/files/The%202011%20Bahraini%20Uprising%20-%20Women's%20Agency,%20Dissent%20and%20Violence.pdf

BIBLIOGRAPHY

Alkadiri, Raad, "Oil and the Question of Federalism in Iraq," *International Affairs*, 86, 6 (November 2010), pp. 1315–28; doi:10.1111/j.1468–2346.2010.00945.x

Alshehabi, Omar, "Divide and Rule in Bahrain and the Elusive Pursuit for a United Front: The Experience of the Constitutive Committee and the 1972 Uprising," *Historical Materialism: Research in Critical Marxist Theory*, 21, 1 (2013), pp. 94–127.

Ambrosio, Thomas, "Beyond the Transition Paradigm: A Research Agenda for Authoritarian Consolidation," *Demokratizatsiya*, 22, 3 (2014), pp. 471–95.

Amrov, Sabrien, and Alaa Tartir, "Subcontracting Repression in the West Bank and Gaza," *The New York Times*, 26 November 2014; https://www.nytimes.com/2014/11/27/opinion/subcontracting-repression-in-the-west-bank-and-gaza.html (accessed 13 April 2017).

Applied Research Institute, Jerusalem, "An Nabi Salih Village Profile," Bethlehem: 2012.

Arafeh, Nur, Dana El Kurd, Munir Nuseibeh, Victor Kattan, and Tareq Baconi, "Trump, Jerusalem, and the Future of Palestine," Al-Shabaka, 18 December 2017.

Ashly, Jaclynn, "Nabi Saleh: 'It's a silent ethnic cleansing,'" Al Jazeera, 4 September 2017; http://www.aljazeera.com/indepth/features/2017/07/nabi-saleh-silent-ethnic-cleansing-170702123734851.html (accessed 5 December 2017).

Balcells, Laia, "The Consequences of Victimization on Political Identities," *Politics & Society*, 40, 3 (7 November 2011), pp. 311–47; doi:10.1177/0032329211424721

Barany, Zoltan D., and Robert G. Moser (eds), *Is Democracy Exportable?*, Cambridge: Cambridge University Press, 2009.

Barnard, Anne, David Halbfinger, and Peter Baker, "Talk of a Peace Plan That Snubs Palestinians Roils Middle East," *The New York Times*, 3 December 2017.

Bartu, Peter, "Wrestling with the Integrity of a Nation: The Disputed Internal Boundaries in Iraq," *International Affairs*, 86, 6 (November 2010), pp. 1329–43; doi:10.1111/j.1468–2346.2010.00946.x

Beaumont, Peter, "Israel–Palestine: Outlook Bleak as Wave of Violence Passes Six-Month Mark," *The Guardian*, 31 March 2016; https://www.theguardian.com/world/2016/mar/31/israel-palestine-violence-knife-attacks-west-bank-gaza (accessed 12 May 2017).

——— "UN Votes Resoundingly to Reject Trump's Recognition of Jerusalem as Capital," *The Guardian*, 21 December 2017.

Beinin, Joel, "Neo-Liberal Structural Adjustment, Political Demobilization, Neo-Authoritarianism in Egypt," in Laura Guazzone and Daniela Pioppi (eds), *The Arab State and Neo-Liberal Globalization*, pp. 19–46. Reading, UK: Ithaca Press, 2012.

Bellin, Eva, "The Robustness of Authoritarianism in the Middle East: Exceptionalism in Comparative Perspective," *Comparative Politics*, 36 (2004), pp. 139–57.

Bennet, James, "A New Mideast Battle: Arafat vs. Hamas," *The New York Times*, 6 December 2001; http://www.nytimes.com/2001/12/06/world/mideast-flare-up-news-analysis-a-new-mideast-battle-arafat-vs-hamas.html (accessed 12 May 2017).

Bishara, Azmi, "'A double responsibility': Palestinian Citizens of Israel and the Intifada," *Middle East Report*, 217 (Winter 2000), pp. 26–9.

Bishara, Azmi, Sara Scalenghe, Steve Rothman, and Joel Beinin, "On Palestinians in the Israeli Knesset: Interview with Azmi Bishara," *Middle East Report*, 201 (October–November 1996), pp. 27–30.

Black, Ian, and Seumas Milne, "Palestine Papers Reveal MI6 Drew Up Plan for Crackdown on Hamas," *The Guardian*, 25 January 2011; https://www.theguardian. com/world/2011/jan/25/palestine-papers-mi6-hamas-crackdown (accessed 25 January 2011).

Blaydes, Lisa, and Drew A. Linzer, "Elite Competition, Religiosity, and Anti-Americanism in the Islamic World," *American Political Science Review*, 106, 2 (May 2012), pp. 225–43; doi:10.1017/s0003055412000135

Blinken, Antony, "How Rex Tillerson Did So Much Damage in So Little Time," *The New York Times*, 30 November 2017.

Blum, William, *Killing Hope: US Military and CIA Interventions since World War II*, London: Zed Books, 2014.

Bohan, Caren, "US Says Saudi Forces in Bahrain 'not an invasion,'" Reuters, 14 March 2011; http://www.reuters.com/article/us-bahrain-usa-invasion-idUSTRE72D6RB 20110314.

Brathwaite, Kirstin J. H., "Repression and the Spread of Ethnic Conflict in Kurdistan," *Studies in Conflict & Terrorism*, 37, 6 (June 14, 2014), pp. 473–91; doi:10.1080/1 057610x.2014.903451

Broning, Michael, *Political Parties in Palestine: Leadership and Thought*, Basingstoke: Palgrave Macmillan, 2013.

Bronner, Ethan, and Michael Slackman, "Saudi Troops Enter Bahrain to Help Put Down Unrest," *The New York Times*, 14 March 2011; http://www.nytimes. com/2011/03/15/world/middleeast/15bahrain.html (accessed 9 May 2017).

Brownlee, Jason, *Democracy Prevention*, New York: Cambridge University Press, 2012.

Brumberg, Daniel, "Islam Is Not the Solution (or the Problem)," *The Washington Quarterly*, 29 (2005), pp. 97–116.

Bullock, Tom, "The Palestinian Faction Fatah: A Primer," NPR, 13 January 2007; http://www.npr.org/templates/story/story.php?storyId=6659712 (accessed 12 May 2017)

Burnat, Emad, and Guy Davidi (dirs), *5 Broken Cameras*, Palestine: Burnat Films, 2011.

Bush, Sarah, "Forms of International Pressure and the Middle East," Project on Middle East Political Science, 21 August 2015.

———— "Varieties of International Influence and the Middle East," *PS: Political Science & Politics*, 50, 3 (12 June 2017), pp. 668–71; doi:10.1017/s1049096517000361

Bush, Sarah, and Amaney Jamal, "Anti-Americanism, Authoritarian Politics, and Attitudes about Women" Representation: Evidence from a Survey Experiment in Jordan," *International Studies Quarterly*, 59, 1 (2014), pp. 34–45; doi:10.1111/isqu.12139

Bush, Sarah S., Aaron Erlich, Lauren Prather, and Yael Zeira, "The Effects of Authoritarian Iconography: An Experimental Test," *Comparative Political Studies*, 49, 13 (6 April 2016), pp. 1704–38; doi:10.1177/0010414016633228

Calvert, Randall L., Mathew D. Mccubbins, and Barry R. Weingast, "A Theory of Political Control and Agency Discretion," *American Journal of Political Science*, 33, 3 (1989), pp. 588–611; doi:10.2307/2111064

Canache, D., J. Mondak, and M.A. Seligson, "Meaning and Measurement in Cross-National Research on Satisfaction with Democracy," *Public Opinion Quarterly*, 65, 4 (2001), pp. 506–28; doi:10.1086/323576

Carmeli-Pollak, Shai (dir.), *Bil'in Habibti*, Tel Aviv: Claudius Films, 2006.

Chacar, Henriette, "Trump's Jerusalem Announcement Sparked Deadly Violence: From Israel," The Intercept, 18 December 2017.

Cheslow, Daniella, "Palestinian Nonviolence: Is the Budrus Model Still Viable?," *The Christian Science Monitor*, 10 December 2010.

Chomsky, Noam, *The Fateful Triangle: The United States, Israel and the Palestinians*, London: Pluto Press, 2016.

Chulov, Martin, "Iran Repopulates Syria with Shia Muslims to Help Tighten Regime's Control," *The Guardian*, 13 January 2017; https://www.theguardian.com/world/2017/jan/13/irans-syria-project-pushing-population-shifts-to-increase-influence (accessed 12 May 2017).

Claassen, Ryan L., and Benjamin Highton, "Policy Polarization among Party Elites and the Significance of Political Awareness in the Mass Public," *Political Research Quarterly*, 62, 3 (9 September 2008), pp. 538–51; doi:10.1177/1065912908322415

Cohen, Roger, "The Story of Palestinian Prime Minister Salam Fayyad," *The New York Times*, 14 February 2013.

Collier, Paul, and Anke Hoeffler, "Greed and Grievance in Civil War," World Bank Policy Research Paper 2355, Washington, DC: World Bank, 2000.

Collier, David, Henry E. Brady, and Jason Seawright, "Sources of Leverage in Causal Inference: Toward an Alternative View of Methodology," in Henry Brady and David Collier (eds), *Rethinking Social Inquiry: Diverse Tools, Shared Standards*, Lanham, MD: Rowman & Littlefield, 2004.

"Congressional Record from October 25, 2000," 106th Congress, 2nd session, issue 146, no. 135: 24316–317.

Corstange, Daniel, "Anti-American Behavior in the Middle East," *Journal of Politics*, 78, 1 (2016), pp. 311–25; doi:10.2139/ssrn.2444102

Corstange, Daniel, and Nikolay Marinov, "Taking Sides in Other People's Elections:

The Polarizing Effect of Foreign Intervention," *American Journal of Political Science*, 56 (2012), pp. 655–70.

Croissant, Aurel, and Stefan Wurster, "Performance and Persistence of Autocracies in Comparison: Introducing Issues and Perspectives," *Contemporary Politics*, 19 (2013), pp. 1–18.

Crow, David, "Citizen Disenchantment in New Democracies: The Case of Mexico," PhD diss., 2009.

Cunningham, Kathleen Gallagher, "Actor Fragmentation and Civil War Bargaining: How Internal Divisions Generate Civil Conflict," *American Journal of Political Science*, 57, 3 (18 March 2013), pp. 659–72; doi:10.1111/ajps.12003

Dalton, R., "Political Support in Advanced Industrial Democracies," in Pippa Norris (ed.), *Critical Citizens; Global Support for Democratic Governance*, pp. 57–77, Oxford: Oxford University Press, 1999.

Dana, Tariq, "Lost in Transition: The Palestinian National Movement after Oslo," in Mandy Turner (ed.), *From the River to the Sea*, London: Lexington Books, 2019.

——— "Social Movements in the Palestinian Territories," presentation, Arab Center for Research and Policy Studies Seminar Series, Doha, Qatar, 15 November 2017.

——— "Social Struggle and the Crisis of the Palestinian Left Parties," Rosa Luxemburg Foundation, March 2016.

Daraghmeh, Mohammed, "Abbas' Government Sued over Alleged CIA-Backed Wiretapping," AP News, 6 February 2018; https://apnews.com/1433ee22ec3343 878be9c78368dfd500 (accessed 6 February 2018).

Davies, James, "Toward a Theory of Revolution," *American Sociological Review*, 6 (February 1962), pp. 5–19.

Deger, Allison, "After Building a Protest Movement, West Bank Village of Nabi Saleh Steps Back from Weekly Friday Protests," Mondoweiss, 9 September 2016; http:// mondoweiss.net/2016/09/building-movement-protests/ (accessed 6 December 2017).

Dodge, Toby, "State and Society in Iraq Ten Years after Regime Change: The Rise of a New Authoritarianism," *International Affairs*, 89, 2 (March 2013), pp. 241–57; doi:10.1111/1468–2346.12016

Dower, Paul Castañeda, Victor Ginsburgh, and Shlomo Weber, "Colonial Legacy, Polarization and Linguistic Disenfranchisement: The Case of the Sri Lankan War," *Journal of Development Economics* (2016); doi:10.1016/j.jdeveco.2016.12.006

Druckman, J. N., and A. Lupia, "Preference Formation," *Annual Review of Political Science*, 3, 1 (2000), pp. 1–24; doi:10.1146/annurev.polisci.3.1.1

Dumper, M. "Policing Divided Cities: Stabilization and Law Enforcement in Palestinian East Jerusalem," *International Affairs*, 89, 5 (2013), pp. 1247–64.

Easterly, William, Shanker Satyanath, and Daniel Berger, "Superpower Interventions and Their Consequences for Democracy: An Empirical Inquiry," National Bureau of Economic Research Working Paper no. 13992, May 2008.

BIBLIOGRAPHY

Eckel, Catherine C., and Philip J. Grossman, "Managing Diversity by Creating Team Identity," *Journal of Economic Behavior & Organization*, 58, 3 (January 2005), pp. 371–92; doi:10.1016/j.jebo.2004.01.003

Ehrenreich, Ben, "Is This Where the Third Intifada Will Start?," *The New York Times*, 15 March 2013; http://www.nytimes.com/2013/03/17/magazine/is-this-where-the-third-intifada-will-start.html (accessed 5 December 2017).

Eid, Haidar, "Withdrawal from Participation as a Palestinian Strategy?," Al-Shabaka, 9 December 2013; https://al-shabaka.org/commentaries/%D8%A7%D9%84%D8%A7%D9%86%D8%B3%D8%AD%D8%A7%D8%A8-%D9%85%D9%86-%D8%A7%D9%84%D9%85%D8%B4%D8%A7%D8%B1%D9%83%D8%A9-%D9%83%D8%A7%D8%B3%D8%AA%D8%B1%D8%A7%D8%AA%D9%8A%D8%AC%D9%8A%D8%A9-%D9%81%D9%84%D8%B3/?platform=hootsuite

El Kurd, Dana, "The Legacy of Repression: Polarization in the Palestinian Territories," *Middle East Law and Governance*, 10, 3 (October 2018).

——— "Mobilization across Class in the Palestinian Territories," in Alaa Tartir and Timothy Seidel (eds), *The Power of Rules and the Rule of Power in Palestine*, New York: Palgrave Macmillan, forthcoming.

El-Affendi, Abdelwahab, "Making Peace Gambles Work: The Oslo Accords, the Sudanese 'Comprehensive Peace Agreement' and Their 'Spirals of Insecurity,'" *Journal of Peace, Conflict, and Development*, 17 (2011), pp. 1–22.

Elman, Miriam, "Spoilers of Peace and the Dilemmas of Conflict Resolution," in Nimrod Goren and Miriam Elman (eds), *Spoilers of Peace and the Dilemmas of Conflict Resolution*, pp. 7–17, Tel Aviv: Israeli Institute for Regional Foreign Policies, 2012.

El-Meehy, Asya, "Relative Deprivation and Politics in the Arab Uprisings," Social Justice & Development Policy in the Arab World Research Report, May 2014.

Erlanger, Steven, "Victory Ends 40 Years of Political Domination by Arafat's Party," *The New York Times*, 26 January 2006; http://www.nytimes.com/2006/01/26/international/middleeast/victory-ends-40-years-of-political-domination-by.html (accessed 12 May 2017).

Esteban, Joan-Maria, and Debraj Ray, "On the Measurement of Polarization," *Econometrica*, 62, 4 (July 1994), pp. 819–51.

Ezrow, Natasha, and Erica Frantz, "State Institutions and the Survival of Dictatorships," *Journal of International Affairs*, 65, 1 (2011).

Fearon, J. D., "Self-Enforcing Democracy," *The Quarterly Journal of Economics* (2011), pp. 1661–708.

Finkel, S. E., A. Pérez-Liñán, and M. A. Seligson, "The Effects of US Foreign Assistance on Democracy Building, 1990–2003," *World Politics*, 59, 3 (2007), pp. 404–39; doi:10.1017/s0043887100020876

Finnemore, Martha, *National Interests in International Society*, Ithaca, NY: Cornell University Press, 1996.

Fiorina, Morris P., Samuel J. Abrams, and Jeremy Pope, *Culture War? The Myth of a Polarized America*, Boston, MA: Longman, 2011.

Fish, M. Steven, "Islam and Authoritarianism," *World Politics*, 55 (2002), pp. 4–37.

Fraihat, Ibrahim, "Why Saudi–Israeli Normalization Could Be Dangerous," Huffington Post, 22 November 2017.

Franklin, Stephen, "West Bank Islamic Groups Show Militant and Softer Faces," *Chicago Tribune*, 17 August 1997; http://articles.chicagotribune.com/1997–08–17/news/9708170258_1_hamas-leaders-islamic-groups-militant (accessed 12 May 2017).

Gandhi, Jennifer, and Ellen Lust-Okar, "Elections under Authoritarianism," *Annual Review of Political Science*, 12, 1 (2009), pp. 403–22; doi:10.1146/annurev.polisci.11.060106.095434

Gengler, Justin, "Bahrain's Sunni Awakening," Middle East Research and Information Project, 17 January 2012; http://www.merip.org/mero/mero011712

——— *Group Conflict and Political Mobilization in Bahrain and the Arab Gulf*, Bloomington, IN: Indiana University Press, 2015.

George, Alexander, and Andrew Bennett, *Case Studies and Theory Development in the Social Sciences*, Cambridge, MA: MIT Press, 2007.

Gerring, John, *Social Science Methodology: A Unified Framework*, Cambridge: Cambridge University Press, 2013.

Gerster, Karin, and Helga Baumgarten "Palestinian NGOs and Their Cultural, Economic and Political Impact in Palestinian Society," Rosa Luxemburg Foundation, December 2011.

Gervasoni, Carlos, "A Rentier Theory of Subnational Regimes: Fiscal Federalism, Democracy, and Authoritarianism in the Argentine Provinces," *World Politics*, 62, 2 (2010), pp. 302–40.

Ghalyon, Burhan, "Has the Syrian Revolution Ended?," Al-Araby Al-Jadeed, 10 January 2017; https://www.alaraby.co.uk/opinion/2017/1/9/%D9%87%D9%84-%D8%A7%D9%86%D8%AA%D9%87%D8%AA-%D8%A7%D9%84%D8%AB%D9%88%D8%B1%D8%A9-%D8%A7%D9%84%D8%B3%D9%88%D8%B1%D9%8A%D8%A9-5

Gilligan, Michael, "Is Enforcement Necessary for Effectiveness? A Model of the International Criminal Regime," *International Organization*, 60 (October 2006), pp. 935–67.

Gleditsch, Kristian, and Michael D. Ward, "Diffusion and the International Context of Democratization," *International Organization*, 60, 4 (2006), pp. 911–33.

Gobel, Christian, "Authoritarian Consolidation," *European Political Science*, 10 (2011), pp. 176–90.

Goette, Lorenz, David Huffman, and Stephan Meier. "The Impact of Group Membership on Cooperation and Norm Enforcement: Evidence Using Random Assignment to Real Social Groups," *American Economic Review*, 96, 2 (May 2006), pp. 212–16; doi:10.1257/000282806777211658

Goldenberg, Suzanne, "Rioting as Sharon Visits Islam Holy Site," *The Guardian*, 28 September 2000.

Goldenberg, Tia, "Growing BDS Movement Raises Alarm among Israeli Leaders," *Haaretz*, 7 July 2015.

Gourevitch, Peter, "The Second Image Reversed: The International Sources of Domestic Politics," *International Organization*, 32, 4 (Autumn 1978), pp. 881–912.

Graham-Harrison, Emma, "How Sinai Became a Magnet for Terror," *The Observer*, 7 November 2015; https://www.theguardian.com/world/2015/nov/08/sinai-magnet-for-terror (accessed 1 May 2017).

Greene, Kenneth F. *Why Dominant Parties Lose: Mexico's Democratization in Comparative Perspective*, Cambridge: Cambridge University Press, 2009.

Grim, Ryan, and Glenn Greenwald, "US Senate's First Bill, in the Midst of the Shutdown, Is a Bipartisan Defense of the Israeli Government from Boycotts," The Intercept, 5 January 2019.

Grimm, Jannis, and Cilja Harders, "Unpacking the Effects of Repression: The Evolution of Islamist Repertoires of Contention in Egypt after the Fall of President Morsi," *Social Movement Studies* (27 June 2017), pp. 1–19; doi:10.1080/1474283 7.2017.1344547

Gurr, Ted Robert, *Why Men Rebel*, Princeton: Princeton University Press, 1970.

Gurr, Ted, and Raymond Duvall, "Civil Conflict in the 1960s," *Comparative Political Studies*, 6, 2 (1973), pp. 135–69; doi:10.1177/001041407300600201

Hafner-Burton, Emilie, "Trading Human Rights: How Preferential Trade Agreements Influence Government Repression," *International Organization*, 59 (July 2005), pp. 593–629.

Hama, Hawre, and Megan Connelly, "Kurdistan's Struggle for Sovereignty: State, Societal, and Human Security," Case Analysis, Doha: Arab Center for Research and Policy Studies, September 2017.

Han, Hahrie, "The Organizational Roots of Political Activism: Field Experiments on Creating a Relational Context," *American Political Science Review*, 110, 2 (May 2016), pp. 296–307; doi:10.1017/s000305541600006x

Hawkins, Darren G., and Wade Jacoby, "How Agents Matter," in Darren G. Hawkins (ed.), *Delegation and Agency in International Organizations*, pp. 199–228, New York: Cambridge University Press, 2006.

Hawkins, Darren G., David Lake, Daniel Nielson, and Michael Tierney, "Delegation under Anarchy; States, International Organization, and Principal–Agent Theory," in Darren G. Hawkins (ed.), *Delegation and Agency in International Organizations*, pp. 3–38, New York: Cambridge University Press, 2006.

Healy, Jack, and Namo Abdulla, "Iraqi Kurdistan, Known as Haven, Faces Unrest," *The New York Times*, 23 February 2011; Accessed December 19, 2017. http://www.nytimes.com/2011/02/24/world/middleeast/24kurd.html (accessed 19 December 2017).

Hertog, Steffen, "Segmented Clientelism: The Politics of Economic Reform in Saudi Arabia," PhD diss., University of Oxford, 2006.

Hetherington, Marc J., "Review Article: Putting Polarization in Perspective," *British Journal of Political Science*, 39, 2 (April 2009), pp. 413–48; doi:10.1017/s0007123408000501

Hilal, Jamil, "The Palestinian Left and the Multi-Layered Challenges Ahead," Rosa Luxemburg Foundation, 19 August 2010; http://www.palestine-studies.org/institute/fellows/palestinian-left-and-multi-layered-challenges-ahead (accessed 12 May 2017).

——— "PLO Institutions: The Challenge Ahead," *Journal of Palestine Studies*, 23, 1 (Autumn 1993), pp. 46–60.

Hill, Seth J., and Chris Tausanovitch, "A Disconnect in Representation? Comparison of Trends in Congressional and Public Polarization," *The Journal of Politics*, 77, 4 (October 2015), pp. 1058–75; doi:10.1086/682398

Hockstader, Lee, "Arafat Says Crackdown on Hamas Not Over," *The Washington Post*, 4 November 1998; https://www.washingtonpost.com/archive/politics/1998/11/04/arafat-says-crackdown-on-hamas-is-not-over/51986192–8a00–401a–9a16–2fd57e9a8a12/?utm_term=.bd3292be6dd0 (accessed 12 May 2017).

Holland, Jack, "Why Is Change So Hard?," in Michelle Bentley and Jack Holland (eds), *Obama's Foreign Policy: Ending the War on Terror*, pp. 1–16, New York: Routledge, 2014.

Holmes, Amy Austin, *Social Unrest and American Military Bases in Turkey and Germany since 1945*, New York: Cambridge University Press, 2014.

Horwitz, Murray, and Jacob Rabbie, "Individuality and Membership in the Intergroup System," in Henry Tajfel (ed.), *Social Identity and Intergroup Relations*, pp. 241–71, Cambridge, MA: Cambridge University Press, 1982.

Hudson, Alexander, "When Does Public Participation Make a Difference? Evidence from Iceland's Crowdsourced Constitution," *Policy & Internet*, 10, 2 (18 December 2017), pp. 185–217; doi:10.1002/poi3.167

Huntington, Samuel, *The Clash of Civilizations and the Remaking of World Order*, New York: Simon & Schuster, 1996.

Hyde, Susan D., "The Observer Effect in International Politics: Evidence from a Natural Experiment," *World Politics*, 60, 1 (October 2007), pp. 37–63; doi:10.1353/wp.0.0001

Hyde, Susan D., and Nikolay Marinov, "Information and Self-Enforcing Democracy: The Role of International Election Observation," *International Organization*, 68, 2 (2014), pp. 329–59.

Ikenberry, G. John, *After Victory*, Princeton: Princeton University Press, 2001.

Institute for Palestine Studies Chronologies; http://www.palestine-studies.org/jps/chronologies

Ishaq, Nasser and Pekka Hakala. Area C: More than 60 % of the occupied West Bank threatened by Israeli annexation. Brussels: Directorate-General for External Policies of the Union Policy Department, European Parliament. Accessed June 2019. http://www.europarl.europa.eu/RegData/etudes/briefing_note/join/2013/491495/EXPO-AFET_SP(2013)491495_EN.pdf

Iyengar, Shanto, and Sean J. Westwood, "Fear and Loathing across Party Lines: New Evidence on Group Polarization," *American Journal of Political Science*, 59, 3 (July 2015), pp. 690–707; doi:10.1111/ajps.12152

Jamal, Amal, *The Palestinian National Movement: Politics of Contention, 1967–2005*, Bloomington, IN: Indiana University Press, 2005.

Jamal, Amaney, *Barriers to Democracy: The Other Side of Social Capital in Palestine and the Arab World*, Princeton: Princeton University Press, 2007.

——— *Of Empires and Citizens: Pro-American Democracy or No Democracy at All?*, Princeton: Princeton University Press, 2012.

Jamal, Ben, "This Ruling Allows Councils to Boycott Israel: It's a Crucial Victory," *The Guardian*, 26 June 2017.

Jones, T. C., "America, Oil, and War in the Middle East," *Journal of American History*, 99, 1 (2012), pp. 208–18; doi:10.1093/jahist/jas045

Josua, Maria, "Cooptation as a Strategy of Authoritarian Legitimation; Success and Failure in the Arab World," paper presented at 6th ECPR General Conference, Reykjavik, August 2011.

Jüde, Johannes, "Contesting Borders? The Formation of Iraqi Kurdistan's De facto State," *International Affairs*, 93, 4 (July 2017), pp. 847–63; doi:10.1093/ia/iix125

Kalyvas, Stathis N., and Matthew Adam Kocher, "How 'Free' Is Free Riding in Civil Wars? Violence, Insurgency, and the Collective Action Problem," *World Politics*, 59, 2 (January 2007), pp. 177–216. doi:10.1353/wp. 2007.0023

Karam, Karam, "An Analysis of Political Change in Lebanon in the Light of Recent Mobilization Cycles," in Laura Guazzone and Daniela Pioppi (eds), *The Arab State and Neo-Liberal Globalization*, Reading, UK: Ithaca Press, 2012.

Katzman, Kenneth, "Bahrain: Reform, Security, and US Policy," Congressional Research Service, Federation of American Scientists. April 13, 2017. https://fas.org/sgp/crs/mideast/95–1013.pdf.

Kedourie, Elie, *Democracy and Arab Political Culture*, 2nd edn, London: Frank Cass, 1994.

Kessler, Judd, and Lise Vesterlund, "The External Validity of Laboratory Experiments: The Misleading Emphasis on Quantitative Effects," in Guillaume R. Fréchette and Andrew Schotter (eds), *Handbook of Experimental Economic Methodology*, pp. 391–406, New York: Oxford University Press, 2015.

Khalidi, Rashid, *Palestinian Identity: The Construction of Modern National Consciousness*, New York: Columbia University Press, 1997.

Khalil, Osamah, *America's Dream Palace: Middle East Expertise and the Rise of the National Security State*, Cambridge, MA: Harvard University Press, 2016.

Khan, Mushtaq Husain, "Introduction," in Inge Amundsen, George Giacaman, and Mushtaq Husain Khan (eds), *State Formation in Palestine: Viability and Governance during a Social Transformation*, New York: Routledge, 2004.

Khodr, Zeina, "Syria Deal: 'Population Swap' or 'Sectarian Cleansing?,'" Al Jazeera, 15 August 2015. http://www.aljazeera.com/blogs/middleeast/2015/08/syrian-deal-population-swap-ethnic-cleansing-150815160046670.html

Khoury, Jack, "Founder of Islamic Movement in Israel, Abdallah Nimr Darwish, Dies at 69," *Haaretz*, 14 May 2017; https://www.haaretz.com/israel-news/founder-of-islamic-movement-in-israel-dies-at-69–1.5471950 (accessed 3 February 2018).

Khoury, Jack, Amir Tibon, and Noa Landau, "Palestinians Say No Compromise on Tax Funds, Even in Face of Economic Collapse," Haaretz.com, 30 April 2019.

King, G., J. Pan, and M. E. Roberts, "How Censorship in China Allows Government Criticism But Silences Collective Expression," *American Political Science Review*, 107, 2 (2013), pp. 326–43.

Kirkpatrick, David, "Tapes Reveal Egyptian Leaders' Tacit Acceptance of Jerusalem Move," *The New York Times*, 8 January 2018.

Koehler, John O., *Stasi: The Untold Story of the East German Secret Police*, Boulder, CO: Westview Press, 1999.

Kuran, Timur, "Now Out of Never: The Element of Surprise in the East European Revolution of 1989," *World Politics*, 44, 1 (1991), pp. 7–48.

Kutyla, Scarlett, "Tulkarem Chemical Factory Exploits Palestinian Labour and Health," Middle East Monitor, 19 September 2014; https://www.middleeastmonitor.com/20140919-tulkarem-chemical-factory-exploits-palestinian-labour-and-health/

Laffont, Jean-Jacques, and David Martimort, *The Theory of Incentives*, Princeton: Princeton University Press, 2002.

Lagon, M. P., "Promoting Democracy: The Whys and Hows for the United States and the International Community," Council on Foreign Relations, February 2011; http://www.cfr.org/democratization/promoting-democracy-whys-hows-united-states-international-community/p24090

Lake, David A., "Legitimating Power: The Domestic Politics of US International Hierarchy," *International Security*, 38, 2 (2013), pp. 74–111; doi:10.1162/isec_a_00139

——— "The New American Empire?," *International Studies Perspectives*, 9, 3 (20 July 2008), pp. 281–9; doi:10.1111/j.1528–3585.2008.00334.x

——— "The State and International Relations," in Christian Reus-Smit and Duncan Snidal (eds), *The Oxford Handbook of International Relations*, New York: Oxford University Press, 2008.

Lake, David A., and Robert Powell, "International Relations: A Strategic-Choice Approach," in David A. Lake and Robert Powell (eds), *Strategic Choice and International Relations*, Princeton: Princeton University Press, 1999.

Langohr, Vickie, "Too Much Civil Society, Too Little Politics: Egypt and Liberalizing Arab Regimes," *Comparative Politics*, 36, 2 (2004), pp. 181–204.

Le More, Anne, *International Assistance to the Palestinians after Oslo: Political Guilt, Wasted Money*, London: Routledge, 2008.

Levitsky, Steven, and Lucan Way, *Competitive Authoritarianism: Hybrid Regimes after the Cold War*, New York: Cambridge University Press, 2010.

Lia, Brynjar. *Building Arafat's Police: The Politics of International Police Assistance in the Palestinian Territories after the Oslo Agreement*, Reading, UK: Garnet Publishing, 2007.

Lichtenheld, Adam, "Beyond Ethno-Sectarian 'Cleansing': The Assortative Logic of Forced Displacement in Syria," Project on Middle East Political Science, 29 March 2017; https://pomeps.org/2017/03/29/beyond-ethno-sectarian-cleansing-the-assortative-logic-of-forced-displacement-in-syria/ (accessed 12 May 2017).

Louër, Laurence, *Transnational Shia Politics: Religious and Political Networks in the Gulf*, New York: Columbia University Press, 2008.

Lucas, Russell E., "Monarchical Authoritarianism: Survival and Political Liberalization in a Middle Eastern Regime Type," *International Journal of Middle East Studies*, 36, 1 (February 2004), pp. 103–19; doi:10.1017/s0020743804361064

Lupu, Noam, and Leonid Peisakhin, "The Legacy of Political Violence across Generations," *American Journal of Political Science*, 61, 4 (October 2017), pp. 836–51.

Lyne, Mona M., Daniel Nielson, and Michael Tierney, "Who Delegates? Alternative Models of Principals in Development Aid," in Darren G. Hawkins (ed.), *Delegation and Agency in International Organizations*, pp. 41–76, New York: Cambridge University Press, 2006.

Malik, Hamdi, "Turkmens Unite against Kurdish Designs on Kirkuk," Al-Monitor, 13 October 2017; https://www.al-monitor.com/pulse/originals/2017/10/kurdish-referendum-turkmen-kirkuk.html (accessed 19 December 2017).

Mann, Michael, *The Rise of Classes and Nation-States, 1760–1914*, New York: Cambridge University Press, 1993.

Marczak, Bill, John Scott-Railton, Sarah McKune, Bahr Abdul Razzak, and Ron Deibert, "Hide and Seek: Tracking NSO Group's Pegasus Spyware to Operations in 45 Countries," The Citizen Lab, 5 November 2018; https://citizenlab.ca/2018/09/hide-and-seek-tracking-nso-groups-pegasus-spyware-to-operations-in-45-countries/

Martens, Bertin, Uwe Mummert, Peter Murrell, and Paul Seabright, *The Institutional Economics of Foreign Aid*, New York: Cambridge University Press, 2002.

Matar, Haggai, "Mustafa Tamimi: A Murder Captured on Camera," 972 Magazine, 11 December 2011; https://972mag.com/mustafa-tamimi-a-murder-captured-on-camera/29459/ (accessed 5 December 2017).

McAdam, Doug, Mayer Zald, and John McCarthy (eds), *Comparative Perspectives on*

Social Movements: Political Opportunities, Mobilizing Structures, and Cultural Framings, Cambridge: Cambridge University Press, 1996.

McCaffray van Den Toorn, Christine, "Internal Divides behind the Kurdistan Referendum," Carnegie Endowment for International Peace, 11 October 2017; http://carnegieendowment.org/sada/73359 (accessed 19 December 2017).

McCarty, Nolan Matthew, Keith Taylor Poole, and Howard Rosenthal, *Polarized America: The Dance of Ideology and Unequal Riches*, Cambridge, MA: MIT Press, 2006.

McDaniel, Richard. "No 'Plan B': US Strategic Access in the Middle East and the Question of Bahrain," Foreign Policy at Brookings, 2013; https://www.brookings.edu/wp-content/uploads/2016/06/24-us-strategic-access-middle-east-bahrain-mcdaniel.pdf

McGreal, Chris, "US Forces Israel to Lift Siege of Arafat," *The Guardian*, 30 September 2002.

Mclauchlin, Theodore, and Wendy Pearlman, "Out-Group Conflict, In-Group Unity?," *Journal of Conflict Resolution*, 56, 1 (25 December 2011), pp. 41–66; doi:10.1177/0022002711429707

Migdal, Joel S. (ed.), *Boundaries and Belonging: States and Societies in the Struggle to Shape Identities and Local Practices*, Cambridge: Cambridge University Press, 2004.

Milner, Helen, "Why Multilateralism? Foreign Aid and Domestic Principal–Agent Problems," in Darren G. Hawkins (ed.), *Delegation and Agency in International Organizations*, pp. 107–39, New York: Cambridge University Press, 2006.

Murphy, Dan, "Israel, US, and Egypt Back Fatah's Fight against Hamas," *The Christian Science Monitor*, 25 May 2007; http://www.csmonitor.com/2007/0525/p07s02-wome.html (accessed 12 May 2017).

Nashif, Nadim, "Surveillance of Palestinians and the Fight for Digital Rights," Al-Shabaka, 23 October 2017.

Nassar, Tamara, "Israel Arrests Community Leaders in Attempt to Quell Protests over Jerusalem," Electronic Intifada, 18 December 2017.

Natali, Denise, "The Spoils of Peace in Iraqi Kurdistan," *Third World Quarterly*, 28, 6 (September 2007), pp. 1111–29; doi:10.1080/01436590701507511

Nexon, Daniel H., and Thomas Wright, "What's at Stake in the American Empire Debate?," *American Political Science Review*, 101, 2 (May 2007), pp. 253–71; doi:10.1017/s0003055407070220

O'Donnell, Guillermo A., and Philippe C. Schmitter, *Transitions from Authoritarian Rule*, Baltimore, MD: Johns Hopkins University Press, 1986.

O'Toole, Megan, and Nigel Wilson, "A Record Year of Home Demolitions in East Jerusalem," Al Jazeera, 2017; https://interactive.aljazeera.com/aje/2017/jerusalem-2016-home-demolitions/index.html

Obeid, Hassan, "Student Political Groups Face Crackdown in West Bank," *Al-Monitor*, 24 December 2014; http://www.al-monitor.com/pulse/fr/contents/

articles/originals/2014/12/student-movement-palestinian-authority-west-bank.
html

Olson, Mancur, *The Logic of Collective Action*, Cambridge, MA: Harvard University Press, 1965.

Oz, Hassan, "Undermining the Transatlantic Democracy Agenda? The Arab Spring and Saudi Arabia's Counteracting Democracy Strategy," *Democratization*, 22, 3 (2015), pp. 479–95.

Palestinian Central Bureau of Statistics Archives; http://www.pcbs.gov.ps/site/lang__en/507/default.aspx

Palestinian Economic Policy Research Institute, "The Economics of Agriculture in the Qalqilya and Tulkarem Districts: Improving the Profitability of Farmers Affected by the Separation Wall," Jerusalem: MAS, 2005.

Pape, Robert A., "The Strategic Logic of Suicide Terrorism," *American Political Science Review*, 97, 3 (August 2003), pp. 343–61; doi:10.1017/s000305540300073x

Pappe, Ilan, *Forgotten Palestinians: A History of the Palestinians in Israel*, New Haven: Yale University Press, 2014.

Parkinson, Sarah Elizabeth, "Organizing Rebellion: Rethinking High-Risk Mobilization and Social Networks in War," *American Political Science Review*, 107, 3 (2013), pp. 418–32.

Parmar, Inderjeet, "The US-Led Liberal Order: Imperialism by Another Name?," *International Affairs*, 94, 1 (1 January 2018), pp. 151–72; doi:10.1093/ia/iix240

Pearlman, Wendy, "Emotions and the Microfoundations of the Arab Uprisings," *Perspectives on Politics*, 11 (21 June 2013), pp. 387–409; doi:10.1017/s1537 592713001072

——— *Fragmentation and Violence: Internal Influences on Tactics in the Case of the Palestinian National Movement, 1918–2006*, Cambridge, MA: Harvard University Press, 2007.

——— "From Palestine to Syria: Three Intifadas and Lessons for Popular Struggles," *Middle East Law and Governance*, 8, 1 (19 July 2016), pp. 91–103; doi:10.11 63/18763375–00801004

——— "Precluding Nonviolence, Propelling Violence: The Effect of Internal Fragmentation on Movement Protest," *Studies in Comparative International Development*, 47 (2012), pp. 23–46.

Peceny, Mark, and Christopher K Butler, "The Conflict Behavior of Authoritarian Regimes," *International Politics*, 41, 4 (2004), pp. 565–81.

Pecquet, Julian, "Bahrain Bristles as US Threatens to Move Fleet," US News & World Report, 19 May 2015; https://www.usnews.com/news/articles/2015/05/19/bahrain-bristles-at-threat-to-move-5th-fleet

Pérez-peña, Richard, "Netanyahu's Talk of West Bank Annexations Is a Blow to Peace But No Surprise, Palestinians Say," *The New York Times*, 8 April 2019.

Phillips, Christopher, "After the Arab Spring: Power Shift in the Middle East?," LSE

Ideas, May 2012; http://www.lse.ac.uk/IDEAS/publications/reports/SR011.aspx (accessed 1 May 2017).

Pickering, Jeffrey, and Emizet F. Kisangani, "Diversionary Despots? Comparing Autocracies' Propensities to Use and to Benefit from Military Force," *American Journal of Political Science*, 54, 2 (2010), pp. 477–93.

Pickering, Jeffrey, and Mark Peceny, "Forging Democracy at Gunpoint," *International Studies Quarterly*, 50, 3 (11 September 2006), pp. 539–60.

Plotke, D., "Representation Is Democracy," *Constellations*, 4, 1 (1997), pp. 19–34; doi:10.1111/1467–8675.00033

Powell, Robert, "Taking Sides in Wars of Attrition," *American Political Science Review*, 111, 2 (14 May 2017), pp. 219–36; doi:10.1017/s0003055416000782

Prusher, Ilene, "Israeli Arabs' Rising Voice of Opposition," *The Christian Science Monitor*, 26 October 2006; https://www.csmonitor.com/2006/1026/p06s01-wome.html (accessed 3 February 2018).

Putnam, Robert, "Diplomacy and Domestic Politics: The Logic of Two-Level Games," *International Organization*, 42, 3 (1988), pp. 427–60; doi:10.1017/s0020818300027697

———— *Making Democracy Work: Civic Traditions in Modern Italy*, Princeton: Princeton University Press, 1993.

Rafizadeh, Majid, "For Syria's Minorities, Assad Is Security," Al Jazeera English, 16 September 2011; http://www.aljazeera.com/indepth/opinion/2011/09/2011912135213927196.html

Rhodes-Purdy, M., "Beyond the Balance Sheet: Performance, Participation and Regime Support in Latin America," PhD diss., 2015.

Ricks, Jacob I., and Amy H. Liu, "Process-Tracing Research Designs: A Practical Guide," *PS: Political Science & Politics*, 51, 4 (October 2018), pp. 842–6; doi:10.1017/s1049096518000975

Robin, Corey, *Fear: The History of a Political Idea*, New York: Oxford University Press, 2004.

Romano, David, "Iraqi Kurdistan: Challenges of Autonomy in the Wake of US Withdrawal," *International Affairs*, 86, 6 (November 2010), pp. 1345–59; doi:10.1111/j.1468–2346.2010.00947.x

Rosen, Armin, "A Middle-Class Paradise in Palestine?," *The Atlantic*, 11 February 2013.

Rubin, Barry M., *The Transformation of Palestinian Politics: From Revolution to State-Building*, Cambridge, MA: Harvard University Press, 1999.

Rubin, Barry M., and Judith Colp Rubin, *Yasir Arafat: A Political Biography*, New York: Oxford University Press, 2003.

Ryan, Curtis R., *Jordan in Transition: From Hussein to Abdullah*, Boulder, CO: Lynne Rienner, 2002.

Salloukh, Bassel F., "Overlapping Contests and Middle East International Relations:

The Return of the Weak Arab State," *PS: Political Science & Politics*, 50, 3 (12 June 2017), pp. 660–3; doi:10.1017/s1049096517000348

Sambanis, N., J. Schulhofer-Wohl, and M. Shayo, "Parochialism as a Central Challenge in Counterinsurgency," *Science*, 336, 6083 (17 May 2012), pp. 805–8; doi:10.1126/science.1222304

Sarsour, Shaker, Reem Naser, and Mohammad Atallah, "The Economic and Social Effects of Foreign Aid in Palestine," Palestine Monetary Authority, Research and Monetary Policy Department, November 2011.

Sayigh, Yezid, "Inducing a Failed State in Palestine," *Survival*, 49, 3 (July 2007), pp. 7–39; doi:10.1080/00396330701564786

Scott, James, and Carie A. Steele, "Sponsoring Democracy: The United States and Democracy Aid to the Developing World, 1988–2011," *International Studies Quarterly*, 55 (2011), pp. 47–69.

Sever, Ayşegül, "'Power Led' Outside Intervention in Kurdish Politics in Iraq and Turkey in the Early 1970s," *Middle Eastern Studies*, 49, 2 (March 2013), pp. 263–79; doi:10.1080/00263206.2012.759100

Sharp, Jeremy, "US Foreign Aid to Israel," CRS Report no. RL33222; https://fas.org/sgp/crs/mideast/RL33222.pdf

Shlaim, Avi, *The Iron Wall: Israel and the Arab World*, New York: W. W. Norton, 2000.

Siddiqui, Rukhsana, "Failed Insurrections and Ethnic Cleavages: A Comparative Study of Zaire and Sri Lanka," *Peace Research*, 24, 1 (February 1992), pp. 37–56.

Simmons, B. A., and A. Danner, "Credible Commitments and the International Criminal Court," *International Organization*, 64, 2 (2010), p. 225; doi:10.1017/s0020818310000044

Slater, Dan, and Sofia Fenner, "State Power and Staying Power: Infrastructural Mechanism and Authoritarian Durability," *Journal of International Affairs*, 65 (2011), pp. 15–29.

Smith, Anthony D., *Myths and Memories of the Nation*, Oxford: Oxford University Press, 1999.

Snider, Erin A., "US Democracy Aid and the Authoritarian State: Evidence from Egypt and Morocco," *International Studies Quarterly*, 62, 4 (27 December 2018), pp. 795–808.

Stacher, Joshua, "Fragmenting States, New Regimes: Militarized State Violence and Transition in the Middle East," *Democratization*, 22, 2 (23 March 2015), pp. 259–75; doi:10.1080/13510347.2015.1010810

Stansfield, Gareth, "The Reformation of Iraq's Foreign Relations: New Elites and Enduring Legacies," *International Affairs*, 86, 6 (November 2010), pp. 1395–409.

——— "The Unravelling of the Post-First World War State System? The Kurdistan Region of Iraq and the Transformation of the Middle East," *International Affairs*, 89, 2 (March 2013), pp. 259–82; doi:10.1111/1468-2346.12017

Stedman, Stephen John, "Spoiler Problems in Peace Processes," *International Security*, 22, 2 (Autumn 1997); doi:10.2307/2539366

Stein, Ken, "The Intifada and the Palestinian Uprising of 1936–1939: A Comparison," in Robert Freedman (ed.), *The Intifada: Its Impact on Israel, the Arab World, and the Superpowers*, Gainesville, FL: University Press of Florida, 1991.

Stork, Joe, "The Significance of Stones: Notes from the Seventh Month," in Zachary Lockman and Joel Beinin (eds), *Intifada: The Palestinian Uprising against Israeli Occupation*, Boston, MA: South End Press, 1989.

Stork, Joe, and Jim Paul, "Arms Sales and the Militarization of the Middle East," *MERIP Reports*, 112, 5 (1983); doi:10.2307/3010847

Stravers, Andrew, and Dana El Kurd, "Importing Autocracy: Regime Type and US Military Bases," forthcoming.

——— "Strategic Autocracy: American Military Forces and Regime Type," *Journal of Global Security Studies*, forthcoming.

Strickland, Patrick, "Wisconsin Governor Signs Anti-Boycott Israel Order," Al Jazeera, 28 October 2017.

Svolik, Milan, "Authoritarian Reversals and Democratic Consolidation," *American Political Science Review*, 102 (May 2008), 153–68.

——— *The Politics of Authoritarian Rule*, New York: Cambridge University Press, 2012.

Tabar, Natalie, and Lauren Bari, "Repression and Nonviolent Protest in the Occupied Palestinian Territory: Case Study on the Village of al-Nabi Saleh," Ramallah: Al-Haq Institute, 2011.

Tarrow, Sidney G., *Power in Movement: Social Movements and Contentious Politics*, Cambridge: Cambridge University Press, 1998.

Tartir, Alaa, "The Evolution and Reform of Palestinian Security Forces 1993–2013," *Stability: International Journal of Security & Development*, 4, 1 (10 September 2015); doi:10.5334/sta.gi

——— "How US Security Aid to PA Sustains Israel's Occupation," Al Jazeera, 2 December 2016; http://www.aljazeera.com/indepth/features/2016/11/security-aid-pa-sustains-israel-occupation-161103120213593.html (accessed 13 April 2017).

——— "The Palestinian Authority Security Forces: Whose Security?," Al-Shabaka, 16 May 2017.

Taylor, Michael, "Rationality and Revolutionary Collective Action," in Michael Taylor (ed.), *Rationality and Revolution*, pp. 63–91, Cambridge: Cambridge University Press, 1988.

Tétreault, Mary Ann, "The Winter of the Arab Spring in the Gulf Monarchies," *Globalizations*, 8, 15 (2011), 629–37.

Tezcür, Güneş Murat, "Ordinary People, Extraordinary Risks: Participation in an Ethnic Rebellion," *American Political Science Review*, 110, 2 (May 2016).

Tibi, Bassam, "Why They Can't Be Democratic," *Journal of Democracy*, 19, 3 (2008), pp. 43–8.

Tilly, Charles, *From Mobilization to Revolution*, Reading, MA: Addison-Wesley, 1978.

Tucker, Aviezer, *The Legacies of Totalitarianism: A Theoretical Framework*, Cambridge: Cambridge University Press, 2015.

Turner, Mandy, "No 'Plan B' Because 'Plan A' Cannot Fail: The Oslo Framework and Western Donors in the OPT, 1993–2017," in Mandy Turner (ed.), *From the River to the Sea*, London: Lexington Books, 2019.

UN Office for the Coordination of Humanitarian Affairs Archives; http://archive.ochaopt.org/

Urbinati, N., and M. E. Warren, "The Concept of Representation in Contemporary Democratic Theory," *Annual Review of Political Science*, 11, 1 (2008), pp. 387–412; doi:10.1146/annurev.polisci.11.053006.190533

Vanderhill, Rachel, *Promoting Authoritarianism Abroad*, Boulder, CO: Lynne Rienner, 2012.

Vine, D., *Base Nation: How US Military Bases Abroad Harm America and the World*, New York: Metropolitan Books, Henry Holt & Co., 2015.

Voller, Yaniv, "Kurdish Oil Politics in Iraq: Contested Sovereignty and Unilateralism," *Middle East Policy*, 20, 1 (Spring 2013), pp. 68–82; doi:10.1111/mepo.12004

Vreeland, J. R., "Political Institutions and Human Rights: Why Dictatorships Enter into the United Nations Convention against Torture," *International Organization*, 62, 1 (2008); doi:10.1017/s002081830808003x

Waak, Erika, "Violence among the Palestinians," *The Humanist* (January–February 2003); https://web.archive.org/web/20030211052937/http://www.thehumanist.org/humanist/articles/waakjf03.htm (accessed 12 May 2017).

Westervelt, Eric, "President Abbas Shuts Islamist Charities in W. Bank," NPR, 21 September 2007; http://www.npr.org/templates/story/story.php?storyId=14586528

Weyland, Kurt, "Autocratic Diffusion and Cooperation: The Impact of Interests vs. Ideology," *Democratization*, 24, 7 (2017), p. 1237.

———— "Risk Taking in Latin American Economic Restructuring: Lessons from Prospect Theory," *International Studies Quarterly*, 40, 2 (June 1996), pp. 185–207; doi:10.2307/2600956

Wildeman, Jeremy, "Neoliberalism as Aid for the Settler Colonization of the Occupied Palestinian Territories after Oslo," in Alaa Tartir and Timothy Seidel (eds), *Palestine and Rule of Power*, Cham: Palgrave Macmillan, 2019.

Williams, Jennifer, and Javier Zarracina, "The Growth of Israeli Settlements, Explained in 5 Charts," Vox, 30 December 2016.

Wohlforth, William C., "The Stability of a Unipolar World," *International Security*, 24, 1 (Summer 1999), pp. 5–41; doi:10.1162/016228899560031

Wood, Elisabeth Jean, *Insurgent Collective Action and Civil War in El Salvador*, New York: Cambridge University Press, 2003.

Wright, Joseph, "How Foreign Aid Can Foster Democratization In Authoritarian Regimes," *American Journal of Political Science*, 53, 3 (2009), pp. 552–71.

Yom, Sean, *From Resilience to Revolution: How Foreign Interventions Destabilize the Middle East*, New York: Columbia University Press, 2016.

Yom, Sean, and Mohammad Al-Momani, "The International Dimensions of Authoritarian Regime Stability: Jordan in the Post-Cold War Era," *Arab Studies Quarterly*, 30 (2008), pp. 39–60.

Yom, Sean L., and F. Gregory Gause, "Resilient Royals: How Arab Monarchies Hang On," *Journal of Democracy*, 23, 4 (October 2012), pp. 74–88; doi:10.1353/jod.2012.0062

Younes, Ali, "Jordanians Demand Closure of US Embassy in Amman," Al Jazeera, 8 December 2017; http://www.aljazeera.com/news/2017/12/jordanians-demand-closure-embassy-amman-171207170857947.html (accessed 5 February 2018).

Zaller, John R., *The Nature and Origins of Mass Opinion*, New York: Cambridge University Press, 1992.

Zenko, Micah, "US Military Policy in the Middle East: An Appraisal," Chatham House, 7 December 2018; https://www.chathamhouse.org/publication/us-military-policy-middle-east-appraisal (accessed 24 February 2019).

Zunes, Stephen, and Emily Schwartz Greco, "The Rise of Hamas," Foreign Policy in Focus, 22 June 2007; http://fpif.org/the_rise_of_hamas/

INDEX